AMERICAN IMMANENCE

INSURRECTIONS: CRITICAL STUDIES IN RELIGION,
POLITICS, AND CULTURE

INSURRECTIONS: CRITICAL STUDIES IN RELIGION, POLITICS, AND CULTURE

Slavoj Žižek, Clayton Crockett, Creston Davis, Jeffrey W. Robbins, Editors

The intersection of religion, politics, and culture is one of the most discussed areas in theory today. It also has the deepest and most wide-ranging impact on the world. Insurrections: Critical Studies in Religion, Politics, and Culture will bring the tools of philosophy and critical theory to the political implications of the religious turn. The series will address a range of religious traditions and political viewpoints in the United States, Europe, and other parts of the world. Without advocating any specific religious or theological stance, the series aims nonetheless to be faithful to the radical emancipatory potential of religion.

For the list of titles in this series, see page 239.

AMERICAN IMMANENCE

DEMOCRACY FOR
AN UNCERTAIN WORLD

MICHAEL S. HOGUE

Columbia University Press
New York

Columbia University Press
Publishers Since 1893
New York   Chichester, West Sussex
cup.columbia.edu
Copyright © 2018 Columbia University Press
All rights reserved

ISBN: 978-0-231-17232-5 (cloth)
ISBN: 978-0-231-17233-2 (paper)
ISBN: 978-0-231-54711-6 (ebook)
LCCN: 2017049987. A complete CIP record is available from
the Library of Congress.

Cover design: Jordan Wannemacher

TO SHARON WELCH—COLLEAGUE,
MENTOR, AND FRIEND

CONTENTS

ACKNOWLEDGMENTS

Writing this book has been a process of inquiring how to make sense of, and how to make use of, what is left of the "religious" in my experience of the world. It turns out that what is left is an excess, an immanent excess—a luminous world of more-than-human experience and creativity, of beauty and trouble that vibrate with the questions of meaning, value, and desire that we are blessed and burdened to answer with the shape of our lives.

Since the shape of one's life is never individual, and since no one writes alone, I would like to thank my colleagues, friends, and family whose encouragement and support have made it possible for me to write this book. Thanks to Jeffrey Robbins, Clayton Crockett, and Wendy Lochner for their interest in this project from the beginning. In a series known primarily for its work in continental philosophy of religion, I am grateful that they made space for a study that explores the relevance of American philosophies of religion to the changing political and planetary climates of our time. I would also like to thank my Meadville Lombard staff and faculty colleagues, especially to President Lee Barker and Provost Sharon Welch, who made it possible for me to take a sabbatical as I began to develop this project. I express deepest gratitude also to Professors Günter Thomas and William Schweiker, who saw the promise in this project, kindly included me in the scholarly community of the Enhancing Life Project, and asked (and will continue to ask) many challenge questions. The

Enhancing Life Project grant provided by the John Templeton Foundation, and administered by the University of Chicago, made completion of this project possible. During seminars in Banff, Berlin, and Chicago, I learned a great deal from the thirty-five international Enhancing Life scholars. I would also like to thank Dean Bell for his friendship, for sharing coffee and family stories, and for always pushing me to imagine theories of resilience and vulnerability in new ways. Lea Schweitz, thank you for being a friend and a writing-buddy during the early phases of this book. And thank you, Heike Springhart, for your friendship and for your hospitality at the Vulnerability and Theology conference in Heidelberg in 2016. I have learned most of what I know about pragmatic naturalism, radical empiricism, and process philosophy through colleagues and friends at the Institute for American Philosophy and Theology. I am grateful especially to the wisdom and support of Victor Anderson, Robert Corrington, Donald Crosby, Gary Dorrien, Nancy Frankenberry, William Hart, Andrew Irvine, Robert Neville, Michael Raposa, Jerry Stone, and Wesley Wildman. Of course, none of these scholar-friends is responsible for any interpretive errors in what follows. Thank you also to William Connolly, Catherine Keller, and Carol Wayne White for demonstrating the political and social significance of American philosophies of religion and for conversations and email exchanges which, unbeknown to you, inspired me through some tenuous places in the project. I also thank Cecelia Cancellaro for helping me at a crucial stage of conceptual development and Sarah Prickett for her help with formatting, bibliography, and indexing.

Last but never least, I owe my family my deepest gratitude. Sara, thank you for your patience with me as I took longer than I had planned to finish this book. Thank you for tolerating my many inopportune disappearances into the office to jot notes or add sentences or references. Thank you to my children, Kincade (age seventeen), Mikaela (age seven), and Kamryn (age six), for keeping me laughing and bringing me "back to Earth" many times a day—may your hearts always know the possibility of a more beautiful world.

AMERICAN IMMANENCE

INTRODUCTION

I n his landmark book on American civil religion, written nearly a half-century ago, the celebrated American sociologist Robert Bellah observed that "Once in each of the last three centuries America has faced a time of trial, a time of testing so severe that not only the form but even the existence of our nation have been called into question."[1] Spanning the eighteenth, nineteenth, and twentieth centuries, these three American trials stand as transformative crises in history's longest-running national experiment in democracy. Through the first trial, the American Revolution, which gave birth to the nation, the raw and rough-hewn colonists united together in the name of liberty to assert their independence from imperial Britain. Although the colonists were victorious against all odds, the founding independence of the new nation was grounded in a deep moral contradiction: freedom for the colonists was achieved while the genocide of Native Americans and enslavement of Africans continued unabated; independence from empire was won by colonizers and slaveholders who became agents of a new empire.

The vicious moral paradox of the first trial thus sowed the seeds of the second trial, the Civil War. During this second trial the young nation threatened to fracture as the echo of its inaugural cry of liberty rebounded against the brutality of chattel slavery. The principal question of this second trial was the scope and integrity of freedom within the national polity—should life, liberty, and the pursuit of happiness be the unalienable birthright of all "men," regardless of race and class? Although the struggle for women's rights remained for the future, Union victory in the Civil War emancipated the slaves and extended nominal freedom to them. This freedom was a promissory note that immediately came up delinquent, for from the first years of Reconstruction through the decades of Jim Crow segregation, African Americans continued to be economically exploited, racially marginalized, and politically oppressed. It took a third trial, the civil rights movement, for the nominal freedom achieved through the second trial to become more substantially realized. While the civil rights movement led by Martin Luther King Jr. may have come to an end nearly fifty years ago, the struggle for the rights, dignity, and freedom of minority and oppressed groups has been unfolding ever since. In recent years, great gains have been made for gays and lesbians, culminating in the Supreme Court's ruling that affirmed the right of same-sex couples to marry.

Although civil rights gains have been made in recent decades, the United States is currently in the throes of a virulent uprising of antiblack racism, white ethnonationalism, and Islamophobia. As I was finishing this book, in fact, the world watched in dismay as "the people" of the United States elected the billionaire reality television star Donald J. Trump to become their next president. Although he lost the popular vote by a significant margin (nearly three million votes), he won the Electoral College by appealing to the economic and racial grievances of white voters in the rust belt states (Michigan, Ohio, Indiana, Wisconsin, and Pennsylvania). Along with 80 percent of evangelical Christians (!) and majorities of voters in traditional Republican strongholds, these white rust belt voters, rural and suburban, blue and white collar, cast their vote for a misogynistic populist who ran a "posttruth" campaign that scapegoated Muslims, Mexican immigrants, and African Americans for all the ills of a globalizing world.[2] Although there will be many analyses of how and why this happened, my view is that the election of Donald J. Trump as president of the United States is a vivid sign that we are living amid a fourth major trial of American democracy. Trump is a symptom of the problem of democracy in an uncertain world.

Considering this, two interrelated premises motivate my work in this book. The first is that in order most fully to understand this fourth trial of democracy, it is important to interpret it within the context of the

Anthropocene paradox. The Anthropocene paradox is constituted by a set of mutually amplifying planetary, religious, and political climate changes that are radically unsettling our world. In other words, the fourth trial of democracy has global and ecological as well as national and political implications. The second premise is that the cultural conditions of this paradox open a conceptual space in which to reimagine a more resilient and radically democratic political theology. This is because although the Anthropocene literally signifies the beginning of a human geological epoch for the Earth, it also signals the end of the idea of the human difference from the rest of nature. By making the Earth *homo imago* we have discovered that we are *terra bēstiae*. While the Anthropocene is the greatest trial the human species has ever faced, it also provokes creative moral, political, and religious possibilities. By unsettling some of the most settled human-centered habits of meaning and value, it forces us to rethink many of the root questions of moral, religious, and political life. These include, among others, questions about value, meaning, power, and common life. Since these are some of the deepest questions we can ask of ourselves, as individuals, as communities, and as a species, the way we interpret and answer them has tremendous implications. Our conceptions of the worth and beauty of life, our own lives as well as the lives of others, and our understanding of our responsibilities to human and more-than-human others, both in the present and into the future, are entangled with our understanding of the depth and scope of moral value, the limits and purposes of human power in relation to the more-than-human powers of the rest of nature, the sources and forms of human meaning, and the ideals and institutions of common life. In short, by revealing to us the complexity and vulnerability of life and how deeply embedded and dependent our human systems are in relation to the ecological systems of Earth, the Anthropocene paradox provokes new ways of imagining the tasks of moral, religious, and political life.

With these premises in mind, my purpose in this book is to explore how the Anthropocene paradox provokes profound questions at the intersection of the theological and the political and compels us to reimagine the frame, ethos, and aim of the theopolitical. My argument is twofold: first, insofar as the Anthropocene is both a perilous human age for the Earth and an age of ecological possibility for humans, it calls us to set in motion a deeply democratic, ecologically attuned, and spiritually vital political theology; and second, the philosophical and theological lineages of what I will refer to as the tradition of "American immanence" provide critical resources for responding to that call. In the uncertainties of the Anthropocene, and in relation to the global rise of right-wing authoritarian figures such as Trump, many of us may feel less assured of the efficacies of democracy. But I will argue that democracy is best understood as a politics of and for a world of uncertainty—uncertainty gives life to democracy and in an increasingly uncertain world we need more and better democracy. Since the theological and philosophical lineages of American immanence emerge out of an understanding of the world as ontologically uncertain, as creatively open-ended, they provide a robust theopolitical infrastructure for a more resilient democracy.

At the heart of the Anthropocene is the anthropogenic climate crisis, whose diffused causes and uneven effects are connected to a myriad of other crises. This is what I meant earlier by suggesting that the Anthropocene is constituted by multiple, mutually amplifying planetary, religious, and political climate changes. Economic insecurity and inequality are forbidding; the causality of our social and environmental crises is nonlinear and its effects are uneven and unjust; we are terrorized by intensifying ecological emergency as well as by the rise of nationalist, xenophobic, and religious extremism; our religious and moral traditions have frayed as a result of their passage through modernity; and the secular foundations of Western modernity are being challenged by the rise of fundamentalisms from within, as well as from without. The symbolic and cultural, the personal and the political, and the ecological and geophysical conditions of human life are as uncertain and unstable as they have ever been. To live in a time of turbulence such as this is to live in a context of insecurity and in a condition of vulnerability. But cultural, social, and political disruptions can also become the basis for revolutionary systemic change—as we have witnessed in recent years with the Occupy movement, the Arab spring, the #BlackLivesMatter movement, and the global Climate Justice movement. The entangled challenges of the Anthropocene also create the possibility of new ways of living out our human lives in a deeply pluralistic, more-than-human, socioecological world.

My hypothesis in this book is that a theology rooted in the pragmatic naturalist, radically empirical, and process lineages of the American immanental tradition provides resources for reimagining the frame, ethos, and aim of the theopolitical, and that it can do so in ways that are attuned to the complexity, gravity, and urgency of our entangled crises.[3] A theology of immanence, in the contexts in which I will elaborate it, signifies the idea that nature is all, that the beauty, depth, terror, and mystery of nature are the sole context for the emergence of being and becoming, knowing and valuing.[4] A theology of immanence is fundamentally committed to the idea, as William David Hart eloquently puts it, "that *nature is all there is*," that "the whence and wherefore of all things is nature," and thus that nature "is both the things that emerge" and the processes through which they emerge.[5] But to say that "nature is all" is not to say that nature is undifferentiated. Although I will discuss this at more length in chapters 3 and 4, it is important to say up front that I will often use shorthand to refer to the forms and patterns of differentiation in nature. At times, I will use the medieval distinction between *natura naturans* (nature naturing, or nature creating) and *natura naturata* (nature natured, or created nature), and at other times I will refer to nature's patterns, processes, and precarities.[6] I use these sets of terms in a general way to emphasize four fundamental points: (1) that nature is all; (2) that nature is differentiated; (3) that nature is in process; (4) that the value of the things and relations of nature emerges out of their vulnerability.

Within this immanental theological frame, there is no outside of nature, nature is infinite and inexhaustible and it is without center or periphery. Nature includes innumerable possible forms of experience and centers of value, but no center of value is at the center of all the rest and no form of experience encompasses all the others. And yet among these innumerable possibilities, the political theology I develop in this book is particularly focused on questions of human and more-than-human experience and value in relation to the vulnerability of planetary life. I will argue for a bifocal political theology. By "bifocal" I mean that this political theology includes two different but integrated lenses, one that focuses on the horizon of planetary life and another that focuses on the particularities of democratic community. As such, a bifocal theopolitics aims to hold together several complementary contrasts, including what ultimately orients us and what immediately concerns us, the future as well as the present of life, the breadth of planetary and global systems along with the depth and intensity of local life. While the politics of "resilient democracy" provides the immediate and local lens, an immanental theology of "world loyalty" provides the lens for the ultimate and planetary.

Coordinated by the creativity of relational power rather than the ideality of unitary and oppositional power, this bifocal political theology offers an inclusive and pluralistic alternative to exclusive and monopolistic political theologies. But my claim is not that this political theology is a solution to the fourth trial of democracy or a global answer to the planetary challenges of the Anthropocene. In fact, to argue that any one proposal is sufficient to our challenges would conflict with the peculiarities of the challenges we face and would run counter to some of the ideas I advance. This then is less of a systematic argument than an invitation to consider a morally catalytic, spiritually invigorating, communally grounded, radically democratic intervention into the root contexts, causes, and conditions of our complex challenges. The philosophical infrastructure and theological framing of the American immanental tradition invite us to imagine and enact more socially just, ecologically attuned, and politically enlivened forms of common life.

This invitation is informed by the view that our ideas about religion, politics, and nature have always influenced one another. These ideas are examples of what William E. Connolly refers to as "cluster concepts" and what Raymond Williams referred to as "keywords."[7] For Connolly, a "cluster concept" is a word or term whose meanings must be interpreted in "complex connection with a host of other concepts to which it is related."[8] For Williams, "keywords" are "significant, binding words in certain activities and their interpretation" and are also "significant, indicative words in certain forms of thought."[9] Cluster concepts and keywords signify across general and specialized vocabularies, and through this dynamic movement they simultaneously become more deeply significant and contested. As concepts, *religion*, *politics*, and *nature* function in this complex way. Reflecting and amplifying this dynamic interplay of signification, the realities to which these concepts point are also interrelated. Religious values, beliefs, and practices have framed the way people have organized the political structure and norms of their common life, and the institutional forms and values that interlink political, moral, and religious life have been framed in relation to ideas about the nature of nature.

Two intrarelated assumptions about nature drive the human-centered patterns of thinking and behavior and meaning and value that have led us into the Anthropocene and the climate crisis: the idea that humans and nature are ontologically distinct from each other and the idea that nature is a fixed and stable backdrop to the dynamism of human culture and history. These assumptions about nature and humans have numerous sources but in modern Western thought they are rooted in what Alfred North Whitehead refers to as the "bifurcation of nature." As I will explore at more length in chapter 3, this bifurcation posits a deep opposition between the world of human minds and the world of nature. It is rooted in the metaphysics of substance dualism and enables the habit of categorizing things as either mental or physical. It also reinforces a host of conceptual and ontological oppositions that have plagued modern Western political and religious thought and practice, including, among others, the oppositions between human and animal, culture and nature, self and other, God and world, transcendent and immanent, and religious and secular. In addition to being philosophically and theologically unimaginative and scientifically suspect, the bifurcation of nature and related dualisms are also unsettled by the conditions of the Anthropocene paradox. The unsettling of these ideas opens a space in which to rethink the relations between nature, religion, and the political on the other side of the bifurcation.

Within this space, I critically juxtapose two American theopolitical traditions, a dominant and a dissenting tradition. The dominant tradition supports the theopolitics of American exceptionalism and is rooted in the Puritan religious imagination and posits a transcendent, Providential God as the external source of creation and as the antecedent foundation of all that is good.[10] While religious reverence for sovereign, unitary power leads historically to the legitimation of diverse forms of concentrated human power, the "redeemer symbolic" at its core sanctifies extractive cultural and economic practices and the externalization of social and ecological costs. The extraction of diverse forms of value and the externalization of diverse costs are justified as the going price and prerogative of American exceptionalism.

If the dominant tradition grows out of a theological exception that grounds it, the dissenting tradition of American immanence, rooted in pragmatic naturalism, radical empiricism, and process philosophy, supports a pluralistic theopolitics that refuses exceptions of all kinds, theological and otherwise. The tradition of American immanence rejects the metaphysics of being and the ontology of inside and outside, and honors nature as the sublime all-inclusive context and all-pervasive dynamic of being and becoming, meaning and value. It interprets moral value as emergent and contextual rather than antecedent and foundational. It understands ethics and politics as provisional and negotiated rather than absolute and imposed. It rejects the symbol of God as unitary, sovereign, supernatural, and transcendent, but clears the way for a diffused, vulnerable, natal, and immanental understanding of the sacred. And this clearing opens to a path that leads to the possibility of "resilient democracy" as a mode of theopolitics and a form of religious and spiritual liberation.

Where the dominant tradition's idolization of omnipotence sanctifies sovereignty and legitimates monopolistic power, the dissenting tradition's commitment to the immanence of the sacred ennobles shared and cooperative power and supports an ethics and politics that is collaborative, democratic, and ecological; whereas the dominant tradition's faith in God as a singularly supreme Being encourages exclusionary modes of faith and absolutist beliefs, the dissenting tradition finds religious depth and value in the adventure of provisional convictions and the practice of remaining inquisitively open to change; while the dominant tradition's political theology informs exceptionalist national and cultural identities, xenophobic exclusions, and the externalization of social and ecological costs, the dissenting tradition supports radically relational views of self, community, and economy. Critically, the American immanental tradition nurtures a spirit of dissidence and resists the religious constraints and social and environmental injustices of the dominant American political theology. Constructively, it offers a theopolitical frame for an ecologically attuned, politically engaged, spiritually vital, and environmentally and socially just mode of democratic life.

Though circumstances are grave they also provide fertile ground for radical change. My contribution toward an emancipatory way forward revolves around the theopolitical potential of the tradition of American immanence. As a scholar informed by pragmatism, I am committed to the view that our ideas about the common good and our commitments to its realization emerge out of culturally formatted habits, values, and practices. Methodologically, then, the theopolitical work of critiquing and constructively reimagining the symbols, meanings, and practices of cultural systems is indispensable to the tasks of political and social change. Critical cultural intervention into the symbolic depths of social and political systems is a crucial aspect of reconstructing them. This is not to say that either critique or cultural intervention is sufficient to achieve revolutionary social and political change. There must also be lament, protest, resistance, witness, and the positive prefiguring of an alternative ecology of blessing, compassion, and justice. But part of the work of change entails demystifying the theopolitical symbols that legitimate our crises and deconstructing the social, economic, and environmental injustices that infuse them. It also entails imaginatively constructing and bringing to visibility a countervailing frame of theopolitical symbols and practices, which I seek to do by shaping the dissenting tradition of American immanence into a socially and spiritually resonant framework that promotes democratic practices and communities.

While the Anthropocene paradox provides a critical context for this book, I have chosen an American theopolitical focus for several reasons. First, and most simply, as a scholar and educator who works with American pragmatist, naturalist, and process philosophies of religion, I have come to believe that these traditions contain theopolitical potential that is relevant to contemporary challenges. Radical empiricism and process thought can help us to see and engage the creativity of complex life in new ways, and pragmatic naturalism, as a mode of thinking and valuing, can catalyze this creativity. A second reason for my American focus is that the United States exerts a hegemonic influence not only on global human affairs but also on the planetary ecological condition. As an engaged intellectual committed to environmental, economic, and social justice, I strive to practice a mode of theology that is contextually, critically, and constructively activated. Insofar as the dominant American theopolitical tradition aids and abets diverse forms of social, economic, and environmental injustice, I view the critique of this tradition and constructive response to it as vocational responsibilities. My third reason for choosing this focus is that I take the American ideals of freedom, equality, and democracy seriously enough to think that they ought to be more fully realized, that they can be more broadly shared, and that the Anthropocene paradox amplifies the urgency of this need. One way to go about this, in addition to the ongoing work of building a more inclusive multicultural and multiracial politics, is to extend what John Dewey referred to as the "way of life" of democracy to its social, economic, and ecological registers. This book seeks to make a modest contribution to that work through a critique of the theopolitical tradition that impedes that way of life and the construction of a political theology that seeks to catalyze it.

There has been a great deal of new work in political theology in recent years.[11] There are several plausible explanations for this but some of the most important provocations include the deepening financial corruption of democracy, the increasingly acute social and ecological contradictions of neoliberal capitalism, and the fracturing of the secularist ideological grounds of liberalism. In other words, the theopolitical revival has emerged out of the postliberal and postsecular fissures in the political forms, values, and foundations of liberal modernity. By "postliberal" I refer to activist resistance to the financialization of politics, the corporatization of democracy, and the philosophical critique of some of liberalism's core normative assumptions. By "postsecular" I refer to the combined effects of the social persistence of religion through modernity, to postcolonial critiques of "secular" rationality, and to debates about the meanings of "religion" as a scholarly category.

The postsecular can be understood as a time in which the religious traditions, meanings, purposes, and desires that orient human groups have been and are being "fragilized" and radicalized because of their passage through modernity.[12] Global dynamics simultaneously shrink the experiential distance between different cultures and amplify consciousness of cultural difference. The religious meanings, purposes, and desires that have traditionally oriented human life are being relativized through increasing cultural interconnectedness. We are deconstructing and reconstructing, hybridizing and queering traditional markers of racial, gender, and sexual identity. Through the globalization of communication and social technologies, from the Internet and cable news to social media, we experience the world as simultaneously shrinking and expanding— our virtual and actual contacts with far-off places and peoples are more frequent, simultaneously deepening, and, oddly, domesticating the feel of difference. This means that a plurality of people around the world are engaged across cultural and other forms of difference at the very moment when the religious traditions through which questions of difference and identity have often been negotiated are themselves being transformed. The instabilities and uncertainties of these global dynamics lead some to turn to orthodoxy and tradition and others to experiment with new religious and spiritual options. The rise of new forms of fundamentalism and the swelling ranks of the "spiritual-but-not-religious" are both aspects of the postsecular historical condition. In these ways, the postsecular does not signify the return of religion, since religion never made an exit, but the innovation of new forms of religion and new modes of religiosity.

The postsecular also refers to a vigorous debate that has led historians and philosophers of religion in recent years to begin to radically question the very idea of "religion" as a scholarly concept and a universal human cultural category.[13] By contesting the Eurocentric, largely Protestant, and colonial origins of "religion" as an academic construct, this debate deeply unsettles many aspects of the scholarly study of religion. Critics rightly question historical, comparative, and social-scientific studies of religion that make use of a culturally and historically contingent concept while making universalizing claims across historical and cultural contexts. Whether understood as a historical condition or a scholarly debate, or as a combination of the two, the postsecular has implications for liberalism.

As a system of political and economic institutions and practices, liberalism is formally and functionally dependent upon a categorical distinction between the religious and the secular. If the religious and the secular are defined by way of an opposition, and this opposition is foundational to liberalism, then to provincialize religion is, mutatis mutandis, to provincialize the secular. Postsecular and postliberal criticism thereby combine to provoke new thinking about the frame, ethos, and aims of a culturally and convictionally pluralistic theopolitics that supports a more socially, economically, and ecologically just democratic way of life.

However, as I indicated earlier I am primarily interested in the emergence of a third space of theopolitical thought signified by the Anthropocene paradox, which marks both an end to the idea of the human as separate from nature and the beginning of a new human age for the

Earth. While the broader revival in political theology is spurred on by postliberal and postsecular provocations, there is also a need and opportunity for political theology to take up this paradox. My thesis, as already stated, is that the American immanental tradition offers a unique set of resources for this work. One reason for this is that it emerges historically in direct response to transformed understandings of the human relation to nature, not unlike those illuminated by the Anthropocene. By interpreting the human within the complex creativity of evolutionary processes rather than as the center of God's creation, by understanding nature as the dynamic context rather than the static backdrop of human history, and by providing ways of thinking and relating to the sacred as immanent, finite, and emergent, the tradition of American immanence provides a useful theopolitical frame for a context of ecological endangerment.

The tradition of American immanence is a mansion with many rooms. It has housed secular as well as religious humanisms, pragmatic and religious naturalisms, classical and prophetic pragmatisms, empirical and speculative process philosophies. It includes aspects of the work of philosophers such as William James, Alain Locke, Jane Addams, John Dewey, and Alfred North Whitehead, as well as theologians such as Henry Nelson Wieman, Bernard Meland, and Bernard Loomer. Contemporary thinkers who work across philosophical and theological lines and draw from psychoanalytic, literary, cognitive scientific, comparative, phenomenological, social-ethical, and other methodologies include Robert Corrington, Donald Crosby, William Dean, Robert Neville, Jerome Stone, and Wesley Wildman. Feminist, ecofeminist, and African American exemplars include, among others, Victor Anderson, Nancy Frankenberry, William Hart, Catherine Keller, Anthony Pinn, Sharon Welch, and Carol White. Philosophers and theorists such as William Connolly, Judith Green, John Ryder, Jeffrey Stout, and Umberto Unger have also sharpened, critiqued, and extended aspects of the tradition in important ways.

It would be impossible to do justice to all of these thinkers. So rather than striving for the impossible, I will interpret the philosophical infrastructure of immanence through close attention to aspects of the work of Dewey, James, and Whitehead. And I will interpret the theological frame of immanence by engaging Wieman and Loomer along with several more recent thinkers and ideas. But to activate the immanental tradition theo-politically, I will also creatively integrate new ideas drawn from systems theory and the multidisciplinary discourses of vulnerability and resil-ience. This integrative work is consistent with the empirical and interdis-ciplinary nature of the tradition. The American immanental thinkers were deeply engaged with the scientific discourses of their own time, and work on vulnerability, resiliency, and systems is an important contempo-rary expression of the blending of natural and social sciences. These dis-courses also offer new resources for resisting the dominant tradition of American political theology and for imagining and beginning to realize more radically democratic forms of common life. As the tradition of American immanence is relevant to the Anthropocene paradox because it emerges out of the breakdown of the ontological difference between humans and the rest of nature, theories of vulnerability and resilience are relevant to American immanence because they enable a way to think crit-ically and constructively across social and ecological systems.

Throughout my writing process, I have been very conscious of what it means to contribute to an insurrectionist theology. As Clayton Crockett has defined it, "Insurrectionist Theology refuses political neutrality, and works not only to critique contemporary corporate capitalism, but to offer ways of thinking and possibilities of living beyond capitalism. We refuse any simple opposition between the religious and the secular, and we argue that both are implicated in the world we live in as well as harbor poten-tial to transform it in important ways."[14] In keeping with those ideas, this book presents a strong critique of the dominant American political the-ology and the social and ecological contradictions of neoliberal capital-ism, it advocates for an ecologically attuned democratic politics, and it presents a mode of theology and spiritual life that, by way of its imma-nental "world-loyalty," creatively inhabits contemporary perforations between the religious and the secular.

However, while this book is an experiment in insurrectionist theology in these respects, it can also be thought of as a friendly intervention. While I share the radically democratic ideals of Clayton Crockett and Jef-frey Robbins, two of the principal editors of the series in which this book appears, I explore these ideals through alternative pathways. Where they seek to integrate aspects of the "death of God" stream of American radical theology with theories of radical democracy, I seek to draw the radically democratic, ecological, and theopolitical potential out of the pragmatic naturalist, radically empirical, and process relational lineages of American immanence. The tradition of American immanence emerges out of a sense of the abundant complexity of life and nature rather than in response to the "death of God." For the American immanental tradition, the question of God's life or death, existence or nonexistence, is a question rooted in a category mistake. Of course, this is not news for radical theologians who work out of an apophatic or ground-of-being theological framework. For if God is not a being existing among other beings but is the ground or matrix of being as such, then not only does God not exist now, but God never did. The problem is that the "death of God" slogan rhetorically reinstates the categories of existence and nonexistence, thus resurrecting the idea of God as *a* being. By working in the negative image of the God of classical theism, the symbolic and conceptual resources of the "death of God" wing of radical theology remain partially enclosed within the logic of the life of God.

An American immanental theopolitics escapes that logic by replacing mortal concern with the death of a transcendent God with natal concern for the complex creativity immanent within the world and emergent through nature. Another way to say this is that a theopolitics of American immanence seeks to operate in the space of the vital sufficiency of sacred nature in contrast to the scarcity of God's death in history. Perhaps American radical theology should be thought of as having two distinct trajectories: one that works in the wake of the death of God and invokes a god-haunted mood of loss and one that takes ecological flight and is attuned to the vital goodness of vulnerable life in a precarious world. The political theology developed in the chapters that follow emerge through this second trajectory.

I should say a word here about some of the concepts I will be using. As a pragmatist, I think of concepts as tools-under-construction put to work for specific purposes and revised in light of their efficacy in relation to those purposes. The question of the meaning of concepts is thus connected to their functionality. In later chapters, as mentioned earlier, I will make use of a network of concepts drawn from interdisciplinary fields including systems theory and the discourses of vulnerability and resilience. But for now it will be helpful to briefly explain how I will use the concepts of theology, the political, and political theology.

By "theology" I refer to the pragmatic formation, critique, and reconstruction of the symbols, practices, ideals, and institutions that format life-orienting religious meanings, purposes, and desires. This is an emphatically antidogmatic, nonabsolutist mode of theology. So defined, theology is something one does more than something that one has—that is, theology in this view is not equivalent to a system of beliefs, and beliefs are not equivalent to cognitive propositions. When this mode of theology is concerned with belief, it is concerned with "belief" as the unfinalizable pragmatic process of communally forming, critically testing, and creatively transforming religious meanings, purposes, and desires. Theology is thus not a set of truth propositions that one possesses. Theology is not about property but process. It is not limited to critical reflection on the symbol "God." Instead, its objects are those diverse constellations of symbols, practices, ideals, and institutions that orient us ultimately by formatting, or shaping and interconnecting, the religious meanings, purposes, and desires through which human communities negotiate the hazards and graces of vulnerable life in an ambiguous world.

By "the political" I refer to the imaginal space of reason and desire within which political communities negotiate relations of power and value in the context of their common life. Thus defined, the political is not limited to traditional political objects, such as the state or party, or to formal institutions, such as legislative and judicial bodies, or to practices such as voting, protesting, assembling, and organizing. Indeed, the political runs through and around and beneath, is immanent within, and yet not exhausted by, each of these traditional objects, institutions, and practices of politics. To refer to the political as an "imaginal space" is to indicate that it is embedded within the affective, aesthetic, narrative, and ritual registers of life in addition to its explicitly articulated presence in discourses and formal institutions.

By "political theology" I refer to the work of thinking the theological and the political together, with and against each other. It is the critical and constructive engagement of the interplay between the religious symbols and practices that ultimately orient us and the imaginal spaces of reason and desire through which we negotiate relations of power and value in our common life. To indicate that ultimately orienting symbols and practices influence political reason and desire is to hold that they can be and often are transposed across religious and other registers of life. Thus, the religious and the secular are not neatly divisible, the religious is not apolitical and the political is not areligious. To suggest that religious symbols and practices inflect negotiations of power and value and common life is to draw attention to their concrete pragmatic effects.

As the discipline of engaging religious and other concepts of power and value as they inform common life, political theology includes critical and constructive tasks. A primary critical task entails interpreting the forms and migrations of theopolitical symbols and analyzing their role in formatting the imaginal spaces of the political. The critical task of political theology so defined is deeply hermeneutical—it entails demystifying the political imaginary by surfacing and contextualizing the cultural symbols and practices that often covertly shape the relations of power and value that orient common life. A primary constructive task includes the construction, deconstruction, and reconstruction of ultimately orienting symbols and practices that normatively shape the contexts of human experience, individual and collective.

The bifocal political theology I advocate engages both tasks. It offers deep cultural critique of macrodynamics (that is, analysis of the theopolitical formatting of social worlds), while also operating constructively in the fast shape-changing mezzo and micro spaces of contemporary social life. New spaces of democratic possibility are emerging through the postsecular perforations of the religious and the secular, postliberal alternatives to neoliberal capitalism, and the paradox of the Anthropocene. These are natal spaces, sites for the gestating of new meanings, purposes, and desires, new ideals, new concepts of power, value, and common life—as such, they are spaces for the potential birthing of new configurations of the religious, the political, and the theopolitical.

With these introductory comments in place, it will be helpful briefly to outline the structure, sequence, and topics in the chapters ahead. Structurally, I have written this book around a set of interlocking critical, contextual, conceptual, and constructive theses. The critical theses are presented in chapter 1, the contextual in chapter 2, the conceptual in chapters 3 and 4, and the constructive in chapter 5.

My focus in chapter 1 is on the dominant American theopolitical tradition. The critical thesis is that this tradition is antidemocratic, it breeds a politics of opposition, and it has served and continues to serve as a symbolic accomplice in diverse instances of social, economic, and environmental injustice, including the climate crisis. I open the chapter with an interpretation of the water crisis in Flint, Michigan. Alluding to the central ideas of the "father" of modern political theology, the German legal philosopher Carl Schmitt, I argue that the Flint crisis illustrates both the temptation and the problem of making exceptions to democracy in times of emergency. I interpret Flint as a synecdoche of the exceptionalist, extractive, and externalizing logic of the dominant American political theology. I then trace this dominant tradition through its historical migrations, focusing on the settler-colonial period, the time from early national period into the nineteenth century, and then from the nineteenth century to the present. I argue that there is a symbolic theopolitical core that migrates across these periods, which I refer to as the "redeemer symbolic." The logic of the redeemer symbolic, I suggest, is exceptionalist, extractive, and externalizing. In the settler-colonial period this logic manifests as an ecclesial ethnocentrism; in the early national period, it takes the form of ethnocentric nationalism; and in recent years it is present in the ideology of neoliberal market fundamentalism. Whether the agent of exception takes the form of a purified church, a superior race, an ideal nation, or a triumphant market, the exception legitimates the extraction of diverse forms of value and the externalization of diverse forms of cost.[15]

Chapter 2 shifts from a national to a planetary focus. The purpose of this chapter is to articulate the contextual thesis of the Anthropocene paradox—that the beginning of a human age for the Earth also marks the ending of the (primarily modern Western) idea of the human as separate from the rest of nature. I situate this thesis in relation to debates about the Anthropocene within and beyond geology to show how the

Anthropocene paradox unsettles disciplinary paradigms and boundaries. At the center of these debates are questions about the power, value, and responsibilities of humans within nature. I bring these questions to a focus through discussion of the problem of naming a geological epoch for the whole of the species when only some humans in recent history are responsible for, and have benefited from, the economic system that is the source of the problem. I then shift to an analysis of the climate crisis as a wicked problem, focusing on the way its moral and political phenomenology revokes the ideal of certainty as a basis for moral and political action. I argue in this chapter that the Anthropocene and climate wickedness call for a theopolitics that is bifocal, planetary, and local, ecologically attuned, experimental, and deeply democratic.

The conceptual work in chapters 3 and 4 explore, respectively, the philosophical and theological lineages of American immanence as resources for a bifocal political theology. Both chapters include significant interpretive work, intended to serve two purposes. The first is to introduce the American immanental tradition—and pragmatic naturalism, radical empiricism, and process thought in particular—as a robust tradition of thought that has been largely neglected by the revival in political theology. The second purpose is to show how the philosophies and theologies of American immanence emerge out of what were at the time new ways of interpreting the place of human experience, knowledge, and value within nature rather than in opposition to it.

Chapter 3 is focused on Dewey, James, and Whitehead and is organized under the themes of thinking, feeling, and valuing immanence. In relation to these thinkers and themes I trace the antiexceptionalist implications of naturalism, the "revolutionary" idea of nature in process, and the idea that the world is felt before it is known and that one way beyond the binaries and bifurcations of modern Western thought is through an ontology of internal rather than external relatedness and the transformation of ontological oppositions into contrasts. I discuss Dewey's pragmatic naturalism as it emerges out of the "discovery" of nature-in-process and a commitment to the provisional and experimental nature of knowledge and values. I suggest that pragmatic naturalism leads us to think about knowledge and values in a way that privileges conjunctions over correspondence or coherence. In other words, the criterial questions for a pragmatic naturalist epistemology are about how our values and claims to knowledge connect us to the world and advance our projects rather than how they mirror reality or how well they hang together with other traditional claims and values.

In the next section I discuss aspects of William James's radical empiricism and Alfred North Whitehead's process thought. I discuss how James illuminates the importance of interpreting relations as things as well as things in relation, and of relations as disjunctive as well as conjunctive. A world of relational experience is not necessarily a world of harmony! In contrast to the classical empiricism of John Locke and David Hume, in radical empiricism "experience" is not limited to sensory experience or the experience of representational consciousness. At its depth, experience is affective—we feel the world before we know it.

I then turn to Whitehead for an account of what is felt, and how. I work from Whitehead's philosophy of symbolism and perception, through aspects of his cosmology, toward his concept of God. This interpretive arc is important to the task of connecting social criticism and social change to the deconstruction and reconstruction of symbols, which is central to the way I interpret the work of political theology. As a segue to chapter 4, I conclude chapter 3 with an analysis and critique of Whitehead's complex concept of God.

Chapter 4 has two aims, both of which I organize under the theme of divining immanence. The first aim is to explicate representative theological interpretations of the philosophical ideas discussed in chapter 3. I focus especially on what has been referred to as the "Chicago school" of theology and give attention to aspects of Henry Nelson Wieman's and Bernard Loomer's philosophical theologies. I interpret the different ways in which these thinkers construct the object of religious devotion and the focus of theological inquiry. While both reject the God of traditional theism and Christianity, along with the bifurcation of nature at the center of modern Western philosophy, they develop distinct alternatives out of the philosophies of American immanence. Where Wieman replaces the God of ontotheology with an axiological concept of ultimacy, Loomer argues for an aesthetic theology that moves beyond both ontotheology and Wieman's axiotheological alternative.

My second task in chapter 4 is to articulate the constructive immanental theology that frames the theopolitical work in chapter 5. Toward that end, I first present an immanental philosophy of religion, integrating aspects of the American immanental tradition with insights from other thinkers, including the African American philosopher of religion Charles Long and the feminist philosopher of religion Grace Jantzen. I also sketch a theory of religion that draws from systems theory and resilience and vulnerability discourses. While this "theory" of religion is merely suggestive, it provides context for the theology of immanence I articulate in the final section of the chapter. Emerging out of the general idea that nature is all, and the specific idea that the cosmos has no center, the theology of immanence I articulate demystifies religious experience and advocates a "prismatic" theory of value.

In chapter 5, I articulate "resilient democracy" as a theopolitical integration of planetary concern and democratic life. I open with a discussion of the Chinese American philosopher-activist Grace Lee Boggs's important distinction between rebellion and revolution. To illustrate and ground this distinction, I correlate it to aspects of Whitehead's metaphysics and his philosophy of symbolism. Building on Boggs's call for bold imagination, I then argue that the theory of panarchy provides a critical hermeneutic bridge between Whitehead's metaphysics and analysis of the vulnerabilities of socioecological systems. This leads to a critique of the ecological and social contradictions of capitalism and the revolutionary potential emerging out of the convergence of those contradictions. I then shift into a discussion of the vulnerability of power and the power of vulnerability as they relate to the paradox of democracy. Working through this paradox, resilient democracy wagers that justice-making depends on the embrace of creative ambiguity, cross-difference solidarity, and the constructive prefiguring of a more beautiful world. Resilient democracy understands these tasks as an expression of creative loyalty to the world-in-the-making, fidelity to the finitude of human being and knowing, and grateful appreciation for the priceless perishability of all things. In sum, the theopolitics of resilient democracy is organized around four claims: (1) that immanence signifies the beauty, depth, terror, and mystery of nature naturing; (2) that embracing immanence is an act of moral responsibility, spiritual reverence, and theopolitical resistance; (3) that integrating responsibility, reverence, and resistance is essential to the culturing of resilient democratic communities and solidarities; (4) and that the culturing of resilient democratic communities and solidarities is sacred work.

1

AMERICAN EXCEPTIONALISM AND
THE REDEEMER SYMBOLIC

*You said in your soul, I will be empire of empires, overshadowing all else,
past and present, putting the history of old-world dynasties, conquests
behind me, as of no account—making a new history, a history of democracy, making old history a dwarf—I alone inaugurating largeness, culminating time. If these, O lands of America, are indeed the prizes, the
determinations of your soul, be it so. But behold the cost, and already
specimens of the cost.*

—WALT WHITMAN, *DEMOCRATIC VISTAS*

SPOTTING CARL SCHMITT IN FLINT

The residents of Flint, Michigan, who are predominantly African American, working class, and poor, have been drinking water containing toxic
levels of lead—in some instances over thirteen times the level required for
federal intervention.[1] Lead poisoning attacks the brain and central ner-
vous system and its effects can be devastating. The problem began in
April 2014 when an emergency manager appointed by Governor Rick
Snyder switched the city's water source from a Detroit system to the
toxic Flint River. Despite the concerns of local residents and overriding
the authority of democratically elected city officials, the state-appointed

emergency manager made the switch in order to save approximately $5 million dollars. As a result of the calamity that has followed this short-sighted concern for the bottom line, American taxpayers will now have to pay roughly $220 million to repair Flint's infrastructure damages.[2] The human damages of this textbook case of environmental injustice are incalculable.

The Flint tragedy was not inevitable. It is rooted in a series of political decisions, an approach to governance, and an ideology that can be illu-mined by the political theology of Carl Schmitt, the German legal scholar infamously known as Nazism's crown jurist. Schmitt's understanding of the essence of politics and the nature of sovereignty supports a mode of governance that is exceptionalist, oppositional, and decisionist. In other words, it is the antithesis of participatory, pluralist, and procedural democracy. A sovereign, according to Schmitt, is one who has the power to decide when an exception to conventional legal and constitutional norms should be made: "Sovereign is he who decides on the exception."[3] Sovereign power is the supreme power of decision and the defining deci-sion is twofold. It is a decision about what constitutes a state of emergency and the constitutional exceptions warranted within that state. While Schmitt defines sovereignty by way of a decision, he defines the political by way of an opposition. The essential core of politics, according to Schmitt, is the friend/enemy distinction. Political identity is constituted by an "us/them" or "we/they" opposition, and this opposition grounds the nature of the political as such—the political, for Schmitt, is confronta-tional and contested rather than collaborative.

Two of Snyder's early actions exemplify Schmitt's concepts of sover-eignty and the political. In his very first act as governor, only three days after he took the oath of office in February 2011, Snyder issued an execu-tive order that divided Michigan's Department of Natural Resources and the Environment into two separate agencies, the Department of Natural Resources (DNR) and the Department of Environmental Quality (DEQ). The restructuring of governmental departments and bodies is of course not in itself a problem. Indeed, it was not long ago that the Michigan DNR and DEQ had been separate departments. In fact, when Snyder announced the split, they had just recently been integrated. Although Snyder's deci-sion to redivide the departments was dispiriting to state employees who had spent the previous year integrating systems, protocols, and forms, the fact of the division is not the point. The critical issue is about how and why the redivision took place, and whose and which interests were served, and whose and which were not.

Snyder appointed Dan Wyant to lead the DEQ. An entrepreneur, a business consultant, and a past director of Michigan's Department of Agriculture, Wyant reported that he was "excited . . . about creating a new government management model that will improve the services it provides residents and businesses" and that he was "honored to be part of a dynamic team focused on implementing customer service-orientated government."[4] Business practices and principles were central to Snyder's political agenda to "reinvent Michigan," which, as he explained it, entailed "reinventing how state government is organized to provide exceptional value to the taxpayers and citizens it serves."[5] In his previous work in public service Wyant had proven himself to be the right kind of guy for this kind of mission. After all, during his stint as director of the Department of Agriculture, he had created the Environmental Assurance Program, a low-cost project that encouraged farmers and agricultural businesses to comply voluntarily with environmental standards.[6] As one might expect, since the inception of this tax-saving voluntary environmental compliance program, a number of issues have arisen, including a truly explosive problem with manure runoff from factory farms that has been responsible for polluting the waterways of the Great Lakes watershed on a grand scale.[7] Groomed by Wyant's program, however, "proprietors of the farms and their friends in the Capitol" dispute the need for environmental regulation and have said "that voluntary efforts will take care of the problem."[8]

The decision to split the DNR and the DEQ was clearly driven by business and economic interests. But Snyder framed the division in the rhetoric of conservation. As he explained at the time, "Michigan is blessed with an abundance of natural resources and we need to be a leader and innovator in protecting these resources. Recreational fishing, hunting and boating activities alone contribute more than $3 billion annually to our economy. Separating the DEQ and DNR means we can better address these key priorities."[9] But which was the priority? Resource preservation, environmental protection, and the public good? Or business and private interests? Snyder's appointment of Wyant, given his record with the Department of Agriculture, revealed Snyder's priorities. What is more, Snyder's division of the DNR and the DEQ played into a narrative that Republicans like Snyder have used for years in their assaults on environmental regulation—business and environmental interests are essentially opposed to each other. The government stifles economic innovation; governmental regulation is bad for business; and if, as with Michigan, one's primary businesses are environmentally intensive agricultural and recreational industries, then it is especially important to isolate and dilute or constrain environmental regulation. Governor Snyder's division of the DNR and the DEQ instantiates this oppositional framing of environmental and economic interests and replicates the friend/enemy distinction at the core of Schmitt's definition of the political.

Several weeks after his first act, in March 2011, Snyder signed Public Act 4 into law. Known as the Emergency Manager law, Public Act 4 embodied the twofold decision at the heart of Schmitt's definition of sovereignty. First, it granted Snyder the singular authority to determine a "state of exception" in cases of municipal financial exigency and, second, it empowered him, once such a state had been declared, to appoint an emergency manager (or emergency managers) to override democratically elected municipal officials. Citizens resisted these assertions of power and soon repealed Public Act 4 through a referendum. But Snyder then signed Public Act 436 into law a short time later. Aside from one significant difference, this new Emergency Manager law was nearly identical to the one that had been repealed. As with the original, the new law granted an emergency manager powers to "reject, modify or terminate labor agreements," to "strip local officials of their duties and of their pay," and to "sell off assets of a local government or school district."[10] However, unlike the original law, the new one brazenly included an amendment that immunized the law from citizen repeal through the referendum process.[11]

With these powers in place, Snyder appointed an emergency manager with expansive powers to Flint. In April 2014, with a mandate to cut costs, the emergency manager switched Flint's water source from the Detroit Water and Sewage Department to the Flint River. In October of that year, General Motors, who had contributed to the contamination of the river in the first place, stopped using water from the river because it was corroding their pistons.[12] And even though the DEQ insisted that the Flint River water was safe to drink, the state office building in Flint was receiving shipments of fresh bottled water.[13] Despite all of this, and in the face of residents' complaints that the water smelled bad, that it was discolored, and that it was causing rashes and hair loss, the state continued to claim the water was safe to drink.[14]

By leading directly to the lead poisoning of Flint residents, Governor Snyder's actions, and his denials and deflections of responsibility, reveal the antidemocratic dangers of Schmitt's political theology. Despite Snyder's persistent claims that the US Environmental Protection Agency [EPA] and local Flint officials were responsible for the crisis, an independent advisory panel that he, to his credit, appointed found that "The Flint water crisis occurred when state-appointed emergency managers replaced local representative decision-making in Flint, removing the checks and balances and public accountability that come with public decision-making."[15] According to the panel, the Flint water crisis "is a story of government failure, intransigence, unpreparedness, delay, inaction, and environmental injustice," and the governor himself, the DEQ, and the emergency manager are primarily responsible.[16] Snyder's attempt to deflect responsibility for the crisis onto local and federal government officials is as outrageous as the lead poisoning of Flint's residents is tragic. He should not be surprised that the report refuses to blame local officials—after all, he himself granted an emergency manager the power to override their authority. Nor should Wyant and the DEQ be surprised that the report refuses to blame the EPA—after all, the panel's investigation provides evidence that the DEQ "waited months before accepting EPA's offer to engage its lead (Pb) experts to help address the Flint water situation and, at times, DEQ staff were dismissive and unresponsive."[17]

Most damningly, however, the report found that the DEQ actively "worked to discredit and dismiss" local Flint residents and public health advocates who sought "to bring the issues of unsafe water, lead contamination, and increased cases of Legionellosis (Legionnaires' disease) to light."[18] Although Snyder sought to "reinvent Michigan" by implementing a more "customer service–oriented" approach to governance, he has served the residents of Flint something else—a large helping of environmental injustice.[19] And as with many other poor communities and communities of color who have been disproportionately affected by toxic waste and environmental pollution throughout the history of the United States, when the people of Flint raised concerns, pointed to the evidence,

and sought remediation, they were "aggressively dismissed" and "belit-
tled."[20] In forceful terms, the report concludes that

> The facts of the Flint water crisis lead us to the inescapable conclusion
> that this is a case of environmental injustice. Flint residents, who are
> majority Black or African American and among the most impoverished
> of any metropolitan area in the United States, did not enjoy the same
> degree of protection from environmental and health hazards as that pro-
> vided to other communities. Moreover, by virtue of their being subject
> to emergency management, Flint residents were not provided equal
> access to, and meaningful involvement in, the government decision-
> making process.[21]

Although Wyant resigned as director of the DEQ, Snyder has not
resigned, at least not at the time this book went to press. This is in keeping with the Schmittian theopolitical structure of the Flint tragedy. For
by defining the sovereign through the power to decide on (and in) a state
of exception, the sovereign is therefore also defined as immune. The power
to suspend the rule of law is equivalent to the power to transcend the rule
of law, and the power to transcend the rule of law is equivalent to the power
of immunity. To define the sovereign in this way is to define the sovereign
as morally exceptional and legally exempt.

⸎

The story of Flint is a synecdoche of a larger story of the United States—the
state of Michigan (under the Snyder administration) is to Flint what
the United States (in certain respects, and at its worst) is and has been
to the larger world. As the Snyder administration sought to "reinvent
Michigan" and deployed legislative maneuvers to claim a state of exception to save Flint, the United States, throughout its history, has justified
its "messianic imperialism" through appeal to the idea of American
exceptionalism.[22] As Schmitt's political theology illuminates the ideological drivers of the environmental injustice in Flint, the theopolitics
of American exceptionalism helps to illumine diverse aspects of the
"missionary persuasion" that runs throughout American history, from
the colonial period to the climate crisis.[23] As the Snyder administration

deflected responsibility for the Flint crisis, many Americans, including many elected officials, preponderantly Republicans, either deny that humans are driving the climate crisis, minimize the US contribution to the crisis, or deflect responsibility by pointing to other contributing factors.[24] And as the Flint crisis disproportionately impacted African Americans and the poor, so also does the climate crisis disproportionately impact poor people and people of color around the world as well as elsewhere within United States.

The tragedy in Flint did not have to happen. But it is not entirely surprising that it did. Nor is it surprising that it negatively impacted African Americans more than others and that those who are most responsible for it have sought to deny or deflect responsibility. The Flint crisis shows the tragic environmental and social fallout of an antidemocratic political theology of exception. Flint is a symbolic canary in the theopolitical coal mine and offers a compressed analogy of the inadequacies, not to mention the dangers, of the dominant American theopolitical tradition in a time of climate crisis.

With this analogy in mind, I will now turn to an analysis and critique of this tradition, paying particular attention to the connections between the theopolitics of American exceptionalism and what I will define later as the "redeemer symbolic." By tracing the migration of the redeemer symbolic through several of its historical incarnations—colonial and ecclesial, nationalist and neoliberal—I will show how this dominant American political theology is constituted by the very dynamics of extraction and externalization that fuel the climate crisis and planetary ecological emergency.

EXTRACTION AND EXTERNALIZATION IN THE REDEEMER SYMBOLIC

From its beginning, the story of American exceptionalism has effaced itself as a story. As has often been said, since Aristotle at least, all stories (as stories) should have a beginning, a middle, and an end, and the beginning is especially important. Effective stories should begin in medias res, in the middle of things, in the midst of action and the tangle of plot. But the story of American exceptionalism, at least as it is often told, begins ex nihilo, out of nothing. It thus begins, in the fashion of Peter, the disciple of Jesus and the cornerstone of the Christian church, with three denials: a denial of its embeddedness in the contingencies of nature and history, a denial of its entanglement with other stories and other worlds, and, most importantly, a denial of its founding violence. When it is told more truthfully, it begins in medias res, with a genocidal extraction of land and life from the Native American people who had lived and labored in the Americas long before Europeans arrived.

The "redeemer symbolic" is deeply rooted in American history and identity and is a central element within the theopolitics of American exceptionalism.[25] As I define it, it is a constellation of biblical and secular narratives, foremost among which are the stories of Christ as the redeeming savior of the world, which legitimates the extraction of diverse forms of value and justifies the externalization of diverse costs as the price of American exceptionalism. The redeemer symbolic is structured around a moral logic: (1) there is one who (or that) is symbolically invested with saving power; (2) this saving one is an exception and enacts an exception; (3) as an exception, the one who saves is an ontological singularity, a one who (or that) is unlike all other things of its kind, transcends the contingencies and conditions of all other things of its kind, and is immune to the constraints that bind and order all other things of its kind; (4) the exceptions enacted by this transcendent singularity entail the extraction of some kind of value and the externalization of some kind of cost, and are justified as the price of redemption. Whether manifest in the explicitly theological register of John Winthrop's "city upon a hill," or in the nationalist and imperialist registers of the doctrine of Manifest Destiny, or in its later neoliberal economic registers, the moral logic of the redeemer symbolic reverberates throughout the theopolitical story of American exceptionalism.

I will not interpret the redeemer symbolic by attending to what theologians and philosophers have had to say about the idea of redemption. My purpose is not to explore the changing reputations of redemption in the history of Christianity, or to explicate how diverse understandings of redemption are informed by, and in turn give form to, different systematic theological accounts of the nature and work of Christ, or the meanings of atonement, or the relations of justification and sanctification. Nor am

I suggesting that the redeemer symbolic has directly caused any particular event in American history. The logic of linear causation is too crude for interpreting the complex cultural effects of myth and symbol. Instead, my focus is on the cultural, social, political, and ecological impacts of the redeemer symbolic dispersed through American history rather than on an articulated theological concept of redemption. In this framing, I am applying Charles Sanders Peirce's pragmatic maxim to the symbol of redemption.[26] For Peirce, the meanings of concepts are constituted by the sum of their practical effects.[27] Meanings are not reducible to definitions or conceptual analysis. With this pragmatic approach to meaning in mind, I will interpret the practical effects of the redeemer symbolic as expressions of the meanings of American exceptionalism. I will show that when its meanings are interpreted in this way, the redeemer symbolic functions within the story of American exceptionalism to legitimate the extraction of diverse forms of value (for example, land, labor, life) and to justify the externalization of diverse forms of cost (social and ecological, for instance).

I am not suggesting that extraction and externalization exhaust the meaning of the redeemer symbolic in American history, or that the dynamic of extraction and externalization is unique to the theopolitics of American exceptionalism. For one thing, the logic of extraction and externalization is intrinsic to capitalism, and although the United States is a champion of capitalism and has been at the center of the capitalist world system for the last 150 years or so, the extraction of value and the externalization of cost are not uniquely American.[28] For another thing, the Europeans who colonized the territories that became the United States are not the only humans in history to have occupied others' lands and subjugated, enslaved, and dehumanized other people for profit. All through human history diverse human groups have believed that it was their right, duty, or burden to enslave other human individuals and groups and extract value from them in some form of pleasure or profit.

So if the dynamic of extraction and externalization is historically and politically unexceptional, what is the point of critically correlating it to the American redeemer symbolic? Ta-Nehisi Coates expresses the point well: "The banality of violence [throughout human history] can never excuse America, because America makes no claim to the banal. America believes itself exceptional, the greatest and noblest nation ever to exist, a

lone champion standing between the white city of democracy and the ter-
rorists, despots, barbarians, and other enemies of civilization."[29] The
point of correlating the dynamic of extraction and externalization to the
redeemer symbolic and to the story of American exceptionalism is to illuminate this contradiction at the core of the dominant American theopolitical tradition. The story of American exceptionalism is a particular
kind of theopolitical story—it is a story that conceals its founding extrac-
tions and denies its ongoing externalities.

It is especially important now, given the recent rise of increasingly vocal
and virulent white supremacist public discourse, the intensification of
xenophobic nativism, the deepening of Islamophobia, and the recalcitrance
of homophobia, in addition of course to the entangled climate crises of the
Anthropocene, to critically engage the dynamics of exception, extraction,
and externalization in the dominant American theopolitical tradition.

THE EX NIHILO ORIGINS OF
AMERICAN EXCEPTIONALISM

For the Native American writer Thomas King, the "magic" in stories is
not so much in their themes as "in the way meaning is refracted by cosmology."[30] Similarly, for Robert Bellah, "where a people conceives itself to
have started reveals much about its most basic self-conceptions."[31] Drawing these insights together, we see that in the American cosmology, the
ex nihilo metaphor reveals the "magic" of concealment and denial.
The ex nihilo metaphor, as used in the American cosmology, underscores
the ideas of newness, originality, and transcendence. Reflecting on the
significance of the founding, Thomas Paine wrote that "the case and circumstance of America present themselves as in the beginning of the
world. . . . We are brought at once to the point of seeing government
begin, as if we had lived in the beginning of time."[32] Rooted in an Enlightenment appeal to reason as ahistorical, Paine's comments correlate the
ex nihilo "case and circumstance of America" with the historically transcendent, unassailable rationality of the American political experiment.

Before Paine, John Locke imagined America in a biblical cadence,
writing that "In the beginning all the world was America."[33] Interpreting

these ideas, Bellah writes, "America stood for the primordial state of the world. . . . The newness which was so prominent an attribute of what was called the 'new' world was taken not just as newness to its European discovers and explorers but as newness in some pristine and absolute sense: newness from the hands of God."[34] The theme of newness reflects the sense among many early European explorers and settlers that America represented a new beginning, not only for their personal lives, but for human civilization and for the church in particular.

While Paine's ex nihilo metaphor dramatizes the transcendent origins of American exceptionalism and conceals the founding violence, Locke's analogy to the opening of the Gospel of John evokes the plot structure of the redeemer symbolic. Both allusions illustrate the arrogance with which Europeans discounted the cultural and political sophistication of the already-existing indigenous civilizations in North America. At their most benign, the early European colonizers thought of the Native Americans in terms of pure innocence, naked denizens of an Edenic paradise. More commonly, they were viewed as natural savages who needed to be converted to Christianity and domesticated into European folkways or cleared entirely out of the way along with much of the rest of the new world wilderness.

In this regard, as historian Francis Jennings has rightly suggested, American nature in the early phases of colonial settlement was "more like a widow than a virgin. Europeans did not find a wilderness here; rather, however involuntarily, they made one."[35] The earliest European and English settlements, such as Jamestown, Boston, and New Amsterdam, grew upon sites previously occupied by Indian communities. Native Americans were identified as uncivilized wilderness people that needed to be settled along with the land. Thus the so-called settlement of America was a resettlement, the occupation of a land made waste by the diseases and demoralization introduced by the newcomers. Native Americans thus were doubly invaded. They were decimated by European diseases, against which their immune systems were defenseless, which in turn diminished their cultural resistance to colonial exploitation. Their combined biological and cultural disempowerment cleared the way for Europeans' political and ecological conquest of the natural environment. Although the magic of the American ex nihilo cosmology conceals this, it turns out, as I will discuss in the next chapter, that the violence of this founding extraction was registered by the climate.

Puritan consciousness and behavior were also of course profoundly influenced by the biblical story of ancient Israel's exodus from Egypt. For the early Puritan settlers, the biblical Israelites' experience of the desert landscape as a wilderness, the site of trial and struggle, served as a metaphor for their own encounter with North American nature as a wilderness against which to struggle and through which to pass. The entire Puritan colonial venture, from departure from England to arrival in the New World, was freighted with the great theme of freeing Christianity from bondage to error. With all of this at stake, the land and native inhabitants of North America played the role of adversarial foil against which the Puritan theological and ecclesiological drama of liberty was plotted.

This is expressed with white supremacist venom in the infamous Senate speech given by Indiana Republican senator Albert J. Beveridge at the turn of the twentieth century:

> God has not been preparing the English-speaking and Teutonic peoples for a thousand years for nothing but vain and idle self-contemplation and self-admiration. No. He made us master organizers of the world to establish system where chaos reigned. He has given us the spirit of progress to overwhelm the forces of reaction throughout the earth. He has made us adept in government that we may administer government among savage and senile peoples. Were it not for such a force as this the world would relapse into barbarism and night. And of all our race He has marked the American people as His chosen nation to finally lead in the redemption of the world.[36]

Beveridge's quotation illustrates the racialist cast of the theopolitics of redemption and its crossing of sacred and secular planes of meaning; it captures its migrations through theological, political, social, and economic spheres of American life. Through its crossings and migrations, it is held together by the assumption that saving power—whether that power is of God, the nation, or a racial group—is sovereign, invulnerable, and singular.

Though rooted in the biblical imaginary and millennialist thinking that shaped the Puritan mission, the redeemer symbolic and the story of American exceptionalism have migrated through American history from its original theological and ecclesiological contexts to secular political and economic registers of meaning. Each of these registers is freighted with an incriminating history of effects. In its early phase, the emergent theopolitics of American exceptionalism was buttressed by the story of Israel's exodus and the redeemer symbolic justified the extractive colonization of the people, wealth, and land of Native Americans. The trinity of exception, extraction, and externalization also supported the enslavement of Africans upon which the wealth and economic power of the United States are founded. As the Anglo-Saxon supremacist form of exception continues to mold contemporary racism, nativism, and xenophobia, as the Trump regime demonstrates on a regular basis, the logic of extraction continues to factor in to destructive American approaches to the natural environment, from industrial pollution to contemporary climate denial. And as we will see, the redeemer symbolic has also provided a plot structure for American military and economic imperialism, from the Revolutionary War and Civil War to our misadventures in Iraq and the War on Terror, and from the nationalist doctrine of Manifest Destiny in the nineteenth century to the global doctrine of neoliberalism in the twenty-first.

ECCLESIAL REDEMPTION

The story of biblical Israel undergirded the sense of national chosenness carried over to the New World by English Puritans. This sense of chosenness was further reinforced by the covenantal theology of the English reformer William Tyndale. Under the influence of Martin Luther, Tyndale presented several translations of books from the New and Old Testaments in the first half of the sixteenth century. The chronology of these translations reflects Tyndale's increasing conviction that the theme of covenant, especially as crystallized in the blessings and curses pronounced in the book of Deuteronomy, provided the key to understanding God's will for the church in general and for England in particular. The second edition of Tyndale's New Testament translation in 1534 presents his covenantal theology in its strongest form. This translation, along with his translation from 1531 of the Old Testament book of Jonah, in which he asserted that God had sent prophets to England in past times who had been ignored, provided the basis for Tyndale's theology of national covenant, which implied that England, as Israel of old, was God's chosen nation.

The effects of Tyndale's translations cannot be understood apart from the Reformation turbulence that roiled the English monarchies. The monarchy of young Edward VI (1547–1553), generally favorable to the cause of Protestant reform, deserves special mention. Seeking counsel on God's covenantal expectations for England, Edward dispatched his archbishop, Thomas Cranmer, to Zurich to meet with the Swiss reformer Heinrich Bullinger. Echoing Tyndale's covenantal translations, Bullinger tasked the monarch and England with the restoration of the church to its purist primitive form. Corroborating this counsel, the Reformed theologian Martin Bucer's treatise *De Regno Christi* emphatically argued that through its restoration of the original church, England could usher in the Kingdom of Christ. This counsel and the resulting sympathy of Edward for reform were heartening to the growing numbers of Protestants in England. Their hopes were quickly dashed, however, when Edward was succeeded by Mary Tudor (1553–1558). The daughter of Henry VIII (1509–1547) and Catherine of Aragon, Queen Mary was resentful of her father in particular and Protestants in general. Seeking to return England to the Church of Rome, she executed hundreds of English Protestants while others fled to Holland and other Protestant havens. Some of these exiles, radicalized by the actions of "Bloody Mary" and influenced by encounters with John Calvin, became some of England's first Puritans.

Puritanism thus emerged in England as a separatist nationalist movement committed to the restoration of the primitive church. Abandoning the project of reforming England from within, and as a result of increasing royal persecution, some of these separatists carried their convictions with them to the New World in 1620, when the Mayflower's Pilgrims settled Plymouth Colony, and later the Puritan settlement of Massachusetts Bay Colony in 1630. The early Puritan form of the redeemer symbolic is nowhere more famously expressed than by John Winthrop in his sermon "A Model of Christian Charity" from 1630, given aboard the *Arbella*. After pronouncing on the proper Christian relation between individuals and community, the inevitable presence of social inequalities amid spiritual equality, and the importance of mutuality, reciprocity, and the charitable obligations of the rich to the poor, Winthrop concluded his sermon with an account of the blessings and curses of the covenant and the global and historical importance of the Puritan mission:

> The Lord will be our God, and delight to dwell among us, as his own people, and will command a blessing upon us in all our ways, so that we shall see much more of his wisdom, power, goodness and truth, than formerly we have been acquainted with. We shall find that the God of Israel is among us, when ten of us shall be able to resist a thousand of our enemies; when he shall make us a praise and glory that men shall say of succeeding plantations, "may the Lord make it like that of New England." For we must consider that we shall be as a city upon a hill. The eyes of all people are upon us. So that if we shall deal falsely with our God in this work we have undertaken, and so cause him to withdraw his present help from us, we shall be made a story and a by-word through the world. We shall open the mouths of enemies to speake evil of the ways of God, and all professors for God's sake. We shall shame the faces of many of God's worthy servants, and cause their prayers to be turned into curses upon us till we be consumed out of the good land whither we are a going.[37]

Winthrop's sermon crystallizes the meanings of the redeemer symbolic in its early ecclesiological phase. The Puritan errand to "New England" to redeem the church to its purist original form was a grand historical enterprise, to be witnessed by the "eyes of all people." The redeeming project was embedded within a covenant with the sovereign God of Israel who saves those who are obedient to him and curses those who disobey. God is the singular, omnipotent locus of sovereignty, the sovereign of the covenant to whom fealty and obedience were necessary if the church was to be redeemed. And as the introductory parts of Winthrop's sermon specify, covenantal obedience required mutual obligation and service to one another. But this mutualism had boundaries; it was selective and highly exclusive. The plantations were hierarchically ordered, with ministers and magistrates holding positions of greatest power, and then church members, and then others. Sociopolitical hierarchy and economic inequality reinforced each other. It was common for those with more power, those held in highest esteem, to be granted outsized landholdings. In the first generation of Massachusetts Puritans, for example, thirty-two men owned more than fifty-seven thousand acres. Winthrop himself, along with other political and ecclesial elites such as John Endicott, Thomas Dudley, and John Cotton, was among those who received generous land grants such as these. While the community was to be ordered internally by justice and mercy and love of God and neighbor, the obligations of mutual love extended only to those who embraced and exemplified the terms of the covenant as determined by those who held greatest ecclesial, political, and economic power.

In the ecclesial phase of the redeemer symbolic, the redemption in question is the redemption of the church to be brought about by Providence through Puritan example; the sovereign agent of redemption is the God of Israel who will save those who are obedient to his purposes and damn those who are disobedient; and the medium of redemption is covenant. These symbols formatted a political ethos that was radically hierarchical, with magistrates and ministers exerting their sovereignty over all but God. Socially, morally, and theologically, conformity was prized above all other concerns. The "New World" was no place of freedom. Dissenters such as Roger Williams and Anne Hutchinson, despite their Christian piety, were banished from Massachusetts. The threat of externalization became a tool of social order. The decimation of native populations and the theft of their land, along with the harsh internal discipline within the early plantations, were theologically justified as means to the redemptive purification of the church.

REDEMPTIVE NATIONALISM

The redeemer symbolic is also expressed in both spiritual and political forms of American millennialism. The spiritual form of millennialism emerged out of the powerful effects of the Great Awakening, which reversed the religious decline of the second- and third-generation Puritans. Inspired by what he saw as the spiritual regeneration of New England, the Great Awakening theologian Jonathan Edwards reflected that "It is not unlikely that this work of God's Spirit, so extraordinary and wonderful, is the dawning, or at least a prelude of that glorious work of God, so often foretold in scripture, which, in the progress and issue of it, shall renew the world of mankind."[38] For Edwards and others, the spiritual effects of the Great Awakening confirmed that America was the New World chosen by God to become the site of the birthing of a new heaven and earth.

The French and Indian War (1754–1763) further reinforced the millennialist expectations of the Great Awakening. The defeat of the Catholic French, who were aided by Native Americans, justified the idea not only that America was the chosen setting for the thousand-year reign of Christ, but that Anglo-Saxon Protestantism was the purest religious expression of the original church. This explicitly anti-Catholic interpretation of the war presaged two further shifts in American millennialist thinking—the shift from its spiritual to its political form and a shift in the locus of sovereignty from God to nation. These shifts mark a profound migration of the early Puritan vision of a nation chosen by the sovereign God to redeem the church to a secularized, Enlightenment vision of American democracy in which the United States itself, as a nation, was understood as the sovereign agent of redemption.

Ernest Lee Tuveson describes these shifts as a reversal of the Augustinian political theology that had predominated up until that point.[39] For Augustine, the City of God, the mystical communion of the faithful, would not be fulfilled until the end of time. It was an eschatological promise, manifest in part since the resurrection, but not to be fully realized until the consummation of time. The migration of the redeemer symbolic into its nationalist phase marks a reversal of this Augustinian vision. The Declaration of Independence in 1776 and the Revolutionary War added new layers to American millennialism. Not only was America the national setting chosen by God for the thousand-year reign of Christ, not only was Protestantism the favored expression of the original church, but now the freedoms and unalienable rights (of some) and the democratic ideals of the new nation were also signs of God's special favor toward the United States and of the United States' special burden as an agent of redemption in the larger world.

In a sermon from 1783, Ezra Stiles, president of Yale University at the time, expressed the convergence of these millennial themes in a way that simultaneously echoes and politicizes Winthrop's sermon a century and a half before:

> This great American revolution, this recent political phenomenon of a new sovereignty arising among the sovereign powers of the earth, will be attended to and contemplated by all nations. . . . That prophecy of Daniel is now literally fulfilling—there shall be a universal traveling "too and fro, and knowledge shall be increased." This knowledge will be brought home and treasured up in America: and being here digested and carried to the highest perfection, may reblaze back from America to Europe, Asia and Africa, and illumine the world with TRUTH and LIBERTY.[40]

As Richard T. Hughes has argued, Stiles's reflections represent both a continuation and a transformation of the redeemer symbolic: "What remained constant was the expectation that a millennial age would shortly dawn. What changed was the way Americans conceptualized that age."[41] During the settlement and colonial periods, as during the Great Awakening, millennialist expectations and the promise of redemption were interpreted through the prism of divine sovereignty. But through the revolutionary and early national period, the locus of redemption began to shift: "The transition from the sovereignty of God to the sovereignty of the people with their unalienable rights marked a radical shift in the thinking of the American populace. Most of all, it tells us that the old Puritan dream of a distinctly Christian state no longer controlled American expectations. In its place stood a new vision of liberty and democratic self-government, a vision generated not by Puritanism but by the Enlightenment."[42]

This transition is evident in changing ideas about the natural world and the land, as represented, for instance, by Thomas Jefferson and his particular brand of republicanism. As is well known, Jefferson's work as a political champion of democracy was deeply intertwined with his ardent agrarianism. His *Notes on the State of Virginia* presents one of his most eloquent expressions of this ideological convergence. While Jefferson's commentary on the land sometimes draws on biblical imagery, he interprets the significance of American nature in terms of its benefit for moral and political virtue, rather than as a source of religious salvation. Those who labor in the earth, he writes, "are the chosen people of God, if ever he had a chosen people, whose breasts he has made his peculiar deposit for substantial and genuine virtue."[43] From this, Jefferson draws a political conclusion: "Cultivators of the earth are the most virtuous and independent citizens."[44] He thus uses biblical imagery to connect the cultivation of the land to the cultivation of moral and political virtue and the foundations of democracy. Jefferson's thinking about nature thus demonstrates both continuity and difference between colonial and early national American attitudes toward the natural world and, through this, a bridge to a new phase of the redeemer symbolic. For Jefferson, the land had a deeply and primarily political significance: those who cultivate it are themselves being morally cultivated for democratic citizenship. It is more than ironic, then, that Jefferson, who so loved the land and the cultivation of democratic principles, failed to include within his political vision the many thousands of Africans brought to America to work that land as slaves.

As reflected in Jefferson's ideas about nature, the redeemer symbolic crosses over from an explicitly religious register in the contact and colonial eras into a secular Enlightenment political register during the early national period. Correlatively, the locus of sovereignty shifts from God to nation and the symbolic medium is transformed from sacred covenant to social and political contract. As H. Richard Niebuhr describes this crossing, "The old idea of American Christians as a chosen people who had been called to a special task was turned into the notion of a chosen nation especially favored."[45] This calling and task are vividly expressed in the doctrine of Manifest Destiny. Manifest Destiny was a doctrine of territorial extraction and imperial exceptionalism. In its most straightforward terms, it was about the westward expansion of the new United States, a classic colonial doctrine of territorial expansion. But it was about more than territory as well. It was premised on the idea that the ordained purpose of the United States was to spread through sovereign example and imperial expansion the ideals of constitutional democracy to the rest of the world. The journalist John L. O'Sullivan was the first to give literal expression to this idea. His argument for the United States as the "nation of futurity" sets the stage:

The American people having derived their origin from many other nations, and the Declaration of National Independence being entirely based on the great principle of human equality, these facts demonstrate at once our disconnected position as regards any other nation; that we have, in reality, but little connection with the past history of any of them, and still less with all antiquity, its glories, or its crimes. On the contrary, our national birth was the beginning of a new history, the formation and progress of an untried political system, which separates us from the past and connects us with the future only; and so far as regards the entire development of the natural rights of man, in moral, political, and national life, we may confidently assume that our country is destined to be the great nation of futurity. . . .

Yes, we are the nation of progress, of individual freedom, of universal enfranchisement. . . .

We must onward to the fulfillment of our mission—to the entire development of the principle of our organization—freedom of conscience, freedom of person, freedom of trade and business pursuits, universality of freedom and equality. This is our high destiny, and in nature's eternal, inevitable decree of cause and effect we must accomplish it. All this will be our future history, to establish on earth the moral dignity and salvation of man—the immutable truth and beneficence of God. For this blessed mission to the nations of the world, which are shut out from the life-giving light of truth, has America been chosen; and her high example shall smite unto death the tyranny of kings, hierarchs, and oligarchs, and carry the glad tidings of peace and good will where myriads now endure an existence scarcely more enviable than that of beasts of the field. Who, then, can doubt that our country is destined to be the great nation of futurity?[46]

O'Sullivan's vision of the moral innocence, superiority, and destiny of the United States pivots the redeemer symbolic from its sacred covenantal to its exceptional nationalist form. This is evident in his later arguments for the annexations of Texas and California, where he refers to the American "manifest destiny to overspread the continent allotted by Providence for the free development of our yearly multiplying millions."[47] And in an editorial later that year, where O'Sullivan argued for the annexation of

Oregon, he provides an explicitly political rather than a merely territorial purpose to the doctrine when he refers to "the right of our manifest destiny to overspread and to possess the whole of the continent which Providence has given us for the development of the great experiment of liberty and federated self-government entrusted to us."[48]

The idea of Manifest Destiny as articulated by O'Sullivan fully displays the transpositioning of the theological and political registers of the redeemer symbolic, and the transformation of biblical chosenness into national exceptionalism. It ties the revolutionary and early national discourses of rights and liberty back to the earlier Puritan covenantal theology. The right to "overspread" and "possess," or to extract land and life from Native Americans and occupy territories, follows from the premise that the continent has been given to Anglo-Saxons as a covenantal blessing merited by the righteousness of their cause. Along these lines, Jedediah Purdy writes that the "Providential imagination reworked conquest, expulsion, and genocide into a benign account of necessary and lawful progress."[49] Implicit within this rendering of Manifest Destiny is the exculpatory premise of exception, that if the providentially gifted land is indeed used for the further development of "liberty and federated self-government," then the young American nation can rest satisfied with the knowledge that what outsiders might condemn, and what Native Americans experienced as raw imperial ambition, was nothing of the sort. The moral cost of extracting indigenous life and land was justified as an externality necessary to advancing and sustaining the cause of American exceptionalism. Territorial extraction— which led to the displacement, "removal," and slaughter of hundreds of thousands of Native Americans and an unprovoked, transparently imperial war with Mexico and the theft of its northern half—was legitimated through the intersecting theological and secular political registers of the redeemer symbolic. As Richard Hughes powerfully puts this, although Puritans in the seventeenth century "understood that chosenness was due entirely to God's will and initiative," rather than their own righteousness, by the nineteenth century "God had become a puppet in the hands of the American people who had placed on God an indisputable claim. The assumption seemed to be that God could hardly refuse to choose America, since the nation so manifestly exemplified God's will."[50]

As the Puritan idea of redemption is transformed into the doctrine of Manifest Destiny, the aspirational virtues of covenant are displaced by claims to special privilege, colonial extraction, and imperial expansion. And as predestined salvation was understood by early Puritans to be manifest visibly through the righteousness of the saints, American exceptionalism was understood as morally meritocratic. In the nationalist phase of the redeemer symbolic, the nations of the world were to be redeemed by the witness of the American Republic, the sovereign agent of this redemption was the government of the United States, and the medium of covenant was transubstantiated into the imperialist doctrine of Manifest Destiny. On the home front, the redemptive mission of the "great experiment of liberty and federated self-government" justified the extraction of Native American land and the price of exception entailed that the moral cost of devastating Native American life would be externalized.

REDEMPTIVE CAPITALISM: FROM ECONOMIC MORALISM TO THE MONETIZATION OF THE REDEEMER SYMBOLIC

In the decades following its birth, the young United States turned its attention to the work of building the nation by settlement, exploiting its natural resources, and developing a market economy. The view of the wilderness as adversary waned; instead, Americans increasingly regarded the land as a stock of resources and as a metaphor for the nation's status as a model of enlightened democracy. Though the wilderness came to be valued in these new ways, its original inhabitants, the Native Americans, continued to be exploited. Andrew Jackson, seventh president of the United States, drew a clear connection between the land and a rationale for oppressing peoples regarded as outside the national body politic. Jackson is as infamous for his policy of Indian Removal, the forced evacuation of Native Americans from their ancestral lands, as he is famous for heralding the spreading market revolution, with its appetite for natural resources and demand for transport routes.[51] He brought these themes into combination in the rhetorical question he posed in his First Annual

Message to Congress (December 8, 1829): "What good man would prefer a country covered with forests and ranged by a few thousand savages to our extensive Republic, studded with cities, towns, and prosperous farms, embellished with all the improvements which art can devise or industry execute?"[52] This question was in many ways answered by the powerful rise of American manufacturing and industrialization, a swelling urban population, and westward expansion, all features of the period following Jackson's election to the presidency.

The most explicit connections between the redeemer symbolic and industrial capitalism go back to the years just after the Civil War. Both the South and the North thought their causes divinely favored, but the North won and viewed their victory in redemptive terms, the saving of the Union. After the war, however, the redeemer symbolic quickly took on an economic valence. While the war devastated the slave-economy in the South, the economy of the North quickly prospered. The infrastructure of the northern military-industrial complex paved the way for the American industrial revolution, led to the rise of American manufacturing power, and fueled the global ascendancy of American capitalism. The enslavement of African bodies and the extraction of value from their labor are the roots of American economic power. Although "the idea that the commodification and suffering and forced labor of African Americans is what made the United States powerful and rich is not an idea that people necessarily are happy to hear," as Edward E. Baptist writes in his recent book, "it is the truth."[53] Continuing, he writes:

> From 1783 at the end of the American Revolution to 1861, the number of slaves in the United States increased five times over, and all this expansion produced a powerful nation. For white enslavers were able to force enslaved African-American migrants to pick cotton faster and more efficiently than free people. Their practices rapidly transformed the southern states into the dominant force in the global cotton market, and cotton was the world's most widely traded commodity at the time, as it was the key raw material during the first century of the industrial revolution. The returns from cotton monopoly powered the modernization of the rest of the American economy, and by the time of the Civil War, the United States had become the second nation to undergo large-scale industrialization.[54]

Indeed, as Ta-Nehesi Coates writes, the extraction of value from black bodies is an American economic tradition:

> As slaves we were this country's first windfall, the down payment on its freedom. After the ruin and liberation of the Civil War came Redemption for the unrepentant South and Reunion, and our bodies became this country's second mortgage. In the New Deal we were their guestroom, their finished basement. And today, with a sprawling prison system, which has turned the warehouse of black bodies into a jobs program for Dreamers and a lucrative investment for Dreamers; today, when 8 percent of the world's prisoners are black men, our bodies have refinanced the Dream of being white. Black life is cheap, but in America black bodies are a natural resource of incomparable value.[55]

The migration of the redeemer symbolic into its economic register was aided by two other historical circumstances, rising economic inequality and ethnic and class prejudice. This was the period that gave rise to significant wealth and income inequality at the turn of the century. It was the time of the Robber Barons, the Carnegies, Vanderbilts, and Rockefellers, personifications of the Gilded Age. It was also a time of massive Southern and Eastern European immigration into the United States. These immigrants took up many of the low-paying manual labor and factory jobs during this period, thus constituting the ethnic white base of the American working class. Northern European and Anglo-Saxons thought of Southern and Eastern Europeans as ethnic and cultural inferiors already. The division of labor in the industrial North only reinforced this ethnic prejudice. This structure of ethnic and class prejudice mirrored the racial dynamics in the South, where African slaves had been freed only to find themselves indentured to white landholders, whose racial superiority complex was circularly reinforced by the oppressive impoverishment-by-design of the sharecropping system. In both the North and the South, then, political and economic power were concentrated among ethnically and racially privileged white elites, while poverty and economic struggle became the condition of the ethnically marginalized and the racially oppressed. As a result, white supremacy was tautologically reinforced by the structuring of racial and ethnic privilege and prejudice into the socioeconomic system.

These dynamics aided and abetted the transformation of the redeemer symbolic into a moralistic economic ideology that assumed, all evidence to the contrary, that the free enterprise system was a level playing field and an equal-opportunity employer. The moral correlate of this assumption is that poverty and wealth are indices of effort and ingenuity, rather than the contingent effects of economic policy, social prejudice, and political power. This economic moralism was an offshoot of Puritan covenantal theology, according to which "business success was a sign of God's providence and a token of benediction for mastery over others."[56] William Lawrence, the Episcopal bishop of Massachusetts, gave voice to this conviction in 1901: "To seek for and earn wealth is a sign of a natural, vigorous and strong character. . . . In the long run, it is only to the man of morality that wealth comes. . . . Godliness is in league with riches."[57] This assertion reflects the persistent and pervasive prejudice in American society that money is a moral metric and that wealth is convertible with moral worth—while poverty and unemployment are the wages of moral vice and irresponsibility, riches are sure to flow from righteousness.

The moralized economic form of the redeemer symbolic provided the cultural groundwork for the formation of American neoliberalism, a synthesis of the "unalienable rights" of life, liberty, and the pursuit of happiness with the economic principles of deregulation, privatization, and free trade. The George W. Bush administration's 2002 National Security Strategy (NSS), which presented what came to be known as the "Bush Doctrine," illustrated the transformation of the Puritan strategy of redeeming the church through evangelical witness into the neoliberal missiology of American hegemony. Although the doctrine is best known for its vigorous expression of neoconservative principles—the unilateral assertion of American power, an apocalyptic moral dualism of "us" and "them" (or friend/enemy), and the exceptional claim of preemptive "first strike"— these principles were inspired by an equally vital neoliberalism, as illustrated by this account of the American national security interest:

A strong world economy enhances our national security by advancing prosperity and freedom in the rest of the world. Economic growth supported by free trade and free markets . . . allows people to lift their lives out of poverty, spurs economic and legal reform, and the fight against corruption, and . . . reinforces the habits of liberty. . . . We will use our economic engagement with other countries to underscore the benefits of policies that generate higher productivity and sustained economic growth, including ... pro-growth legal and regulatory policies to encourage business investment, innovation, and entrepreneurial activity; tax policies—particularly lower marginal tax rates—that improve incentives for work and investment.[58]

With respect to the correlations among these principles, the NSS declared that the faith of Americans and indeed the rest of the world need not be blind. Reflecting Francis Fukuyama's thesis in *The End of History and the Last Man* that, with the collapse of state socialism, liberal capitalism had established itself as the spiritually sublated and self-evidently superior form of political economy, the NSS asserted that "The lessons of history are clear: market economies, not command-and-control economies with the heavy hand of government, are the best way to promote prosperity and reduce poverty. Policies that strengthen market incentives, that deregulate, privatize, and liberate trade, are deemed to be relevant for all economies—industrialized countries, emerging markets, and the developing world."[59] Of course it is conveniently not mentioned that the lessons of history also indicate that these policies lead to oligarchic concentrations of wealth and power, increasing economic inequality and social fragmentation, the disempowerment of working classes and the emergence of a permanent underclass, the rise of precarious workers, and the ecologically reckless, intensified extraction of fossil fuels and the fomenting of climate injustice.

However, before the NSS came out, Bush telegraphed what would become its guiding principles with some of his more peculiar comments immediately after 9/11. Though the claim that he told Americans to "go shopping" seems to be apocryphal, he did say, in a speech on September 27, 2001, that "one of the great goals of this nation's war is to restore public confidence in the airline industry. It's to tell the traveling public: Get on board. Do your business around the country. Fly and enjoy America's great destination spots. Get down to Disney World in Florida. Take your families and enjoy life, the way we want it to be enjoyed."[60] And several weeks later, on October 17, 2001, he solicited California business leaders to support an appeal for "trade promotion power," which would allow his administration to enact its trade vision by limiting congress to the passive role of either affirming or denying trade accords. In a speech filled with frequent references to the American entrepreneurial spirit, tax rebates, low interest, and cheap energy, he assured his audience that the United States would defeat terror "by expanding and encouraging world trade."[61]

The NSS consolidated these sentiments into a security doctrine by strategically conflating political and moral freedom with the market principles of competitive production, trade, and exchange: "If you can make something that others value, you should be able to sell it to them. If others make something that you value, you should be able to buy it. This is real freedom."[62] As William Finnegan provocatively wrote at the time, this construction of "real" freedom "makes vulgar Marxism look subtle and humane. The only 'real freedom' is commercial freedom. Free speech, a free press, religious freedom, political freedom, all these are secondary at best. There is a lockstep logic here, an airbrushed history, that suggests a closed intellectual system—the capitalist equivalent, perhaps, of Maoism or Wahhabism."[63] Although Finnegan sharply critiques the Bush doctrine's mirroring of the ideological systems it opposes, he doesn't acknowledge the theological roots of its "closed system" or its moral and political dualism. For the righteous ecclesial exclusivism of Puritan theology is expressed here in the registers of neoliberal triumphalism and neoconservative apocalyptic. Though the context and idiom are different, the genetic imprint is clear. Hughes explicates the structural identities as follows:

> If God had singled out America as his chosen instrument among all the nations of the earth, then America had every right to engage in economic expansion. If God blessed the righteous with wealth and cursed sinners with poverty, then it stood to reason that God *required* economic expansion. If capitalism was rooted in the natural order of things, then American economic expansion partook of the natural order as well. If America was a Christian nation, then the work of economic expansion was an act of Christian charity. And if part of the American mission was to hasten the redemption of the world and the final golden age, then economic expansion was . . . a significant part of the redemptive process.[64]

The monetization of the redeemer symbolic, illustrated by the Bush doctrine, also played a role in debates between Republicans and Democrats during the 2012 presidential campaign, when President Barack Obama suggested that Republican budget priorities amounted to a thinly veiled form of social Darwinism. The analogy was accurate insofar as Republicans sought to continue to slash taxes for the wealthy, deepen cuts to social welfare, and further deregulate the very business and financial sectors that had led to the economic recession in 2008. In Darwinian idiom, Republican fiscal policy magnifies the power of the wealthy by creating an environment that selects for their interests. And given the ferocious financial distortions of American electoral politics unleashed by the Supreme Court's decision in *Citizens United* to conflate money with political speech and to equate associations with individuals, unequal economic empowerment reproduces unequal political power.[65] The result of this, as Jeffrey Stout writes, is that although the people "retain the right to vote . . . their effective political voice appears to be dwindling as rapidly as the average wage earner's share in the common wealth."[66]

Though Obama has cited the influence of Reinhold Niebuhr's Christian realism on his political philosophy, H. Richard Niebuhr's interpretation of American Protestantism in *The Kingdom of God in America* better describes the roots of this economic ideology. For this Niebuhr, the structural logic of American government is thoroughly Calvinist. If God's power and goodness are sovereign and absolute, then the value and trustworthiness of all human institutions are relativized. This suspicion of human institutions produces an obvious dilemma when it comes to building a nation and establishing a government. As Niebuhr argues, "The dilemma of Protestantism [is that it] had no will to power and in view of its positive principle [divine sovereignty] could have none, for supreme power belonged only to God and evil resulted from every human arrogation of his dominion. . . . As a theory of *divine* construction the Protestant movement was hard put to it to provide principles for human construction [of systems of social and political order]."[67] Given the theological claim that human institutions cannot be trusted and that unchecked power tends to absolutize itself, the safest way to establish a government is to diffuse power by distributing the tasks of governance across different branches and giving the people the right to elect their representatives. The American system of divided government is a politically institutionalized means for coping with the "dilemma of [Calvinist] Protestantism."

But why were these same ideas not integrated with equal foresight into American capitalism? Why didn't the champions of governmental "checks and balances" advocate also for the economic application of this principle? Niebuhr's explanation for this was that American capitalism in the eighteenth century was "a relatively modest and harmless thing whose growth toward an absolutism like that which church and state had exercised could not be foreseen."[68] But to the extent that corporate power now vastly exceeds the powers of church and state, American capitalism needs its own countervailing "checks and balances." Although it can be argued that the free market incorporates democratic principles through its inclusive and competitive entrepreneurialism, structural integration of the system of "checks and balances" requires the *internal* democratization of businesses and corporations. For the American economy to become more truly democratic, workers and stakeholders, not merely executives and shareholders, should be granted power sufficient to "check and balance" the tendency of the power of capital to concentrate.

By electing Donald J. Trump to the presidency, the United States has moved even further away from fulfilling this democratic ideal. Indeed, as the journalist Julian Borer observes, Trump is approaching the presidency "in the spirit of a tycoon making a new acquisition, overseeing the merger of Trump Inc and America Inc—a merger in which it is far from clear which would be the senior partner."[69] In this sense, the election of Trump is the apotheosis of the neoliberal phase of the redeemer symbolic. The redeemer symbolic comes full circle: the free market is revered as sovereign, transcendent, and providential; corporate tax cuts and deregulation provide the keys to the Kingdom of God; government is the Whore of Babylon; affluence is a sign of righteousness; and American capitalism has become a sacred crusade.

❦

While the election of Trump epitomizes the neoliberal transubstantiation of the redeemer symbolic, neoliberalism itself functions as the dominant cultural ideology of the Anthropocene. As Adrian Parr provocatively puts this, "Environmental degradation is the concrete form of late capitalism."[70] Sustained by a pervasive social ethic and political logic, the neoliberal form of late capitalism incarnates the dangerously unsustainable human and environmental impacts of an exceptionalist, extractive, and externalizing theopolitics. As a social ethic, neoliberalism treats the market as the model of all other social relations. Neoliberalism is committed to the proposition that, as David Harvey writes, "human well-being can best be advanced by liberating individual entrepreneurial freedoms and skills within an institutional framework characterized by strong property rights, free markets and free trade."[71] Interpersonal life and associational life are formatted in competitive, transactional, and contractual terms, and the language of interests, shareholders, and cost-benefit analyses takes the place of the language of moral responsibility and the common good. By minimizing the social welfare functions of the state and assuming that the market is the most efficient, rational, just means for allocating goods and services, the political logic of neoliberalism is driven by the imperative to deregulate the market and to privatize public services. But the political logic of neoliberalism is not antigovernmental in an absolute sense. Although social, environmental, and consumer regulations are anathema to the neoliberal mindset, the neoliberal construct of the free market depends on the state to create and protect legal entities such as corporate personhood and to open new markets through global trade agreements. While assaulting the social welfare functions of the state with one hand, neoliberal actors and institutions aggressively lobby the state to support their own welfare with the other.

Although neoliberalism as a cultural ideology reflects these general characteristics, there really is no such thing as neoliberalism in general. Neoliberalism is not a singular thing. It is a history of various motivations, policies, philosophical orientations, and effects. William Davies, who aptly describes neoliberalism as the "disenchantment of politics by economics," argues that neoliberalism should be interpreted in terms of three distinct but overlapping historical phases.[72] He refers to the first phase, from the late 1970s through the 1980s, as "combative neoliberalism." This is the period of neoliberalism's emergence and consolidation, represented by the theoretic vision of Friedrich Hayek and by the center-right policies of Reagan and Thatcher. Combative neoliberalism took form as a "self-conscious insurgency . . . aimed at combating and ideally destroying the enemies of liberal capitalism" and as a set of policies and tactics, especially antilabor legislation, "aimed at undermining the possibility of socialism."[73] As Davies rightly notes, the ideological structure of neoliberalism, rooted in the binary opposition of liberal capitalism and socialism, reflects the friend/enemy logic in Schmitt's concept of the political.

After the fall of the Berlin wall in 1989, and in the absence of a coherent socialist opposition, neoliberalism enters what Davies refers to as its "normative" phase, which lasts until (and precipitates) the global financial crisis of 2008. As Davies explains, "Once the horizons of political hope had been delimited to a single political-economic system . . . the neoliberal *telos* became a constructivist one, of rendering market-based metrics and instruments the measure of all human worth, not only inside the market but, crucially, outside it as well."[74] The neoliberal project during this phase entails demonstrating not only the productivity and efficiency but also the fairness of neoliberalism, as reflected by the application of strict cost-benefit analyses and corporate accounting methodologies in the nonprofit sector, social services, and philanthropy. Because the normative project required a more socially interventionist mode of government, it was driven by the center-left political logic of the "Third Way." The irony of the morally driven normative phase of neoliberalism is that its implosion in 2008 was brought about in large part due to the morally unscrupulous accounting and auditing culture that pervaded the financial sector.

The Great Recession fomented concerns with the national debt, which the previous decades of neoliberal tax cuts had massively inflated, and led to the austerity policies that constitute neoliberalism's current phase, which Davies defines as "punitive." By tethering "economic dependency and moral failure" to debt, punitive neoliberalism justifies the governmental and societal unleashing of "hatred and violence upon members of their own population."[75] As Davies observes, and as I argued at the beginning of this chapter, the Schmittian structure of this phase of neoliberalism is such that "the 'enemies' targeted now are largely disempowered and internal to the neoliberal system itself."[76] This is precisely what we see in the Flint crisis.

The Flint crisis brings the human and environmental dangers of neoliberalism into dramatic relief. While Governor Snyder's aspiration to "reinvent Michigan" by instituting a new "government management model" based on best business practices and principles perfectly exemplifies the political ethos of neoliberalism, his effort to advance a customer service–oriented approach to governance illustrates the neoliberal social ethic. This political logic and social ethic paved the way to the Flint tragedy. Although the externalization of human and environmental costs is necessary to sustaining the neoliberal illusion of a free and fair market, the Flint tragedy shows not only that externalities always end up costing someone somewhere, but that they are often internalized by— and, in this case, literally ingested by—those who are already the most vulnerable.

In these ways, then, the Flint tragedy reveals the concrete human and environmental impacts of neoliberalism. It also offers a prismatic view of the mutual refractions of the exceptionalist, extractive, and externalizing themes of the dominant American political theology. It shows that sovereign power exercised in and through a state of emergency exception, even in the name of redemption (or "reinventing Michigan"), can cause harm on a scale that creates new emergencies. It also reveals the diverse ways in which the logic of extraction manifests itself, including through the extraction of democratic voice and process. While the physical costs of the Flint crisis will be embodied by the people of Flint through the long-term effects of lead poisoning, the political costs of the democratic extraction will be manifest through deepened citizen cynicism and a metastasizing sense of political disempowerment. Thus the people of Flint are what Walt Whitman described, in the epigraph for this chapter, as "specimens of the cost" of the theopolitics of American exceptionalism. While this chapter has focused in on some of the human "specimens of the cost" of American exceptionalism, in the next chapter I will expand out to a broader view of the planetary and more-than-human "specimens of the cost" of human species exceptionalism.

2

THE ANTHROPOCENE AND
CLIMATE WICKEDNESS

The shape of the Anthropocene is a political, ethical and aesthetic question. It will answer questions about what life is worth, what people owe one another, and what in the world is awesome or beautiful enough to preserve or (re)create.

—JEDEDIAH PURDY[1]

I t has only been a little more than a half-century since the publication of the famous images of Earth from outer space "Blue Marble" (1972) and "Earthrise" (1968). And it has only been a little more than a quarter-century since the American writer and climate activist Bill McKibben announced the "end of nature" in 1989.[2] But as a result of the intensifying pace and deepening ecological impacts of human interventions over these years, an alternative set of images and ideas comes to mind. Rather than picturing the Earth as a ball of bold blue suspended in the void of black space, we now see the Earth as a hall of mirrors. For wherever we look into Earth's systems, whether geological, hydrological, or atmospheric, we see a peculiar image reflected back. What we see, rather than the end of nature, is the end of the idea of the human as set apart from nature.

To live in this context is to live in the time of the Anthropocene, literally a human age in the history of the Earth in which the human and the nonhuman, the political and the planetary, the economic and the ecological, and the human present and the future of life have become vividly and inextricably entangled. Evoking these entanglements, the Anthropocene is a sign of a paradox: as a result of the collapse of the ontological difference between the human and the Earth, this human age for the Earth has become an ecological age for us. By making the Earth *homo imago*, by terraforming our own self-image into the Earth, we have discovered ourselves as earth creatures, *terra bēstiae*.

In becoming creators of a geological age we have crossed over from a biocultural to a geophysical form of agency, a phenomenological and moral threshold at least as profound as that which was crossed when we first saw a portrait of Earth hanging in space. This crossing is a radical thought. As Jedediah Purdy has observed, "There is no more nature that stands apart from human beings. There is no place or living thing that we haven't changed. Our mark is on the cycle of weather and seasons, the global map of bioregions, and the DNA that organises matter into life."[3] But to say that there is no more nature apart from the human is also to say that there is no more human apart from nature. To the extent that the difference between the human and the rest of nature has been an organizing opposition of modern Western thought—and has formatted other organizational binaries such as outside/inside, object/subject, environment/organism—the Anthropocene paradox opens a space for rethinking fundamental philosophical, theological, and political questions.

As a way to enter into this space, in this chapter I will explore some of the debated meanings of the Anthropocene and analyze several accounts of the moral and political phenomenology of the climate crisis. The purpose of this is to present a critical context for the conceptual and constructive work of the next chapters, which interpret the relevance of the philosophies and theologies of American immanence to the Anthropocene paradox. As I suggested in the introduction, one important reason the American immanental tradition is relevant to the present is that it too emerged in response to changing ideas about the nature of nature and the human place in nature. In particular, the philosophical and theological lineages of American immanence affirm, in different ways, that human being, knowing, and valuing are not creative exceptions in nature but that nature itself is a creative process that includes human creativity as one of its emergent expressions. But the task of this chapter is to show why the moral and political urgencies of the climate crisis and the Anthropocene make it more important than ever to engage and activate this and other ideas associated with the American immanental tradition.

ON THE ANTHROPOCENE

The term *Anthropocene*, which literally means "human age," signifies two ideas. First, it signals that the Earth is or has moved "out of its current geological epoch, called the Holocene."[4] This in itself is an unsettling idea, for the relatively stable climate of the Holocene made human civilization possible—it made agriculture possible, which made settlement possible, which made cities possible. The normal CO_2 range during the Holocene, which covers roughly twelve thousand years, fluctuated between 260 and 285 ppm. But we have just crossed over to 400 ppm, and given the way the carbon cycle works, no matter how much or how quickly we cut emissions, no one alive today will see CO_2 levels drop below this level. In short, everything that humans know and experience as civilization was made possible by the climate stability of the Holocene, and so, to be moving out of the Holocene is a very big deal. The second idea signaled by the term *Anthropocene* is at least as disturbing. It is the claim "that human activity is largely responsible for this exit from the Holocene,. . . that humankind has become a global geological force in its own right."[5] In other words, the point is not only that we have exited the Holocene, the geological niche in the history of the Earth that has been uniquely hospitable to human civilization, but that we have shown ourselves the door. While it is generally agreed that the Anthropocene refers to these two ideas, this is where broad consensus ends. While scholars within geology debate when and how to mark the precise beginning of the Anthropocene, scholars in the humanities and social sciences debate what the Anthropocene means for us morally, politically, and culturally, and whether or not the term *Anthropocene* is an appropriate name for the new epoch.

For example, the geologists Mark Maslin and Simon Lewis of University College London have argued that the beginning of the new geological epoch coincides with the imperial conquest of the Americas in the late fifteenth century.[6] As the fossil record indicates, this time frame marks the beginning of a profound and unprecedented exchange of species between the "Old World" and "New World." It also marks the beginning of events that led to a significant drop in atmospheric CO_2 levels by 1610. According to Maslin and Lewis, the combined planetary impacts of the transcontinental exchange of species, or the Columbian Exchange, and the CO_2 dip in 1610 mark "an unambiguous event after which the impacts of human activity became global and set Earth on a new trajectory."[7]

This argument stands apart from and overlaps with other Anthropocene arguments in several respects. While most accounts of the Anthropocene correlate it with *increased* anthropogenic CO_2 concentrations, Maslin and Lewis date the beginning of the Anthropocene in reference to *decreased* CO_2. But how could human activity cause a dip in atmospheric CO_2 concentrations? Maslin and Lewis argue that the drop in CO_2 levels was caused by the rapid reforestation that followed in the wake of the deaths of millions of indigenous peoples in the Americas: "the near-cessation of farming across the continent and re-growth of Latin American forests and other vegetation removed enough carbon dioxide from the atmosphere to produce a pronounced dip in CO_2 seen in Antarctic ice core records." [8] In other words, as David Biello interprets this, "The atmosphere recorded the mass death, slavery and war that followed 1492. The death by smallpox and warfare of an estimated 50 million native Americans—as well as the enslavement of Africans to work in the newly depopulated Americas—allowed forests to grow in former farmlands."[9] Just over a century after Columbus landed on the shores of Watlings Island, "the growth of all those trees had sucked enough carbon dioxide out of the sky" to cause a sufficient drop in atmospheric CO_2 levels to start a little ice age.[10]

Maslin and Lewis's account of the Anthropocene coincides with what David E. Stannard describes as "the most massive act of genocide in the history of the world."[11] This is actually an understatement. While it was thought as recently as the 1950s that the population of the whole of the Western hemisphere in the fifteenth century was just over eight million, it is generally agreed now that the area north of Mexico alone was home to between eight million and twelve million indigenous people. The hemispheric population estimates, meanwhile, range between seventy-five million and 145,000,000. These are staggering numbers, and current scholarship indicates that within a few generations after European contact in 1492, the population of the Americas had declined by 95 percent. Thus a low estimate for the number of indigenous people who died or were killed as a direct result of European contact is seventy-one million. This is nearly ten times as many people as were thought to have lived in the whole of the Western hemisphere just a generation ago. To put this in perspective, this means that there were at least 500 percent more indigenous deaths after European contact than the *combined* total of people killed in the Jewish Holocaust (1933–1945), the Armenian genocide (1915–1916), the Assyrian genocide (1915–1923), the Cambodian genocide (1975–1979), the Romani genocide (1935–1945), and the Rwandan genocide (1994). While microbes carried over by Europeans certainly caused many of these deaths, this fact has too often been used to deflect moral responsibility— death by disease has been deployed "to exonerate individuals, parties, nations, of any moral blame."[12] The reality is that "From almost the instant of first human contact between Europe and the Americas firestorms of microbial pestilence *and* purposeful genocide began laying waste the American natives."[13] Maslin and Lewis's argument, in effect, is that the atmosphere recorded and memorialized what history has denied— the American holocaust became a climatic event.

Other theories of the Anthropocene, however, argue that it should be dated to the beginning of the Industrial Revolution in the mid- to late eighteenth century. This argument is nearly the inverse of the 1610 argument. Propelled by the mass burning of newly discovered fossil fuels, the Industrial Revolution generated not only a human population explosion but also an explosion of CO_2 emissions. Ever since that time, human population growth, increasing economic production, and higher carbon emissions have mutually amplified one another. For example, since the beginning of the Industrial Revolution the global human population has grown from approximately one billion to well over seven billion, energy use has increased 4000 percent, economic production has increased 5000 percent, the amount of land under intensive human use has nearly tripled, and atmospheric CO_2 concentrations have increased from 277 ppm in 1750 to over 400 ppm in 2016.[14]

There is no doubt that the Industrial Revolution marked a dramatic turning point in the human relationship to the Earth. But part of the story includes the period sometimes referred to as the Great

Acceleration.[15] As a result of the massive global buildup of manufacturing capacity during World War II, the decades since 1950 have seen especially sharp increases in population, production, and global environmental impact. For example, while it took two hundred years for the population to grow from one billion to approximately three billion between 1750 and 1950, it took only fifty years for the population to double after 1950. Since then economic production has increased exponentially, the number of motor vehicles has increased from forty million to over seven hundred million, and global trade, communication, and transportation flows have profoundly accelerated. After World War II, the World Bank and the International Monetary Fund were created in order to generate, manage, and administer postwar recovery. The global influence of these institutions and the ascendant economic power of the United States combined to move the world into the neoliberal phase of capitalism, as described at the end of the previous chapter. Central to the story of the Great Acceleration, then, is how postwar economic globalization amplified the planetary impacts of the increased production and population brought about by the Industrial Revolution.

It is critically important to acknowledge, however, that although many of the environmental and climate impacts of the Industrial Revolution and Great Acceleration have been global, the drivers of those impacts were regional. The economic and technological centers of the industrial whirlwind were located in Europe, the United Kingdom, and the United States. As distinct from one another as the 1610 proposal and the Industrial Revolution and Great Acceleration arguments may be, they all implicitly identify the Anthropocene as a colonial phenomenon driven by the for-profit extraction of resources, whether land or fossil fuels, and the externalization of ecological and social costs. In the 1610 case, the Anthropocene is an expression of classic colonialism, the imperial conquest of territory and people. In the cases of the Industrial Revolution and the Great Acceleration, the Anthropocene begins with industrially scaled environmental impacts and is then amplified by neocolonial economic policies. In other words, all three cases show that the exit from the Holocene was not caused by the whole of the human species, but by certain members of it. And yet while the geological arguments themselves demonstrate this, they do not question the naming of the epoch after the whole of the species. As I will discuss shortly, this disjunction is not lost on the debates in other fields about the moral, political, and cultural meanings of the Anthropocene. But before turning to those debates, it is important to look a little more deeply into the conflict within geology.

What accounts for the various competing arguments for dating the Anthropocene within geology? What explains the different ways geologists are seeing and interpreting the data? According to Clive Hamilton, the diversity of Anthropocene proposals reflects a paradigm shift unfolding in geology.[16] The shift is from a paradigm organized by the concepts and methods of environmental science to the altogether different paradigm of Earth System theory. The environmental science framework views the Earth as an aggregate of multiple environmental systems, including, for example, the systems and subsystems of the lithosphere, atmosphere, hydrosphere, and biosphere. The Earth System framework, on the other hand, views the Earth itself as a complex adaptive system—a planetary ecological metasystem. While the environmental science model interprets geological data through the unilateral and bilateral influences of environmental systems upon one another, the Earth System model interprets geological data through the multilateral feedback loops between lower-level environmental systems and the higher-level Earth System as a whole.

These two models imagine the Earth in fundamentally different ways. As Hamilton writes, "The gulf between the two remains, even if the local environments of ecological thinking are aggregated up to the 'global environment.' The global environment is not the Earth System."[17] Hamilton is right that there is an ontological difference between a multiplicity or an aggregate of systems, on the one hand, and a metasystem or a system collective, on the other. In a system collective the component systems interact not only with one another but also with the metasystem with which they are intertwined. The subsystems and the metasystem mutually influence one another. In dialectical interplay the metasystem exerts downward causal influence on the subsystems while the subsystems exert upward causal influence on the metasystem.

The differences between the Earth System (metasystem) framework and the environmental science framework amount to two fundamentally different ways of interpreting the Earth and how it functions. These alternatives have different epistemic and methodological underpinnings that influence alternative ways of dating the Anthropocene but also competing rationales and criteria for adjudicating the diverse proposals. In the environmental science framework, the planetary geological, chemical, and hydrological systems influence one another. In the Earth System framework, these systems not only influence one another but also impact the larger Earth System as a whole, and vice versa. The distinct epistemic underpinnings of these competing images of the Earth are correlated to the contrast between ontologies of internal and external relatedness, which I will discuss in the next chapter. It turns out that our ways of imagining phenomena on a planetary scale and our metaphysical assumptions about the meaning and structure of more fundamental phenomena mutually influence one another—the paradigm shift that may be currently underway in geology has deep philosophical roots and precedent.

Beyond the methodological shifts and debates in geology, however, scholars in other fields question the moral, political, and cultural meanings of the Anthropocene. These questions frequently pivot around the appropriateness of the name for the epoch. For example, the sociologist Eileen Crist is critical of what she refers to as the "shadowy repercussions of naming an epoch after ourselves."[18] Foremost among these repercussions, on her account, are "a reflection and reinforcement of the anthropocentric actionable worldview that generated 'the Anthropocene' . . . to begin with."[19] Crist argues that to the extent that the discourse of the Anthropocene reinforces this worldview, it "excludes from our range of vision" precisely what we most need to see, "the possibility of challenging human rule" over the Earth.[20] As Crist sees it, the Anthropocene "delivers a Promethean self-portrait: a genius if unruly species, distinguishing itself from the backdrop of merely-living life, rising so as to earn itself a separate name (anthropos meaning 'man,' and always implying 'not animal'), and whose unstoppable and in many ways glorious history" has risen to the level of "Nature's own tremendous forces."[21]

Crist's argument makes two forceful critical points. First, to the extent that the Anthropocene discourse further entrenches the theme of human exceptionalism, it tends to legitimate rather than interrogate the history of human ecological exploitation that has led us out of the Holocene. Second, by slavishly reinforcing the narrative of human mastery, it occludes the human freedom to choose to live differently in the future. Though I am sympathetic to Crist's strong critique of human exceptionalism and the concerns that motivate it, I am suspicious of the idea that the geological discourse of the Anthropocene extends the narrative of human mastery. This line of argument, in my view, conflates the geoscientific description of human geological dominance with a prescription for ongoing human ecological negligence.

An alternative line of argument, presented most strongly and thoroughly by the sociologist Jason W. Moore, challenges the geological task on its own terms.[22] Rather than arguing that the Anthropocene is wrongly named because it gives license to ongoing ecological exploitation, this line of critique argues that the Anthropocene is wrongly named because it misidentifies the dominant geological influence—the dominant geological influence is not the whole of the human species but a particular historical civilizational form. In his critique, Moore argues that one reason for this misidentification has to do with the consequentialist methodology used by geologists to establish geohistorical timelines. Moore argues, for instance, that dating the Anthropocene to the beginning of the Industrial Revolution methodologically privileges the environmental impacts and effects of industrialization rather than the contingent relations of power and capital that gave the revolution the particular form it took.

Moore's argument is important for implicit epistemic and explicit political reasons. On the one hand, by critiquing the consequentialist approach to marking geohistorical time, Moore is implicitly questioning the epistemic structure of the field of geology. The production and organization of knowledge in geology depend on clearly established time frames for the history of Earth. The stratigraphic task entails deciding on objective markers in the geological record for the timelines that shape the structure of the broader field. But objective markers in the geological record are by definition markers of things from long ago, the effects of events and circumstances on timescales that dwarf human history. In other words, the operative historical scale in geology necessitates a consequentialist methodology. The problem is that a consequentialist methodology is prima facie ill suited to the naming of the present. For the consequences and effects of the new geological epoch are still in the making, and the closer one moves toward the geological present, the harder it becomes to precisely designate the origin point for the new time unit. Rather than a precise point in time with an objective imprint in the geological record, the origin begins to take the shape of an event whose effects are still unfolding and are unevenly distributed through the plane of recent human history.

The explicit political significance of this should be obvious. As Moore argues, rather than naming the new geological epoch after the whole of the species, attributing geophysical causality to the whole of human history, and rather than treating the beginning of the Industrial Revolution as the origin point, the new epoch should be named after the civilizational system that has fueled the exit from the Holocene. This new epoch in Earth's history should be named the "Capitalocene." As infelicitous as this name may sound (though it really is no more awkward than "Anthropocene"), it has the merit of taking the geological task seriously enough to propose a name for this new epoch that reflects more precisely the historical processes that have brought it about.

For it is simply not the case that every member of the human species is equally responsible for the CO_2 and other GHG emissions that are driving the climate crisis. The most affluent and industrialized nations in the global North have not only generated far more than their share of carbon emissions; they have also capitalized the most on the economic and technological systems that drive those emissions. For instance, wealthy, developed nations emitted a cumulative total of roughly 900 to 950 billion metric tons of CO_2 between 1800 and 2010.[23] The rest of the world, including rapidly developing countries such as Brazil, India, and China, emitted a cumulative total of only 400 billion metric tons. Although the emissions of wealthy nations in the global North began to escalate rapidly around 1860, the rest of the world's emissions did not begin to escalate until well after World War II. While developed nations account for only 20 percent of the world population, they are responsible for approximately 70 percent of cumulative GHG emissions.[24] As a result of their overwhelming contribution to cumulative emissions, the nations of the global North bear the burden of responsibility for the climate crisis. The nations that have contributed the least are the most immediately and negatively impacted by climate change, while the wealthier, developed nations who have contributed the most will experience some benefits of climate change.[25] These critical facts are simply occluded by naming the geological epoch after the whole of the human species.

Although Moore's and Crist's critiques and the various geological proposals discussed earlier all advance important insights and claims, can they all be true at the same time? Is the Anthropocene a planetary geo-physical reality and the contingent effect of a historical civilizational form? Is it an ecospheric as well as a sociocultural condition, a problem for the whole of the present and future of human life even though it has been caused by a small historical subset of the species?

The postcolonial historian Dipesh Chakrabarty asks the question of what it might mean for human historical self-understanding if elements of all of these truths could be held together at once. He argues that it is "impossible to understand global warming as a crisis without engaging the propositions put forward by [climate] scientists," propositions whose significance pertains to the future of the whole species.[26] But at the same time, "the story of capital, the contingent history of falling into the Anthro-pocene, cannot be denied by recourse to the idea of species, for the Anthro-pocene would not have been possible, even as a theory, without the history of industrialization."[27] Chakrabarty calls us to think the truths of both of these stories together.

As a postcolonial historian, Chakrabarty knows that no particular story tells the whole story of history. Interpreting the meanings of history entails coming to know a multiplicity of stories, not in order finally to know the fullness of history's meaning, but in order more fully to engage the many meanings of the conflicts, contests, and contradictions that ani-mate history. In the case of the Anthropocene, historical understanding entails coming to terms with the contingent political histories of capital-ism and Western modernity along with the planetary history of the cli-mate and the geological agency of the species. This means seeking to hold the universal and the particular together, a perennially difficult philosoph-ical and historical task. Chakrabarty puts the question this way: "How do we relate to a universal history of life—to a universal thought, that is—while retaining what is of obvious value in our postcolonial suspicion of the universal? The crisis of climate change calls for thinking simultane-ously on both registers to mix together the immiscible chronologies of capital and species history."[28]

Whether or not we can mix these histories together, wherever one stands in relation to the critiques and debates of the Anthropocene dis-course, and however the paradigm shift within geology plays out, it is clear that we are living through a time that, as a leading team of geolo-gists has asserted, "represents a new phase in the history of both humankind and of the Earth when natural forces and human forces became intertwined, so that the fate of one determines the fate of the other."[29] In other words, as pointedly described by Christophe Bonneuil and Jean-Baptiste Fressoz, "The Anthropocene is the sign of our power, but also of our impotence."[30] The paradox of this sign is dramatically at play in the moral and political phenomenology of "climate wickedness," to which I will now turn.

CLIMATE WICKEDNESS

The concept of "wicked problems" has arisen in recent years as a way to name a particular type of systemic problem that not only resists but refuses solution. Wicked problems are often exacerbated by the application of conventional problem-solving repertoires since, in many cases, the political and economic contexts of conventional approaches to large-scale problems are indentured to interests that have much to do with the creation of wicked problems in the first place. Since they are structurally embedded in social and economic systems and reinforced and legitimated by cultural values and habits, learning to see wicked problems, let alone taking responsibility for them and engaging them practically, can be exceptionally difficult. The causal structure of wicked problems is non-linear and their effects are uneven—they impact different people in different places in different ways, and so they resist universal, totalizing solutions and "silver bullets."

Furthermore, the scale and complexity of wicked problems mean that our understanding of them is always incomplete, our analyses of how they arise often conflict, and our interpretations of what to do about them are sometimes contradictory. Wicked problems are global problems in the double sense that they impact interconnected societies and nations around the world and are intensified by the various dynamics of globalization. And yet while they tend to be global in scale, they are not experienced or suffered by all people in the same way. Their causes, conditions, and effects are not evenly or symmetrically distributed. Wicked problems are conditioned by the diverse contingencies that shape disparate contextual circumstances. Thus solutions or strategies that might be effective in one set of circumstances not only may be infeasible but could actually be counterproductive in another. This is why the effort of scholars such as Chakrabarty to mix seemingly "immiscible" theoretical and critical analyses is so important. And yet because wicked problems impact so many people (and other species and diverse systems) in so many ways, they tend to provoke strong reactions and positions. The urgency of the threats and the complexity of the risks of wicked problems yield ideological polarization, simplistic thinking, and political reactivity, mindsets that intensify rather than diffuse wickedness.

Consider, as just one example among many, the Syrian refugee crisis, the causes of which are complex and multiple. In addition to the brutal authoritarianism of the Assad regime, and the displacement, death, and destruction caused by ISIS, the causes of the crisis can also be correlated to disruptions to the balance of powers in the Middle East and to environmental and agricultural disruptions caused by an extended draught in the region.[31] The causes of the refugee crisis, in other words, are a mix of local, national, regional, and global social, environmental, and political dynamics. While the US invasion of Iraq is one of the most obvious proximate causes of the regional political disruption, the national environmental and agricultural crisis is a local symptom exacerbated by the planetary climate crisis, for which the United States bears a great burden of responsibility. Through our military and climactic misadventures, the United States has indisputably contributed to the conditions that precipitated the refugee crisis. Despite this, American political discourse and policy have recently become so infected by a viral outbreak of nativist, xenophobic, and anti-Muslim demagoguery that as a nation we disavow our complicity in the crisis and refuse to accept the refugees whose homeland we have helped to unravel. As the Syrian refugee crisis illustrates, wicked problems frequently affect vulnerable communities of poor and oppressed people disproportionately, they emerge out of entangled social, ecological, economic, political, and cultural dynamics, and their nonlinear complexity wreaks havoc with, even as it provokes a desire for, simplistic solutions.

In short, to live in a context of wicked problems is to live in the aftermath of certainty. And of all the wicked problems, the climate crisis is surely the wickedest of them all. While it is physically caused by increased atmospheric concentrations of CO_2 and other greenhouse gases,

THE ANTHROPOCENE AND CLIMATE WICKEDNESS 67

greenhouse gases are not inherently problematic. They have been in the atmosphere since the beginning of life on Earth and are in fact indispensable to the regulation of the Earth's temperatures within a range hospitable to life. CO_2, for instance, is an externalized byproduct of some forms of life, and a condition of possibility for others. This is the central point of James Lovelock's Gaia theory, which imagines the Earth itself as a self-regulating biomorphic system.[32] The carbon cycle, in which CO_2 emissions and other greenhouse gas outputs are balanced by a roughly equivalent absorption by the Earth's natural sinks, such as vegetation and the oceans, is the pivotal cycle within the Earth System's self-regulation. The carbon cycle is the Earth's biomorphic circulatory system. The problem, then, is not CO_2 as such, but the massive increase of carbon emissions since the beginning of the fossil-fueled Industrial Revolution.

As described earlier, the Industrial Revolution magnified economic productivity and led to a human population explosion, both of which required the extraction and burning of more fossil fuels to be sustained. This is an example of a reinforcing feedback loop in which fossil-fueled industrial production and population and economic growth mutually amplify one another in a way that destabilizes the functioning of the carbon system. Over the past couple of centuries, the cumulative CO_2 emissions externalized by this reinforcing feedback loop have overwhelmed the "natural" sinks in the carbon cycle and oversaturated the atmosphere. In other words, the reinforcing industrial feedback loop has spawned a reinforcing climatic feedback loop. Warming air and oceans not only amplify one another but also lead to changing ocean currents and increased ocean condensation, which lead to more moisture in the air, which, in combination with altered ocean currents, leads to more frequent extreme weather events, such as longer droughts in some areas and more intense rainfall and flooding in others.

Meanwhile, the climatic feedback loop has generated tertiary socio-ecological feedback loops such as diminishing water supplies, crop failure, rising numbers of ecological refugees, new migratory patterns, and changing distributions and rates of vector-borne diseases.[33]

If the reinforcing feedback loops interconnecting the industrial and carbon cycles are the externally visible manifestations of climate wickedness, its less visible internal core grows out of the opacity of its moral and political phenomenology. I refer here to the way the climate crisis appears or does not appear as a moral object, and how we experience it, or don't, as a moral problem, as well as to the self-reinforcing dynamics of political and economic power that fuel the crisis and condition divergent moral perceptions and experiences of it.

For example, as I argued in chapter 1, the extraction of value and the externalization of cost are built in to the logic of the redeemer symbolic and the theopolitics of American exceptionalism. In this American context the massive extraction of fossil fuels not only was required by industrialization and the will to global economic power, but also can be interpreted as a geophysical incarnation of the exceptionalist logic of redemption. Through American history, the theopolitics of American exceptionalism and the redeemer symbolic provide reinforcing narrative feedback for the various historical forms of extraction and externalization, whether of land, life, and labor or, in this case, fossil-fuel extraction and CO_2 externalization. As reflected in the Republican chant frequently heard during the 2008 presidential election season, burning coal and drilling for oil came to be seen by many people to be as patriotic and American as apple pie: "Drill, baby, drill!"

As physically tangible as drilling for oil and burning fossil fuels may be, however, the moral and political phenomenology of their atmospheric impacts is much less so. The evolution of the human brain and the structure of human moral psychology are crucial to understanding the challenging moral phenomenology of the climate crisis. As Dale Jamieson writes, "Evolution did not design us to solve or even to recognize this kind of problem. We have a strong bias toward dramatic movements of middle-sized objects that can be visually perceived, and climate change does not typically present in this way. The onset of climate change is gradual and uncertain rather than immediate and obvious."[34] Our inbuilt evolutionary moral biases toward "dramatic movements" and visually perceptible "middle-sized objects," which tend to obscure the moral nature of the climate crisis, are of course only exacerbated when one's immediate environment is insulated from the most dramatic negative impacts of climate change. In short, human moral psychology biases us against seeing, experiencing, and feeling the climate crisis as a moral problem in anything close to the way that we experience very intensely the moral dimensions of interpersonal relations. As the psychologist Daniel Gilbert explains, this is because our brains evolved to respond optimally to what he refers to as PAIN: to *P*ersonal and interpersonal interactions, to *A*brupt rather than gradual change, to *I*ndecent or impious behavior happening *N*ow.[35] This helps to explain why many people, especially those who are least personally, abruptly, immediately, and negatively impacted by climate change, have such a hard time engaging the climate crisis as a moral problem driven by human activity.

The historical sociopolitical contexts through which we innovate, conserve, and transform our moral cultures reinforce the evolutionary moral problem—especially the relations between social complexity and energy use. In his now classic work *The Collapse of Complex Societies*, the anthropologist Joseph Tainter argued that "Energy flow and sociopolitical organization are opposite sides of an equation. Neither can exist, in a human group, without the other, nor can either undergo substantial change without altering both the opposite member and the balance of the equation."[36] Tainter's comparative historical analyses led him to develop a formula: in order to sustain increased social complexity, network density must increase, and when network density increases, so must energy use. In other words, as social systems become more complex as a result of role specialization, demographic diversification, class stratification, and increased territorial scale, they must invest resources in the building up of institutions, bureaucracies, surveillance, and regulatory programs in order to strengthen the ties that bind the society together, and this investment in network density takes lots of energy. While the increased energy needed to sustain social complexity has often been acquired through the conquest of people and territory, since the Industrial Revolution it has been acquired by increasingly extreme methods of fossil-fuel extraction. Tainter's thesis is that social collapse occurs when social systems reach the point of diminishing marginal returns on the energy investment needed to sustain their own complexity.[37] In the context of climate wickedness, this thesis could be rephrased to say that when the externalized costs of an energy regime begin to dramatically heat the planet, something has got to give, and it's time for radical change.

Along the lines of Tainter, the classicist and anthropologist Ian Morris has recently theorized that "Methods of energy capture largely dictate what demographic regimes and forms of organization will work best, and these in turn dictate what kinds of values will flourish."[38] Less concerned with the question of collapse, Morris draws from the work in anthropology and evolutionary psychology to theorize correlations between moral systems and energy regimes. He argues that although evolutionarily foundational moral concerns with such things as fairness and justice, love and hate, respect and loyalty, harm prevention, and a sense of the sacred have remained relatively constant over the past twenty thousand years, they are inflected and prioritized in basically three different ways as a result of the forms of social order made possible by three different historical modes of energy capture—foraging, farming, and fossil-fuels extraction. While foragers value equality over hierarchy and are tolerant of violence, farmers value hierarchy over equality but are less tolerant of violence, and fossil-fuelers value social equality but tolerate wealth inequality and are intolerant of violence.

According to this thesis, then, the social values of foragers, farmers, and fossil-fuelers are calibrated to the scale and complexity of the forms of social order they inhabit, the scale and complexity of social systems are correlative to particular forms of energy, and particular forms of energy correspond to distinct modes of energy extraction. In short, social ethics, social orders, energy forms, and modes of energy extraction reciprocally influence one another. Since these three historical phases unfolded, roughly speaking, through the Holocene, it is pertinent to ask how the Anthropocene paradox will provoke new correlations of ethics, energy, and extraction. And since the climate crisis illuminates the Anthropocene paradox in particular ways, different accounts of the moral and political phenomenology of the climate crisis are relevant to this question.

For Stephen M. Gardiner, the climate crisis constitutes a "perfect moral storm."[39] "What matters most," he writes, "is what we do to protect those vulnerable to our actions and unable to hold us accountable, especially the global poor, future generations, and nonhuman nature."[40] But the problem is not only that the climate crisis is the greatest ethical problem that humanity has ever faced. Nor is it merely that it is difficult for us to morally grasp and politically engage. It is both of these things and more, for the several layers of asymmetrical power that structure it also aggravate human tendencies to moral self-deception and institutional corruption.

Gardiner specifies three layers of asymmetry that constitute this perfect moral storm—global, intergenerational, and theoretical. With respect to the global layer, Gardiner observes that global political and economic asymmetries are such that wealthy nations and the richest within them have used their power "in ways which favor their own concerns, especially over those of the world's poorer nations, and poor people within those nations."[41] As pronounced and significant as this global asymmetry is, however, the intergenerational asymmetry is more severe. The present generation has all the power. Future generations cannot causally impact the present while the present has a profound impact on the future. When the additional complexities of the climate crisis are added, there is no significant historical precedent in ethical theory for engaging moral asymmetries of this magnitude. According to Gardiner, there is a paucity of ethical theory related to questions of "intergenerational ethics, international justice, scientific uncertainty, and the human relationship to animals and the rest of nature."[42] One effect of this is that the nations and people most responsible for the crisis are even "more vulnerable" to the patterns of self-deception and institutional corruption that already attend global and intergenerational asymmetries of power.

This is what we would expect from a wicked problem. As I stated earlier, insofar as wicked problems are not only structurally embedded in social and economic systems but also reinforced and legitimated by cultural values and habits, learning to see them and to take moral responsibility for them can be difficult. Even more maddening than this, however, is that this phenomenological opacity can be leveraged by those who have a vested interest in some aspect of the problem and therefore seek to legitimate inaction and even to foment misunderstanding. While the historians of science Naomi Oreskes and Eric M. Conway have damningly documented corporate instances of this in *Merchants of Doubt*, Gardiner describes the governmental and citizen inaction in developed nations in the following way:

> On the one hand, governments [of developed countries] have persistently had "other priorities," and citizens have failed to see climate change even as a serious environmental problem, let alone one of humanity's largest problems per se. On the other hand, we have seen much hand wringing about the soundness of the science (albeit almost all by nonscientists, or scientists who don't work on climate), active campaigns of disinformation, and a tendency to reduce the issue to tangential matters such as recycling. In short, few seem interested in really dealing

with the problem despite its catastrophic potential. All of this seems difficult to explain away in any normal sense. . . . The temptation to pass the buck on to the future, the poor, and nature is very strong.[43]

As discussed in the previous chapter, and as mentioned earlier, the temptation to "pass the buck" has a theopolitical dimension to it in American history. Through the logic of the redeemer symbolic, the dominant American theopolitical tradition sanctifies the externalization of its environmental, social, cultural, and economic costs, and throughout American history, and into the present, these costs have disproportionately impacted the most vulnerable, the religious outsiders, the racially exploited, the socially marginalized, other species, the land, and the atmosphere. By extracting the value of labor, land, and life from the most vulnerable people and places, the redeemer symbolic turns the externalization of cost into the unavoidable price of American exceptionalism.

Along with Gardiner's "perfect moral storm," the environmental philosopher Timothy Morton's ideas about "hyperobjects" provide another way to think through the Anthropocene and the phenomenological wickedness of the climate crisis. For Morton, the Anthropocene begins with two objects: the steam engine invented in 1784 by James Watt and the atom bomb that was tested in New Mexico and then dropped on Hiroshima and Nagasaki in 1945. The atom bomb and the steam engine are objects that amplified human agency to a planetary scale and thus mark a "logarithmic increase in the actions of humans as a geophysical force."[44] The irony of this, as Morton recognizes and as I have been suggesting, is that these human objects and actions bring an end to certain fundamental ideas about being human and the human relation to the world. On Morton's analysis, they bring an end not only to the idea that humans are at the center of things but also, and much more radically, to the idea that there is a center or an edge to things at all.[45] All three of these ideas have literally been pivotal to Western modernity insofar as they have functioned as conceptual hinges for the ontological bifurcation of humans and nonhumans and culture and nature. By disrupting these ideas, the Anthropocene and the climate crisis "force something on us, something that affects some core ideas of what it means to exist, what Earth is, what society is."[46]

Morton's analysis of the distinctive characteristics of hyperobjects explains why they can force such profound questions upon us. Of the several characteristics he describes, I will discuss two that are especially relevant here.[47] First, hyperobjects are "viscous." The climate, for instance, is attached to everything. There is no getting beyond it. It is so "massively distributed in space and time" that every human act and thought is in some way related to it. The climate is thus not an object that we relate to in a merely external way but is something that fully envelops us. We are to the climate as Jonah is to the whale.[48] The climate as a hyperobject blows through the dualism of subjects and objects and the bifurcation of humans and nature. It thus also troubles the ontology of external relatedness that dominates modern philosophy, as I will discuss in the next chapter. The enveloping viscosity of the climate wreaks epistemic havoc with us. But this havoc becomes uncanny when we recognize that precisely to the extent that we cannot avoid contact with the climate, no particular contact with it in any particular place or time is ever fully an experience of it. Insofar as the climate is everywhere it is nowhere in particular. Morton illustrates this as follows: "When I look at the sun gleaming on the solar panels on my roof, I am watching global warming unfold. . . . Yet I do not see global warming as such. I see this brilliant blade of sunlight, burning the top of my head as I watch it with half-closed eyes reflecting off the burnished, sapphire surface of the solar panels. . . . Yet global warming is not here. Hyperobjects are *nonlocal.*"[49] Thus the flipside of the "viscosity" of the climate is its "nonlocality."

The epistemic havoc created by the viscous and uncanny nonlocality of the climate can be put to sinister use. Viscosity and nonlocality make it possible for climate denialists to say that the human connection to climate change is uncertain. Given the suffering and harm caused by the climate crisis, and the power and profit gained by those most responsible for this suffering and harm, this is a diabolical mystification of science in general, and climate science in particular. As Morton explains this, the nonlocality of the climate illuminates the nature of causality as it is understood in the modern sciences. The unscientific fantasy of direct proof and absolute certainty has given way to the scientific logic of association, correlation, and probability. This is why reports from the Intergovernmental Panel on Climate Change (IPCC) correlate terms such as *likely* and *very likely* to statistical probabilities. The climate denialists' claim that there is no direct empirical proof that isolates human activity as the cause of global warming is a deliberate mystification of the fact that no isolated piece of empirical evidence makes contact with the whole of the history of the climate. As Dale Jamieson writes, "Climate change poses threats that are probabilistic, multiple, indirect, often invisible, and unbounded in space and time."[50] It is true that there is no singular "smoking gun" that proves with absolute certainty that global warming is humanly caused. Climate deniers are right about this in precisely the same sense that lawyers for Big Tobacco were right that there is no isolable direct proof that smoking tobacco always causes cancer. Big Tobacco and Big Oil have deployed unscientific ideas about certainty to deliberately confuse the public understanding of science. In so doing they have pursued their own private gain at an immense cost to the common good and human and planetary health. In this way Big Tobacco and Big Oil epitomize the internalization of profit and the externalization of loss.

To live amid climate wickedness is indeed to live in the aftermath of certainty. In this sense the climate is a synecdoche of a more general epistemic, moral, and ontological condition. As the viscosity and nonlocality of the climate are such that we can neither escape it nor experience it fully, we also cannot "jump out of the universe" to know nature, reality, or the universe as a totality or whole.[51] There is no "view from nowhere" from which to see things as they really are. This may seem like an unremarkable point until one recalls that one of the leading epistemic strategies of modernity is organized around the postulate that a view from nowhere (in particular) is the very condition of possibility of human understanding. Kant responded to Hume's skepticism by arguing that things as they appear to knowers and things as they are in themselves can be correlated to each other by postulating universal categories of human understanding. The very possibility of knowing anything in particular through experience depends on general categories of understanding such as, among others, quantity, unity, existence, and plurality. Knowing is therefore a correlative enterprise and the categories of understanding provide the bridge. In short, the interface between the minds of knowing human subjects and the world of objects is established entirely on the terms and conditions of human minds. For Morton, this Kantian illusion "of a privileged transcendental sphere" in which our "transcendental faculties are

at least metaphorically floating in space beyond the edge of the universe"
is shattered by our encounters with hyperobjects such as the climate.[52]

As viscous and nonlocal, the climate is attached to every particular
and yet can never be fully accessed through any particular. In this way,
then, climate wickedness illustrates the more general condition of our
epistemic vulnerability amid the ontologically irreducible complexity
of nature's patterns and processes. The complexity of *natura naturans*
envelops us, we are entangled within it, it is as close to us as our breath
and yet we can never fully know it. If the Anthropocene is like a hall of
mirrors reflecting the end of the idea of the human as separate from
nature, climate wickedness is a spotlight illuminating the end of certainty and the inescapable ontological, epistemic, and moral vulnerability of human life. As a result of crossing over the epochal boundaries
of the Holocene into the Anthropocene, we find ourselves facing bound-
ary questions related to the conditions of human life and the fundamental political and religious assumptions that orient us in relation to those
conditions.

As the Anthropocene reveals the inescapable entanglements of human
and more-than-human life, of living and nonliving nature, and of human
and natural history, the wickedness of the climate crisis is signified by its
nonlocal viscosity, diffused causality, and asymmetrical effects. While
the entanglements of the Anthropocene entail the end of the idea of the
human as set apart from the rest of nature, the wickedness of the climate
crisis points to the end of certainty. Thus the Anthropocene and climate
wickedness dissolve two of the defining impulses of modern Western
thought and compel us to confront the questions of who we are and what
we can know. While these are certainly not the only questions we should
be asking in this time of epochal turning, they are nonetheless essential.
For the questions of who we are and how and what we can know are intertwined with moral and religious concerns with the worth and beauty of
life, the nature and scope of moral value, the limits and purposes of
power, the forms and depth of human meaning, and the ideals and institutions of common life.

While there are many traditions to which one could turn to engage these questions and concerns, the American immanental tradition offers an especially relevant conceptual context. This is because the ending of the ideal of certainty and the collapse of the opposition between humans and the rest of nature give birth to the American immanental tradition. Within this tradition, as I will articulate it, there is no outside to nature and there is no end to mystery. To be human is to be a creature of nature who can only know nature from the inside, immanently. And rather than enclosing mystery, it turns out that an immanental frame emancipates it.

With these fundamental ideas in mind, the next chapter, on philosophies of the American immanental tradition, is organized around the themes of thinking, feeling, and valuing immanence. I will focus in particular on aspects of John Dewey's pragmatic naturalism, William James's radical empiricism, and Alfred North Whitehead's process philosophy. I will show how Dewey's pragmatic naturalism calibrates the critical and creative powers of inquiry to a mode of immanental thinking and a conjunctive epistemology. I will then discuss how James's affective extension of the empirical broadens the inventory of the empirical to include relations as well as things, and disjunctions as well as conjunctions. Following the work on James, I will trace the way Whitehead crosses the bifurcation of nature by transforming ontological oppositions into contrasts, and by plunging the feeling and valuing of immanence into the ontological depths of things. Let us now turn to the crossing of this bifurcation and the possibilities it opens for rethinking creativity and agency amid the Anthropocene paradox.

3

THINKING, FEELING, AND
VALUING IMMANENCE

American Immanental Philosophies

The American immanental tradition invites us into a world of more-than-human vitality and creativity, a world in which agency and value are distributed through the whole of nature's patterns, processes, and precarities rather than concentrated within or monopolized by a particular species, ethnoracial group, nation, political economy, or concept of God. By affirming the wonder and sublimity of the diverse expressions of creativity and agency in the universe, the American immanental tradition lures us toward more vital and more resonant ways of being in the world, more existentially and spiritually enlivening modes of life.

Whereas the American redeemer symbolic grows out of convergent understandings of biblical covenant, divine sovereignty, and national exception, the American immanental tradition emerges as a post-Darwinian early-twentieth-century response to changing ideas about the nature of nature and the human place within its complexities. It critically interrogates what John Dewey identified as the "whole brood and nest of dualisms" that constitute the modern Western epistemic quagmire—for example, between fact and value, knower and known, nature and culture, human and animal, subject and object.[1] It attempts to cross the alleged ontological opposition between the workings of nature and the thinking of human minds, oppositions reflected in and reinforced by the substance-quality structure of logic and the subject-predicate structure of language, an opposition that Alfred North Whitehead referred to as the "bifurcation of nature."[2] By spanning this bifurcation and thinking beyond these dualisms, the American immanental tradition thinks against the grain of the ontological and epistemic exceptionalisms that have set humans over and against other forms of animal life and human culture, society, and economy over and against the ecological systems upon which they depend. In this way, the philosophies and theologies of American immanence question the "general form" of Western modernity's "forms of thought" and clear a space through which to deconstruct and reconstruct the stories and images that have enclosed the modern Western philosophical and religious imagination.[3] As Robert Cummings Neville has put this, these philosophies and theologies take the "high road around modernism."[4]

In relation to the Anthropocene paradox, crossing the bifurcation of nature and affirming the diffusion of agency, value, and creativity beyond the human world are important for theopolitical reasons as well. For a distributed view of creative agency and value directly challenges the exceptionalist logic of sovereign and unitary power. Ultimately rooted in the ideals of traditional monotheism, this logic of power is also manifest in diverse ways in the dominant American political theology and the redeemer symbolic, as shown in chapter 1. Deconstructing the logic of exceptional power and reconstructing an alternative are critical to more fully understanding and responding to the monumental challenges of life in the Anthropocene. To the extent that the American immanental tradition provides resources for this deconstructive and reconstructive work, it is of profound relevance to the theopolitical conditions of the Anthropocene.

To provide a philosophical context for that relevance, I have divided this chapter into three main sections. In the first, I will interpret John Dewey's pragmatic naturalism as an exemplary mode of immanental thinking; in the second, I will discuss the feeling of immanence through William James's radical empiricism; in the third, I will discuss the valuing of immanence through Alfred North Whitehead's process philosophy. My intention is neither to offer new interpretations of these thinkers nor to intervene within the vast scholarly literature surrounding their work. More modestly, but no less importantly, I will focus on aspects of their philosophies relevant to the constructive theological and theopolitical work in chapters 4 and 5. With this developmental aim in mind, I am particularly interested in the significance of several ideas: that nature is all there is and that it is in process, that we feel the world before we know it, that things are internally intrarelated rather than merely externally inter-related, and that the dualisms that haunt modernity can be overcome through the transformation of ontological oppositions into integral con-trasts. In short, this chapter traces the American immanental critique of epistemic and ontological exceptionalism in order to prepare the way for an exploration of the creative theopolitical possibilities opened up by critique.

THINKING IMMANENCE: JOHN DEWEY'S PRAGMATIC NATURALISM

Pragmatic naturalism can be defined, in general terms, as a melioristic form of naturalism concerned with the purposes of human inquiry and conduct in a world of contingency and probability, rather than with the problems of epistemology in a static world of fixed necessities and cer-tainties.[5] In other words, it conjoins a pragmatic concern with the prob-lems and possibilities of human life with a naturalistic mode of inquiry that constructs provisional hypotheses about how to interpret and evalu-ate the indeterminacies of life in the fully natural world. Pragmatic natu-ralism renders its hypotheses vulnerable by subjecting them to testing within an inquiring community's experiences of the world, with the aim of revising them in order more intelligently to navigate the deeper, broader world of experience. As I will clarify further along, I contrast the phrases *world of experience* and *experience of the world* to mark the criti-cal ideas within the tradition of American immanence that experience is deeper than cognition and more than human and that there are thus diverse "experiences of the world" within a broader, deeper "world of experience." However, all this is to say that pragmatic naturalism is inquisitively engaged with a vital, wholly natural world of experience that is always changing and in which, therefore, knowledge is provisional and hypothetical. Pragmatic naturalism affirms epistemic vulnerability, not only as the condition of knowledge in a changing world but also as the very impetus for ongoing inquiry. The indeterminacy of circumstances and the ambiguities of life mean not only that what we know at any given moment is vulnerable, but also that we should make what we know vulnerable to revision in the light of ongoing experience. Pragmatic naturalism is, therefore, critical of foundationalist philosophies of settled ideas constructed to reinforce the antecedent truths upon which they are based. In contrast to foundationalist commitments to antecedents and precedents, pragmatic naturalism commits to a prospective concern with consequents.

Thus understood, pragmatic naturalism is an integrative mode of immanental thought appropriate to human beings as *terra bēstiae*. It understands humans as organisms subject to the same basic evolutionary dynamics as other "earth creatures" and therefore affirms that human knowing and valuing are evolutionarily emergent capacities constrained and catalyzed by the patterns, processes, and precarities of nature naturing. Pragmatic naturalist inquiry is motivated and limited by the indeterminacies of being a thinking, valuing creature who is both sustained and challenged by the conditions of life in a world of experience whose scope, depth, and mystery exceed what can be known. Pragmatic naturalism participates within and exemplifies the mysteries of nature's unfurling even as it endeavors to understand what it can about this unfurling. However, what is "naturalistic" about pragmatic naturalism and what more specifically is the relevance of John Dewey's pragmatic naturalism to life in the Anthropocene?

In his classic mid-twentieth-century essay, John Randall referred to the emergence of "naturalism" in American philosophy as "post-modern."[6] Although the early days of American philosophical naturalism look nothing like the poststructuralist and deconstructive postmodernism of recent decades, it does represent a kind of revolution, philosophical and otherwise. So, what is the case that Randall makes? His first point is that the emergent naturalism of the time was defined not by a unified set of doctrines but by a "community of temper." The common questions around which this community is organized, and the temper they share in common and through which they engage their common questions, are provoked by a common recognition of the philosophical significance of new scientific understandings of nature and the human place in nature. As Randall describes this, " 'Naturalism' came into vogue as the name for a recognized philosophical position during the great scientific movement of the nineteenth century, which put man and his experience squarely into the Nature over against which he had hitherto been set. The obliteration of the gulf between the nature of the 'natural scientist' and human life was then associated with the discovery of the facts of biological evolution."[7] This understanding of nature and the human place in it led to the breakdown of the long-standing Western idea of nature as a term of distinction, whether the classical Greek distinction between nature and art, or later distinctions between the natural and the supernatural, or the natural and the transcendental, or natural and cultural.

There is a double shift that is important here, each of which is historically and philosophically distinct. The one is the idea of nature as the whole of things or all there is—the view that nature, however else we define it, is the "all-inclusive category," rather than a "term of distinction." Of course this view of nature, broadly understood, has precedent in Western philosophy, for example, in Epicurus and Spinoza. What matters most, Randall suggests, is the integration of this idea of nature-as-all with the insights of evolutionary biology and their philosophical implications. This integration puts the "all" of nature into motion and brings humans and all that humans do into continuity with nature. To say that nature is all, and therefore that humans are included in nature, is one thing. To say that nature is all, and that it is in motion, and that humans are continuous with this dynamic nature, is quite another thing. The epistemic and methodological consequences of this idea are much more profound than with the first idea. For one can say that nature is all, and includes humans, and still understand the human as ontologically distinct within nature, and therefore continue to segregate ways of knowing nature and humans. However, when nature is all and humans are not only included within it but also continuous with it, the ways of knowing nature and humans need not be so rigidly divided. It is the methodological significance of these combined ideas that leads Randall to the view that American philosophical naturalism is best defined as a "community temper" that represents a revolution in modern philosophical thought. Or, as Thelma Lavine put this, alluding to Dewey's principled emphasis on continuity in nature and inquiry, American naturalism should be defined in terms of a continuity of analysis rather than a continuity of genesis.[8] Her point was that naturalism was organized primarily not around a set of doctrines or ideas, but around a method of inquiry. And yet this method of inquiry does issue from a fundamental idea, the break-down not only of the ontological difference *between* humans and nature but also of the human ontological difference *within* nature. Thus with the emergence of American philosophical naturalism we see not only a rejec-tion of the traditional dualisms in the long history of Western philoso-phy but also a probing beyond the modern Western bifurcation of nature.

John Dewey, who had been Randall's teacher, advanced the naturalis-tic turn in revolutionary ways. The pragmatic naturalism he developed can be interpreted as including two dimensions, critical and creative. Dewey understood critique as a pivotal philosophical task, even as the genesis of philosophical inquiry. He writes: "Philosophy is criticism; crit-icism of the influential beliefs that underlie culture; a criticism which traces the beliefs to their generating conditions as far as may be, [and] tracks them to their results. . . . Such an examination terminates . . . in a projection of them into a new perspective which leads to new surveys of possibilities."[9] As I will show further along, these references to the critical opening up of a "new perspective" and to "new surveys of possibilities" resonate with important aspects of Whitehead's ideas about symbolism and his organic process metaphysics. For Dewey, however, the idea of phi-losophy as critique reflects the Hegelian roots of his thinking. In *Experi-ence and Nature*, he specifically defines philosophy as the "critique of prej-udices," while also acknowledging that we "cannot permanently divest ourselves of the intellectual habits we take on and wear when we assimilate the culture of our own time and place."[10] Though this may be the case, the critique of prejudice is but one element of Dewey's pragmatic naturalism.

Where the critical task of Dewey's thinking reflects the influence of Hegel, its creative movements reflect the transformational impact of Dar-win. Interpreted through Darwin's theory of evolution, Dewey understood inquiry as an aspect of human organismic life related to the creatural work of coping with and navigating environments that sustain as well as imperil creatural life. The creative task of Dewey's pragmatic naturalism instrumentalizes ideas and values and tests their adequacy in relation to the ever-changing dynamics of intersecting social, natural, and histori-cal environments. The criteria of adequacy are pragmatic: Does an idea, or hypothesis, help to clarify a problematic context of some kind, and do particular beliefs and values orient us in our purposeful engagement of the environments we inhabit? As Dewey puts this, "a first-rate test of the value of any philosophy" is to ask whether it generates results that render "ordinary life-experiences and their predicaments . . . more luminous to us" and our dealings with them "more fruitful."[11] In sum, while the critical movement in Dewey's pragmatic naturalism engages historical contexts of change in order to critique problematic habits and prejudices, the creative task renders ideas, beliefs, and values vulnerable to the questions of whether or not they help to clarify a given context of experience, or move a line of inquiry forward in some fruitful way, or aid us in the purposeful organismic work of navigating, coping with, and intervening within our various human habitats.

Dewey's integration of critique and creativity, rooted in an appreciation for the full ecology of human life, exemplifies a mode of thinking relevant to the indeterminacies of life in the Anthropocene paradox. This is not surprising, since Dewey is well known for his commitment to making philosophy relevant to the practical challenges of human life. Relevance, in his mind, demanded a melioristic attitude and a democratic community of inquiry. He wrote, "The problems with which a philosophy relevant to the present must deal are those growing out of changes going on with ever-increasing rapidity, over an ever-increasing human-geographical range, and with ever-deepening intensity of penetration."[12] As he interpreted them, the problems of the first half of the twentieth century were problems of the sort that called out for a reconstruction of philosophy. The chief philosophical problem, as he understood it, was that philosophy had not yet truly taken up the "new temper of imagination and aspiration" unleashed by "the revolution in our conceptions of nature and in our methods of knowing it."[13] The catalytic agent of this new temper was "the most revolutionary discovery yet made," a paradigmatic shift from the assumption that the nature of reality is constituted by "underlying fixities" to the recognition that what "is actually 'universal' is process."[14] Dewey understood that while the intellectual history of the West was driven by a quest for certainty, the embrace of process required "a consent to contingency," as Nancy Frankenberry has artfully put this.[15]

The discovery of the universality of process and change in nature, known by Dewey through Darwinian evolutionary theory, did not merely result in a new aspect or dimension of our knowledge of reality. Instead, it led to a wholly new way of seeing nature, to wholly new ways of interpreting the place of humans within nature, and thus also to wholly new ways of knowing and valuing. As Dewey wrote, "The conception of evolution is not so much an additional law as it is a face-about. The fixed structure, the separate form, the isolated element, is henceforth at best a mere stepping-stone to knowledge of process."[16] We begin to see that what we have perceived as fixed, separate, and isolated is not a reflection of the reality of things but is instead the effect of a habitual perspective we have taken toward them. With a "change in standpoint," however, "the whole scheme of values is transformed" and we begin to see that "elements are . . . starting-points for new processes; bare facts are indices of change; static conditions are modes of accomplished adjustment."[17] In other words, we begin to identify things and articulate the objects of our experience in terms of unified functions, or common purposes, rather than static compositions or forms.

Although the idea that nature is processive and dynamic was not exclusively Western, Dewey rightly recognized that the modern Western sciences were bringing the ubiquity of process in nature to visibility in new ways. He was also right that these newly visible realities of process had revolutionary philosophical significance, especially given that the major philosophical systems in the history of the West have generally prioritized ideas and values thought to be "fixed, immutable, and therefore out of time; that is, eternal."[18] On one hand, Western philosophy has historically idealized fixity and its epistemic correlates, such as the concern with absolutes, universals, foundations, essences, and certainties. On the other hand, the modern Western sciences were bringing to focus a picture of nature as dynamic, changing, and in process. As Dewey saw it, the incommensurability between the dominant philosophical prejudices of Western philosophy and the disclosures of the modern sciences accounted for "the whole brood and nest of dualisms which have, upon the whole, formed the 'problems' of philosophy termed 'modern.' "[19] Insofar as these dualisms divided unchanging human ideals from the changing processes of nature, and segregated moral from scientific inquiry, these dualisms needed to be critically demystified. Accordingly, for Dewey, "The problem of restoring integration and cooperation between man's beliefs about the world in which he lives and his beliefs about the values and purposes that should direct his conduct is the deepest problem of modern life."[20] Dewey's commitment to a philosophy of relevance therefore led him to call for a "reconstruction in philosophy" that would coordinate how and what we know about the world with the values and purposes that orient us within it.

To undertake this reconstruction, Dewey critically and creatively uses modernity against itself. He understood that this had social and political as well as philosophical significance. Among other things, "The supposed fact that morals demand immutable, extra-temporal principles, standards, norms, ends, as the only assured protection against moral chaos can . . . no longer appeal to natural sciences for its support, nor expect to justify by science its exemption of morals . . . from considerations of time and place—that is, from processes of change."[21] For Dewey, the idea of nature as process demanded a dismantling of the supremacy of unchanging ideas, final causes, and theoretical problems over ideas of change, efficient causes, and practical challenges. But what is more, these conceptual hierarchies were entangled within a history of social hierarchy. Insofar as "the divorce that was set up between mere means and ends-in-themselves . . . is the theoretical correlate of the sharp division of men into free and slave, superior and inferior," the fascination with the fixed and unchanging and with the certain and absolute is interrelated with oppressive social stratification.[22] Dewey's view of intellectual history was contextualized within a dialectical critique of the diverse forces of intellectual and socio-historical change. The metaphysical and epistemological prejudices of Western philosophy reflect and reinforce the habits of dualistic thinking and a whole network of segregations that privileges theory over practice, knowing over doing, mind over body, and the spiritual over the physical. Dewey critiqued these prejudices and habits on two registers, creatural and contingent. The concern with the fixed, for instance, is rooted in an organismic "quest for a peace which is assured, an object which is unqualified by risk and the shadow of fear which action casts."[23] Action always entails an element of risk and provokes fear insofar as the contexts of action are always changing and the consequences of action are often unpredictable. As Dewey evocatively puts this, "Man finds himself living in an aleatory world; his existence involves, to put it baldly, a gamble. The world is a scene of risk; it is uncertain, unstable, uncannily unstable."[24] While this is especially pronounced in a time of wicked problems such as our own, any person who has ever worked with incomplete knowledge, unpredictable conditions, and imperfect material and has experienced unforeseen outcomes can attest to what Dewey has in mind here. Whether we understand fear as "an instinct or an acquisition . . . [it] is a function of the environment. [We fear] because [we exist] in a fearful, an awful world," a world that is "precarious and perilous."[25]

What Dewey is getting at is that the risk of acting in a changing environment is the tinder that fuels the creatural quest for security, that the quest for security fires the philosophical quest for certainty, and the quest for certainty habitually favors thinking, knowing, and theory over acting, doing, and practice. But whereas the quest for security has creatural roots, Dewey held that the quest for certainty is sustained by historically contingent social and class hierarchies and the material conditions that reproduce them. In particular, hierarchies of class privilege reinforce theory's privilege over practice and amplify the dualisms of mind and body, spirit and matter, and the fixed and changing. Dewey writes, "Classic philosophy was conceived in wonder, born in leisure and bred in consummatory contemplation."[26] Although the luxury of philosophical contemplation was "confined to a few," it was held by these few "as an end given spontaneously or 'naturally.'"[27] Theory and speculation were viewed as intrinsically suited to certain classes and kinds of people but not others. The idealist view of thinking as "the final and complete end of nature became a 'rationalization' of an existing division of classes in society."[28] The prejudicial valuing of theoretic knowing over practical doing not only reflected class hierarchies; it also reflected and reinforced a metaphysics that habitually elevated static Being over dynamic becoming. As Dewey put this, "A local and temporal polity of historical nature became a metaphysics of everlasting being."[29] In these ways, then, the classification and ranking of social differences and the creatural quest for security circularly reinforced the epistemic privileging of knowing over doing, the metaphysical priority of Being over becoming, and the idealization of the fixed and the absolute. All of this is what Dewey had in mind when he declared that the idea of nature in process was "the most revolutionary discovery yet made."

For Dewey, then, the revolutionary interpretation of nature-in-process was socially and politically as well as philosophically revolutionary. It represented a shift from a feudal to a democratic metaphysics. The premodern view of nature not only organized different things and phenomena into distinct kinds and classes; it projected "castes in nature" and pictured the universe "on an aristocratic, one can truly say a feudal, plan."[30] In contrast to the feudal idea of nature as a closed system of fixed forms and definite boundaries, the modern sciences disclosed nature as democratically open and as "infinite in space and time, having no limits here or there, at this end, so to speak, or at that, and as infinitely complex in internal structure as it is infinite in extent."[31] As Dewey interpreted this, nature's infinite internal complexity and spatiotemporal extension compelled "the substitution of a democracy of individual facts equal in rank for the feudal system of an ordered gradation of general classes of unequal rank."[32] Given Dewey's appreciation for the dialectical interplay of ideas and sociopolitical conditions, the historical proximity of the modern scientific "democratization" of nature and the sociopolitical emergence of modern democracy was no coincidence to him. The "discovery" of nature as dynamically processive informed a "transfer of interest from the eternal and universal to what is changing and specific," a transfer of philosophical interest that is mirrored socially in "the gradual decay of the authority of fixed institutions and class distinctions and relations, and a growing belief in the power of individual minds, guided by methods of observation, experiment and reflection, to attain the truths needed for the guidance of life."[33] By connecting the universality of process and change in infinite nature to the democratizing of human society, this quotation reflects the importance of critique to the creative dimensions of Dewey's thought, and specifically his understanding of pragmatism.

Where Charles Sanders Peirce advanced pragmatism as a method for clarifying the meaning of concepts, and William James advocated pragmatism as an approach to truth and to the settling of philosophical disputes, Dewey developed his form of pragmatism into a wholesale philosophical mode of engaging the multiple dimensions of the world of experience—from psychology and education to aesthetics, politics, and religion. Along with Peirce, a polymath whose varied professional experiences included applied and laboratory sciences, Dewey was committed to an experimental approach to the production and testing of knowledge within a community of inquiry. But Dewey viewed the whole of human experience as a laboratory. Consequently, Dewey's understanding of the relevant community of inquiry was more broadly democratic than Peirce's. The community of inquiry relevant to a particular problem included all those affected by the problem and with a stake in its resolution. A more broadly inclusive and democratic community of inquiry provided more experience and input to draw upon in order to creatively engage the problem at hand.

Dewey's commitment to this broader community of inquiry reflected his appreciation for James's conception of experience. In his account of the historical development of American pragmatism, Dewey makes the point of noting that James was an empiricist before he became a pragmatist, and that he understood his pragmatism as a necessary extension of his particular form of empiricism.[34] Dewey affirmed James's commitment to the importance of prospective experience, which James famously expressed when he defined the pragmatic attitude as consisting in "looking away from first things, principles, 'categories,' supposed necessities; and of looking toward last things, fruits, consequences, facts."[35] However, while James evocatively articulated the importance of prospective experience, it was Dewey who appreciated its historical and social significance more fully. After all, while James identified pragmatism as a new name for old ways of thinking, Dewey developed his mode of pragmatism into a creative alternative to old habits and as a critical departure from the past. Along with James, Dewey held that pragmatism "does not insist upon antecedent phenomena but upon consequent phenomena; not upon the precedents but upon the possibilities of action."[36] But contrary to the old habit of thinking that the "world is already constructed and determined" and that the task of reason is to sum it up, Dewey's pragmatic naturalism was active, melioristic, and constructive. He held that "the future is not a mere word" but is a set of perils and possibilities that we, quite literally, knowingly bring to life: "The doctrine of the value of consequences leads us to take the future into consideration. And this taking into consideration of the future takes us to the conception of a universe whose evolution is not finished, of a universe which is still, in James' term, 'in the making,' 'in the process of becoming,' of a universe up to a certain point still plastic."[37]

Thus it could be said that in response to modern philosophy's dualistic quagmire, Dewey's pragmatic naturalism reconstructs philosophy into a causally effective and morally accountable mode of inquiry. As a naturalist, Dewey held that nature is all there is, that there is nothing outside of nature, and thus that there are no supernatural causes or agents. As James put this, for Dewey, "There is nothing real, whether being or relation between beings, which is not direct matter of experience.

There is no Unknowable or Absolute behind or around the finite world.... [Nothing is] eternally constant ... but everything is process and change."[38] This image of nature has profound implications for understanding the role of human thinking and valuing within nature. If nature is all there is, and nature is in process, then human knowing and valuing are not only processes within nature, but also efficacious aspects of nature in process. This means not only that knowledge and values can never be settled once and for all, since they are in motion along with the rest of nature, but also, and more profoundly, that human knowing and valuing causally contribute to the unfurling of nature in process.

Dewey's pragmatic naturalism not only activates human inquiry for melioristic purposes but is a causally efficacious expression of nature's own meliorism. As a mode of immanental thinking, pragmatic naturalism is a dynamic expression of *natura naturans*. If inquiry is not merely active but generative, if reasons are not only significant but consequential, if beliefs and values are not only orienting but efficacious and constructive, then what and how we claim to know and value are morally significant with respect to the futures of nature and human life. Dewey expresses this idea when he suggests that the "pragmatic faith" fuses "love of truth and love of neighbor" through the "conviction that consequences in human welfare are a test of the worth of beliefs and thoughts."[39] To the extent that human knowing, valuing, and behavior are integral to the world "in the making," then we are, in part and to varying degrees, morally responsible for the unfolding future of the human and more-than-human world.

Inquiry in a pragmatic naturalist mode is provisional, participative, and pluralistic, and this entails a shift from correspondence and coherence strategies of epistemic justification to a conjunctive strategy. From a pragmatic naturalist perspective, correspondence theories of knowledge are intrinsically regressive and conservative. They are regressive insofar as they adjudicate how accurately knowledge claims reflect an antecedently held image of how things really are and they are conservative insofar as they assume a static world of facts and values. Correspondence is thus an epistemic form of nostalgia. However, the critical point is not that regression, conservatism, and nostalgia are problematic in themselves and in all cases and respects. Instead, the critique is that correspondence prioritizes the status quo in a world of experience that is constantly

changing—correspondence is epistemically insufficient to the processual complexity of the world. But pragmatic naturalism also rejects the
sufficiency of coherentist theories of knowledge. Certainly the production, transmission, and communication of knowledge require a degree
of coherence between particular claims and a larger network of signification. Yet if the problem with correspondence is that its impulses are
epistemically insufficient to the changing dynamics of a world "in the
making," then the problem with coherentism is that it can easily become
exclusionary and polarizing. By reinforcing disciplinary insularities and
rigidifying the disjunctions among explanatory, interpretive, and normative discourses, epistemic coherentism can end up reifying the dualistic quagmires and bifurcations of modern philosophy.

Thus in place of the sufficiency of either correspondence or coherence
theories of knowledge, a pragmatic naturalist mode of immanental thinking is committed to a conjunctive epistemology. A conjunctive epistemology follows from the pragmatic naturalist commitment to a world-in-process and to knowledge and value claims as vulnerable hypotheses open to
revision through experimental testing. In addition to being fundamentally
vulnerable, hypotheses according to this view are also inherently interpretive and contextually conditioned. Rather than correspondence to
some antecedent image of the way things allegedly really are, or coherence within a culturally or epistemically particular network of concepts
and meanings, justification depends on the functional adequacy of claims
as hypothetic guides through the unfolding contexts, challenges, and
possibilities of a world in process. A conjunctive epistemology is thus
contextual and melioristic, progressive and anticipatory.

In sum, pragmatic naturalism is a conjunctive mode of immanental
thinking that thinks nature from the inside and is an expression of
nature's own patterns, processes, and precarities. Since the melioristic
aim of pragmatic naturalism is to clarify and navigate particular experiences of the world within the broader world of experience, it presumes
that a community of inquiry should include the many for whom the problems and possibilities in a given context of experience are relevant. In
keeping with Dewey's interpretation of the modern scientific shift from a
feudal to a democratic cosmos, pragmatic naturalism likewise entails the
embrace of a democratic episteme. A commitment to a democratic episteme is among the more significant aspects of pragmatic naturalism that

I will carry forward into the constructive work ahead. If one of the aims of a theopolitics for the Anthropocene is to be more fully attuned to the complex interdependencies of a world of more-than-human experience, then it is important that it be inclusive of as wide an array of experiences of the world as possible. Along with this democratic epistemology, I will also embrace a spirit of resistance to certainty, a view of the universe as unfinished, and the idea that human knowing and valuing are causally and morally efficacious. In addition to being relevant to the entanglements of the Anthropocene paradox, these commitments also resonate with the nonlinear complexities of wicked problems.

But the question this brings up and which has been begged all along, is the question of what is meant by "experience." Although this is among the most vexed of problems in the history of philosophy, and although there are no singularly right answers to it, it is a central question within the American immanental tradition, as I will now show by interpreting the "feeling" and "valuing" of immanence in the philosophies of James and Whitehead.

FEELING IMMANENCE: JAMES'S
RADICAL EMPIRICISM

I stressed earlier the importance of the contrast between a "world of experience" and the "experience of the world." The point of this contrast is to indicate that the idea of experience in the American immanental tradition is not limited in kind to human experience or in quality to cognitive or sensory experience—that is, the question of experience within the immanental tradition is irreducible to intentional consciousness, or to the mental capacity to form representations of the world. This distinction having been made, however, it nonetheless remains the case, as Whitehead rightly said, that "The word 'experience' is one of the most deceitful in philosophy."[40] So what is this world of experience that is the context for particular experiences of the world? What is its quality, texture, and feel? In what follows I will first trace some of the ways that James responded to these questions, and then, in the next section, I will turn to Whitehead. Again, my aim is not to offer a new way of reading these major thinkers but to interpret select aspects of their philosophies in order to put them to work in the constructive tasks that remain. Given the idea that the Anthropocene paradox calls for a theopolitics that affirms more-than-human value, creativity, and agency, I will attend in what follows to the importance of the ideas that we feel the world before we know it and that the bifurcation of nature can be bridged through an ontology of internal relatedness that transforms dualistic oppositions into integral contrasts.

The feminist philosopher of religion Nancy Frankenberry claims that the epistemological significance of James's radical empiricism is that it eliminates the problems "associated with correspondence views in the theory of knowledge" and broadens the "understanding of experience from a mere modality of cognition to an inclusion of experienced relations, felt transitions, and qualitative feelings."[41] These are of course not unrelated issues. The relational broadening and affectual texturing of experience are what eliminates the problems of representational correspondence, which reflect and reinforce Dewey's "nest of dualisms." Frankenberry illustrates the epistemic significance of James's account of experience by pointing toward its religious implications. In particular, she claims that James's radical empiricism is religiously significant for two main reasons: "(1) it not only permits but demands a nonreductive way to overcome dualisms between 'God' and 'world,' and (2) it flatly opposes the subject-object view of experience that historically has perpetuated the assumption that the religious dimension of experience has to do with a subject experiencing a religious object as an object among others, much as a person experiences a chair or a table."[42] I will return to the theological and theopolitical significance of these ideas further along, but to prepare for that work, it is important to look a little more closely at what James means by radical empiricism and how Whitehead ontologically deepens that meaning.

Broadly speaking, empiricism treats experience as the source and limit of human knowledge. But the meanings of "experience," its breadth and depth, its quality and character, vary with different types of empiricism. Whereas Descartes assumed all experience was conscious representational experience, and the classical empiricisms of John Locke and David Hume defined experience in terms of human sensory data and impressions, James's radical empiricism includes but is irreducible to either conscious or sensory experience. James's radical empiricism amplifies the breadth and depth of these types of empiricism in two ways. First, it deepens the concept of experience by plunging it into the concreteness of precognitive perception rather than limiting it to the abstract cognitive impressions of sensory data. Second, and correlatively, it broadens the inventory of things that can be experienced. James expresses it this way: "To be radical, an empiricism must neither admit into its constructions any element that is not directly experienced, nor exclude from them any element that is directly experienced."[43]

Empiricism is sometimes thought of in reductive terms—only what can be directly experienced, measured, and quantified can be known. The more rigorous the empiricism, the more reductive and eliminative it becomes. But as this quotation indicates, James radicalizes empiricism by moving in the opposite direction—a more radical empiricism is supplemental rather than reductive, additive rather than eliminative. In particular, James writes that for radical empiricism, "the relations that connect experiences must themselves be experienced relations, and any kind of relation experienced must be accounted as 'real' as anything else in the system."[44] Radical empiricism includes in its inventory of experience relations between things and relations-as-things. Radical empiricism posits that relations between individual things are just as real and accessible to direct experience as the cognitively isolated things of isolated sensory perception.

Elsewhere James defines radical empiricism as consisting of a postulate, a claim of fact, and a generalized conclusion.[45] The postulate is that philosophers should only debate things "drawn from experience." The "statement of fact," as mentioned earlier, is that relations between things, as well as things themselves, can be experienced. This means that the postulate that philosophers should only debate things "drawn from experience" dilates rather than diminishes the range of debatable things. But James also emphasizes that experienced relations can be disjunctive as well as conjunctive, discordant as well as concordant, disconnected as well as connected, ruptured as well as resonant. And yet, as James claims in his "generalized conclusion," while all is not harmonious, all is in relation. He writes, "the parts of experience hold together from next to next by relations that are themselves parts of experience."[46] So it is not just that relations can be experienced as well as individual things, both conjunctively and disjunctively, but also that apart from relations, there is no world of experience—the world of experience is continuous and intrarelated. Although this does not mean that it is a world of harmonious relations, it does entail, as James put this, that "the directly apprehended universe needs . . . no extraneous trans-empirical connective support, but possesses in its own right a concatenated or continuous structure."[47] The world of experience holds together on its own—it is the sufficient answer to the question of how things hang together.

Implicitly, James addresses the question of why there is a world of experience with a description of how it is the way it is. Explicitly, he identifies the continuous or concatenated "how" of things with the concept of "pure experience." He writes: " 'Pure experience' is the name which I [give] to the immediate flux of life which furnishes the material to our later reflection with its conceptual categories."[48] While James developed the idea of "pure experience" late in his career, it conceptualizes the "blooming, buzzing confusion" of a newborn baby's synaesthetically overloaded first encounters with the world, which he discussed in his early work *Principles of Psychology*.[49] Pure experience functions within James's radical empiricism as the connective perceptual tissue of the "world of experience" that precedes and exceeds every cognized sensory "experience of the world." Negatively, this means that every experience of the world is an abstraction from the "pure experience" that connectively structures the world of experience. Positively, however, James held that every experience of the world adds to the world of experience. This additive idea served as the basis for his understanding of the world "in the making" and supported his commitment to metaphysical pluralism. As he stated, "The world is in so far forth a pluralism of which the unity is not fully experienced as yet. But, as fast as verifications come, trains of experience, once separate, run into one another; and that is why . . . the unity of the world is on the whole undergoing increase. The universe continually grows in quantity by new experiences that graft themselves upon the older mass; but these very new experiences often help the mass to a more consolidated form."[50] While these are James's words, they clearly resonate with Whitehead's metaphysics, in which creativity, his category of the ultimate, is described as the process whereby "the many become one and are increased by one."[51]

As a way to transition to Whitehead, it is important to say that by deflating the epistemic function of representational consciousness, radical empiricism inflates the epistemic role of feeling. By prioritizing the vaguely felt dimensions of perceptual experience over the cognitive abstractions of sensory perception, James's radical empiricism troubles the neat Cartesian dualism between *res cogitans* and *res extensa*, or between the mental and the physical, as well as the mutual exclusivity of subjects and objects. By affirming affective experience over cognitive and sensory experience, radical empiricism uplifts the epistemic powers of the physical body. Rather than limiting the experiential range of the conscious mind, the body functions as a physiological and emotional register of the immanental depths and the connective tissue of the world of experience. The mental is not enclosed by the physical, but is opened up by it; the body does not imprison the mind but emancipates it. Radical empiricism transposes the opposition between the subjective inside of mind and the objective outside of body into a mutually enriching contrast, thus bringing into view a bridge beyond the bifurcation of nature. I will now turn to a discussion of how Whitehead transforms James's radically empirical postulate, claim, and conclusion into an intrarelated system of symbolic, epistemic, ontological, metaphysical, and theological hypotheses.

VALUING IMMANENCE: WHITEHEAD'S PROCESS PHILOSOPHY

Whitehead's philosophy is notorious for its linguistic inventiveness and conceptual pyrotechnics. As Isabelle Stengers has accurately described it, the language of Whitehead "is a strange tongue . . . that challenges all clear distinctions between description and tale-spinning, and induces a singular experience of disorientation in the heart of the most familiar experiences. It is a language that can scandalize, or else madden, all those who think they know what they know."[52] He innovates many concepts, as we will see, and uses existing concepts in new ways. This conceptual promiscuity is an effect of his radically empirical commitments. As he writes,

> to discover some of the major categories under which we can classify the infinitely various components of experience, we must appeal to evidence relating to every occasion. Nothing can be omitted, experience drunk and experience sober, experience sleeping and experience waking, experience drowsy and experience wide-awake, experience self-conscious and experience self-forgetful, experience intellectual and experience physical, experience religious and experience skeptical, experience anxious and experience care-free, experience anticipatory and experience retrospective, experience happy and experience grieving, experience dominated by emotion and experience under self-restraint, experience in the light and experience in the dark, experience normal and experience abnormal.[53]

As a result of his fidelity to the "infinitely various components of experience," Whitehead's philosophy reverses many of the conceptual polarities and reanimates the sedimented categories that have formed the history of Western philosophy and theology.

For instance, although Whitehead employs the categories of subject and object, subjects and objects are relationally and phenomenally relative aspects of things rather than ontologically discrete kinds of things. Further, and relatedly, while experience is a central aspect of his system, it is a concept of experience that gives rise to subjects rather than one where subjects have experience; subjects and subjectivity do not precede experience but are effects of experience. Although reality is process for Whitehead, this is a notion of process that coalesces and eddies from moment to moment, rather than a process of pure flux and flow. While Whitehead is certainly a philosopher of relations, his philosophy is organized as well around ontologically basic individual things, which he defines as "actual entities" or "actual occasions."

However, while Whitehead works against the grain of the grooves of Western thought in these and other ways, he does not simply reverse or invert them—instead, he transposes and chiastically reorders them. Whitehead's philosophy is many things, but it is not a philosophy of either/or. As with James's radical empiricism, Whitehead's process philosophy is additive and integrative rather than eliminative and segregative. It is a simultaneously speculative, meliorist, and fallibilist metaphysics that strives to integrate rational coherence, pragmatic applicability, and empirical adequacy.[54] It is a "grassroots" metaphysics that dives through the diffused depths of creativity into "a buzzing world, amid a democracy of fellow creatures."[55]

To enter into this buzzing world of creatural democracy, I will follow a path through Whitehead's ideas about symbolism. This path provides an illuminating way into the meanings of Whitehead's metaphysics of creativity. After all, insofar as Whitehead's philosophy is melioristic, it cannot be adequately understood apart from the problem that provoked it, the bifurcation of nature, and his ideas about symbolism help to show why this problem is so important and how it arises. Whitehead's ideas about symbolism are also directly relevant to the definition of theology I outlined in the introductory chapter. Whitehead's account of the interconnections between the structure of social symbolism and the phenomenology of symbolic reference, especially as he articulates this in *Symbolism: Its Meaning and Effect*, underscores the theopolitical relevance of understanding theology as the formation, critique, and revision of life-orienting symbols.[56] While there are of course varieties and levels of symbolism, to be human is as much about being used by symbols as it is about being a creature who uses them. Whitehead shows why and how this is so through an account of the relation between social symbolism and the deeper phenomenology of symbolic reference.

Sounding a little like Dewey, Whitehead states in *Symbolism* that his "main thesis" regarding social symbolism "is that a social system is kept together by the blind force of instinctive actions, and of instinctive emotions clustered around habits and prejudices."[57] The instinctive forces that hold social systems together are transmitted through diverse symbolic forms, such as language, literature, art, and ritual, but these forms operate on two different registers, conceptual and preconceptual. While the conceptual register orients "individuals to specific actions," the deeper preconceptual register of symbolism functions to organize a "miscellaneous crowd into a smoothly running community."[58] Social symbolism on the conceptual level is essentially normative and instrumental—for instance, civic and religious rituals, as modalities of symbolism, simultaneously shape individuals' and communities' concepts of justice and the sacred and also direct them toward certain patterns of behavior rather than others. But at a deeper preconceptual register, social symbolism is connective. It is at this level that social symbolism can transform aggregates of individuals into communities of selves, and it has this power insofar as it connects the "vague ultimate reasons" that orient individuals to an affective register of behavioral instinct, emotion, habits, and prejudice.[59]

The communal ties that bind individuals together are other, or more, than conceptual—community is felt more deeply than it is known. Social symbolism at its depth functions as a vector of feeling that connectively binds individuals into communities. But of course communities and social systems can change and even dissipate, and often precisely because they are made up of individuals with particular ideas and motivations. As Whitehead puts this, social systems have "to face the disruptive elements introduced by . . . claims for individual idiosyncrasies."[60] They must learn to combine "the advantages of social preservation" with "the contrary stimulus of the heterogeneity derived from freedom."[61] Social change is the result, in part, of critical disruptions and disturbances brought about by individuals or factions that often exist on the margins or peripheries of communities. But whether the impetus to change comes through internal critique or external disturbance, some "new element in life renders . . . the operation of the old instincts unsuitable."[62] By presenting a significant contrast of some kind to the existing social order, this "new element in life" exposes, or brings to visibility, the instinctive emotions, habits, and prejudices of the community, as well as their symbolic mediations.

Social systems both depend upon and are destabilized by symbolism. Once exposed by way of disruptive contrast of some kind, the affective depths and the pragmatic register of social symbolism become subject to interpretation, deliberation, evaluative judgment, and potential transformation. The communally binding vectors of feeling as well as the vague ultimate reasons that orient a community are made vulnerable to critique. As Whitehead writes, "societies which cannot combine reverence to their symbols with freedom of revision must ultimately decay either from anarchy, or from the slow atrophy of a life stifled by useless shadows."[63] This idea is central to the theopolitical thesis in this book: by exposing the exceptionalist, extractive, and externalizing logic of the American redeemer symbolic, the Anthropocene paradox and climate wickedness render the dominant American theopolitical tradition vulnerable to radical critique. In short, the Anthropocene paradox is "a new element in life" that renders "the operation of old instincts unsuitable." And so as apolitical as the forthcoming analyses of Whitehead may seem, they are critical to my constructive tasks.

Given Whitehead's account of social symbolism, social change can be catalyzed by the improvised revision of existing symbolic repertoires or the innovative formation or subversive interjection of new symbols. Not coincidentally, Whitehead's metaphysics is an exercise in just this sort of symbolic improvisation, innovation, and interjection. In a very real sense, it can be thought of as a blueprint for deep social change. It critically disrupts an existing order of things, in this case the inherited metaphysical and ontological order that undergirds many of the categories and concepts, the instincts, habits, and prejudices, and the vectors of feeling and vague ultimate reasons that have normatively oriented the history of Western thought. While Whitehead's metaphysics is critical in this sense, it disrupts through innovation—it disturbs an existing metaphysical order by innovatively prefiguring an alternative set of symbols in order to draw attention to, and to advance, a "new element in life." This "new element" presents a contrast to the dualistic categories and substance habits of modern Western philosophy. Given all that has just been said about social symbolism, dominant categories and habits of philosophical traditions are entangled not only with patterns of thinking, but also with the behavioral patterns and institutional forms of human life—from the very concepts of selves and persons to the structures of interpersonal relationships and relations between different cultural groups, from the traditions and institutions that organize and orient political communities to diverse ways of imagining the sacred and the divine, from theories about the nature and direction of the universe to the very elemental feeling of becoming a being among other beings becoming in their own ways. Thus Whitehead's constructive critique of the dominant categories and habits of modern philosophy, and their taproot in the bifurcation of nature and its correlated "nest of dualisms," is a radically interrogative enterprise— it is not only philosophically bold but revolutionary in the multiple senses that Dewey also had in mind.

Basic to all of this is Whitehead's analysis of the phenomenology of symbolic reference. Analogous to the dual registers of social symbolism whereby individuals are bound together into normative communities, Whitehead's analysis of the more fundamental phenomenology of symbolic reference explains how the connections (and disconnections) between mind and world are forged through the fusions (and frictions) of two different modes of perception. Symbolic reference accounts for how the world appears to us as a world. Rather than pragmatically orienting or socially constitutive, the power of symbolic reference is conjunctive: "The result of symbolic reference is what the actual world is for us, as that datum in our experience productive of feelings, emotions, satisfactions, actions, and finally as the topic for conscious recognition when our mentality intervenes with its conceptual analysis."[64] In other words, symbolic reference is the process whereby our particular experiences of the world, whether at the affective or conceptual register, are conjoined with what Whitehead here refers to as the "actual world," and which I have been referring to as the "world of experience," which transcends any particular individual "experience of the world."

The conjunctive power of symbolic reference originates, according to Whitehead, out of "the interplay between two distinct modes of direct perception of the external world, closely connected but distinct."[65] It is important to consider these modes of perception in some detail since the relation between them illuminates how Whitehead bridges the bifurcation. Whitehead refers to these modes of perception as "presentational immediacy" and "causal efficacy." He describes presentational immediacy as precise but trivial and causal efficacy as vague but important. Presentational immediacy is, roughly speaking, sensory perception, the vivid and direct experience "of the immediate world around us . . . decorated by sense data."[66] Through this perceptual mode the world appears as a "community," a "plenum of organisms," an associational "solidarity of actual things," and we experience the world as "definite in our consciousness."[67] And yet, while this sounds very concrete, Whitehead describes it as a "barren" experience. Although perception in the mode of presentational immediacy connects us to an objective community of actual things in the world, this community of things is objectified, or made objective, by abstract sensory inputs such as sound and color, taste and touch.[68] *Objectivity* for Whitehead is not an epistemic or ontological term but a relational one, a point that I will clarify more fully in my discussion of his concept of "actual occasions." Whitehead's claim here is that objectivity is an abstraction projected onto things through perception in the mode of presentational immediacy. And so although perception in the mode of presentational immediacy discloses an objective world, it is a world "concealed under an adventitious show, a show of our own bodily production."[69] While this world we sense is an associational world of solidarities, the "bonds of presentational immediacy arise from within us."[70]

But Whitehead is not an idealist, subjective or absolute. Instead, and in keeping with the radical empiricism of James, and contrary to the classical empiricism of Locke and Hume, he is saying that direct sensory perception is already abstract. Perception in the mode of presentational immediacy reduces the inherent fullness and independent vitality of actual things. The world as it is immediately present in sensory perception is a compressed world, a mere digest of actuality. The world we sense is merely a slice of things. To explain this, Whitehead makes an important distinction between the formal actuality of things and their objectivity. While formal actuality refers to things as they exist "in their own completeness" independently of any perception of them, things are made "objective" through presentational immediacy. Things exist formally (and concretely) in the unity of their own experience. Things are made objective (and abstract) through the presentational immediacy of sensory experience.

And yet Whitehead is not a dualist, either, and so he does not mean by this that some things exist formally and others objectively—these terms do not refer to ontic attributes but to different facets of things' relationships to one another. This is why Whitehead stresses that even though presentational immediacy is abstract, the world it discloses is a world of solidarities and communities. No individual thing exists apart from a functionally active relationship to some other things. Actuality is thus an effect rather than an antecedent cause of activity—things are what they are, even in the formal "unity of their own experience," as a result of relational activity.[71] The reality of things, their actuality as something rather than nothing, is an emergent effect of their intrarelatedness to other things. Things do not first exist and then relate to one another in a merely external way; they are always already internally related.

But in the mode of presentational immediacy, this objective solidarity of things is sensed only in the abstract. The vital solidarity of things, or the active relationality of solidarity, is not sensed—it is felt. It is felt through perception in the mode of causal efficacy, and it is felt nostalgically as a vitality that has always already perished. In direct contrast to presentational immediacy, in which the bonds of connectedness arise from within us, "the bonds of causal efficacy arise from without us" and "disclose the character of the world from which we issue."[72] Where presentational immediacy is a perceptual mode characteristic of higher organisms, perception in the mode of causal efficacy is "the experience dominating the primitive living organisms, which have a sense for the fate from which they have emerged, and for the fate towards which they go."[73] Perception in the mode of causal efficacy is affective rather than sensory and brings us into contact with time's flowing, with the occasional, eventual structuring of experience in time. Rather than the vivid precision of presentational immediacy, perception in the mode of causal efficacy "is vague, haunting, unmanageable."[74] It is haunting because it is "heavy with the contact of the things gone by," it is "the hand of the settled past in the formation of the present."[75]

The haunting vagueness of causal efficacy is important for many reasons. For one, it links Whitehead's empiricism to his rationalism. Through an affective subversion of the limits of both sense and reason, he controverts Hume's reduction of the empirical to direct sensory experience, on the one hand, and Kant's reduction of the rational to the mentally in-built categories of understanding, on the other.[76] By plunging James's radical empiricism into the ontological depths, Whitehead discovers affectional connections beneath and between the rational and empirical. Thus if Whitehead's ideas about social symbolism lead to the claim that community is felt more deeply than it is known, his ideas about symbolic reference lead to the more radical claim that not only is the world felt before it is known, but it is felt before it is sensed. Evocatively describing the relation between feeling and sense, Whitehead writes that "The contrast between the comparative emptiness of Presentational Immediacy and the deep significance disclosed by Causal Efficacy is at the root of the pathos which haunts the world."[77] Put otherwise, what is vaguely felt is the relational flowing of things becoming in time for themselves, and what is hauntingly felt is the persistent perishing of things becoming for others. In this way, through Whitehead's theory of symbolic reference we can begin to feel the bifurcation of nature transposed into a contrast between modes of perception, a contrast that interconnects the difference between any "experience of the world" and the deeper "world of experience." A turn to Whitehead's "actual occasions" will help to materialize this contrast.

For Whitehead, the most fundamental realities in nature are not independent things or substances but individual relational processes, which he refers to as "actual occasions," or "actual entities."[78] They are the "final real things of which the world is made up. There is no going behind actual entities to find anything more real."[79] The structure of actual occasions, as energy events, literally provides a window into all other things, from the things we perceive with our senses even to ourselves as observers, from organs to organisms—they are the "stuff" of the cosmos through which the processes, patterns, and precarities of the cosmos come into view. In other words, Whitehead's metaphysics is holographic—every "occasion is a microcosm of the whole universe."[80] Although actual occasions function metaphysically in a way that is similar to Leibniz's windowless monads, in distinct contrast to monads, actual occasions are "all window."[81]

In one of Whitehead's most compressed and memorable metaphors, he describes actual occasions as "drops of experience, complex and interdependent."[82] By describing actual occasions as "drops" Whitehead is saying that the most ontologically fundamental elements of reality are both individuals and more than individuals, both one and more than one. Actual occasions are not only individual things externally related to one another. Rather they are individuals that are both internally related to one another and to a larger reality of processes. As internally related to one another, or intrarelated, actual occasions include aspects of one another in themselves, and therefore also aspects of the larger processes of reality in which they are included. Actual occasions, as ontologically basic and finally real, are intrarelated individuals included within a larger reality that, through their intrarelatedness to one another, they themselves also partially include.

This larger reality of processes that includes actual occasions and that they partly include within themselves is the whole of experience—actual occasions are "drops of experience" in a vast ocean of experience. Actual occasions are individual experiential events within the unfurling of the larger world of experience. It is not just that experience is not limited to the sensory experience of conscious subjects. As Whitehead puts this, "Consciousness is a variable uncertain element which flickers uncertainly on the surface of experience."[83] But nor is it merely that affective experience precedes or is more basic than both conscious experience and sensory perception. Instead, and paradoxically, the individuality of actual occasions does not precede or preexist experience. They do not undergo experience. Rather, experience occasions the individual, and the individual is one of the occasions of experience.

These "drops of experience" are also "complex and interdependent." With this description Whitehead offers a road sign that simultaneously points the way to the crossing of the bifurcation of the mental and physical and to a detour of the classic metaphysical aporia of the one and the many. To say that actual occasions are complex is to say that they are structural wholes made of interconnected aspects. To use another important concept of Whitehead's, they are "dipolar," comprising mental and physical aspects. This is how Whitehead works around the habits, instincts, and prejudices of substance dualism, according to which the most fundamental things are either physical or mental. As "the final facts" there is no going behind actual occasions; they are the most basic units of creative process. They are what they are because of how they are, which is to say, they are an effect of how they relate to other final facts and the larger processes of reality within which they are included, and which they include within themselves. As Whitehead succinctly states, "How an actual entity becomes constitutes what that actual entity is. . . . Its 'being' is constituted by its 'becoming.' This is the 'principle of process.'"[84]

By interpreting what is most fundamentally real through the structure of an occasion, or through an event ontology, Whitehead indicates not only that to be is to become, but that to be is to become in relation to, with, and even for others. As I have already said, occasions for Whitehead are internally rather than merely externally related to one another. They do not exist only alongside one another, spatially and temporally, but they coconstitute one another, and this coconstitutive internal relatedness is affective, perceptual, and aesthetic. Whitehead develops the concept of "prehension" to signify these dynamics of internal relatedness. In contrast to "comprehension," which connotes cognitive understanding or connectedness, "prehension" signifies the fundamentally perceptual nature of relatedness—prehensions are the feeling vectors through which things are perceptually and aesthetically related to one another.

Whitehead analyzes the vector function of prehensions into three factors: "(a) the 'subject' which is prehending; . . . (b) the 'datum' which is prehended; (c) the 'subjective form' which is how that subject prehends the datum."[85] The "subject" in this case is the occasion with respect to its becoming. Against the habit of substance thinking, the subject is not an entity that already exists. Rather than being an actual thing that precedes prehension, the subject is incipient, a possibility coming-to-be through the dynamics of prehension. In its coming-to-be, this incipient subject selectively prehends relevant data from the proximate past of other occasions that exist objectively in relation to it. To say that these other occasions exist objectively is to say that they have already come-to-be, or, to use two other important concepts from Whitehead, after having "concresced" into "satisfied" subjects in themselves they immediately perish and become objective data for the becoming of others.

But if the occasion is subjectively incipient, or in process of becoming, in what sense is it selecting relevant objective data from other occasions— if "it" is concrescing and coming-to-be, how can "it" decide? This is where the concept of "subjective form" comes in. Subjective form is the particularized vector shape through which the relevant objective datum from the past is affectively integrated into the subject in its becoming. Whereas the affective relation that internally relates the subject coming-to-be to the objective datum of some occasion that has already come-to-be is physical, the subjective form that shapes the particular way in which that physically felt datum is integrated is conceptual. This is why Whitehead describes actual occasions as dipolar, as consisting of physical and mental aspects. Subjective form, then, aesthetically integrates the mental and physical aspects of actual occasions, as well as occasions with one another, and also, as I will soon discuss, with God. So, what accounts for the aesthetic integration of subjective form and where does subjective form come from and how does it arise? Similar to the tripartite structure of prehensions, subjective form is a function of three elements: the particular matrix of relational conditions in which the incipient subjectivity is situated, the possibilities available to it as envisaged by God (which possibilities Whitehead refers to as "eternal objects"), and the causal efficacy exercised through the act of deciding on particular possibilities or eternal objects.

Through these dynamics of subjective formation, an actual occasion comes-to-be or concresces into an individual something; it becomes a subject; it becomes one. At the same time, however, it is not only or merely a subject, and as an individual, it is not only or merely one. Whitehead rejects the Cartesian dualistic habit of thinking of some things as subjects and others as objects. Subject and object are not ontological categories for Whitehead. Instead, an occasion is both subject and object at different times. At the moment an occasion concresces into its own nature as a subject in itself, it becomes an object for others—there is no moment of stasis. Subject and object are relational and phenomenal contrasts rather than opposed ontological categories. Nor is the occasion merely one. Insofar as it is an individual constituted by relational processes, it is a one made of many. And thus the metaphysical opposition between one and many and the ontological opposition between objects and subjects are transformed into the generative contrasts of creative process.

The occasion is an emergent phenomenon born out of the processual, relational unfolding of the creativity of the universe. Actual occasions are occasions of experience, not the experience of intentional or representational consciousness, but the more primal affective and aesthetic experience of becoming a creatively experiencing one in relation to, with, and for the experiential creativity of many. As Whitehead rhythmically describes the process, "The novel entity [actual occasion] is at once the togetherness of the 'many' which it finds, and also it is one among the disjunctive 'many' which it leaves; it is a novel entity, disjunctively among the many entities which it synthesizes. The many become one, and are increased by one."[86] The affective, perceptual, and aesthetic character of the relational processes through which the "disjunctive diversity" of many passes into "conjunctive unity" and then passes again into disjunctive diversity and so on is the expression of Whitehead's category of the ultimate, creativity, and creativity is the principle of novelty in his cosmology. Creativity is the fecund, organic, natal coming-to-be of the universe-in-the making, the unfinalizability of cosmic aesthesis.

As I indicated in the introduction to this chapter, one of the most compelling aspects of Whitehead's philosophy in relation to this project is how it works against the grain of ontological exceptionalism—there is nothing in the cosmos that is not constituted by actual occasions, and there are no relations in the cosmos that are not related in the way that occasions are intrarelated. As Whitehead states this, "God is an actual entity, and so is the most trivial puff of existence in far-off empty space."[87] This ontological antiexceptionalism, however, does not mean that the cosmos is ontologically homogenous. While "the principles which actuality exemplifies all are on the same level," "there are gradations of importance, and diversities of function."[88] These gradations and diversities are a function of the different ways in which actual occasions are ordered. Whitehead describes aggregations or connected pluralities of occasions as nexūs, which constitute the things of ordinary human sense experience—tables, chairs, rocks, but also the atmosphere, persons, and even space. But nexūs themselves are structured in different ways. Some nexūs are structured societies of conformally related occasions, such as hair or rock. Other structured societies are personally ordered, which is to say that their connectedness not only is conformal, but endures with a continuous, serially integrated identity. The distinction between nonpersonally and personally ordered societies turns on the difference between conformal togetherness on the one hand and enduring serial continuity plus conformal relatedness on the other. But whether or not these structured societies are personally or nonpersonally ordered, Whitehead refers to them as enduring objects, the stuff, things, and relations of ordinary human sensory experience.

For my purposes here, it is not important to extend this analysis of the profusion of concepts with which Whitehead elaborates the diverse structures of the cosmos. But I offer this brief summary for three reasons. The first reason is to show that, as I alluded to in my introductory chapter, to say that nature is all is not to say that nature is undifferentiated. Far from being in contradiction with the principle of ontological antiexceptionalism, the unfathomably wild heterogeneity of the cosmos is imagined by Whitehead as instantiating that very principle. Second, these concepts, and the different scales and complexities of order they signify, underscore how deeply relational the cosmos is, from the quantum structure of actual occasions themselves to the animate and inanimate objects of sensory experience. Everything exists in, as, and through relationship—cells, stones, and storms as well as selves and civilizations are all intrarelated societies of different kinds. Third, these concepts help to illuminate not only how Whitehead's vision breaks through modern Western dualism and bridges the bifurcation of nature, but also how it points beyond the anthropocentric prejudices of the Western philosophical and religious imagination. The human is not at the center of Whitehead's cosmology insofar as the human is not the only experientially active catalyst of creativity in the universe. The experience of creativity and the creativity of experience are diffused throughout the cosmos. No species or kind of thing has a monopoly on creativity; no species or kind of thing is an exception; no species or kind of thing stands unaffectedly outside the creative processes of reality.

This embargo on ontological exceptionalism leads into a discussion of Whitehead's concept of God. As a way to move into this discussion, recall my earlier description of Whitehead's philosophy as holographic. I hope that the preceding analyses have helped to clarify this idea. Consider, for example, the structural similarities between Whitehead's theory of symbolic reference and the dynamic of prehension. Recall that Whitehead's theory of symbolic reference builds upon two different but intrarelated modes of perception, presentational immediacy and causal efficacy. In my interpretation of this, I showed how symbolic reference serves a vector function that interconnects mind and world and individuals and collectives. The dynamic of prehension functions in a similar way, but on a different level. Symbolic reference describes, at the level of organismic consciousness, the perceptual transfer of always already past aspects of the "world of experience" into the conceptual immediacy of a particular "experience of the world." Similarly, the dynamic of prehension describes the affectual transfer of data from some proximately past occasion into the integrative becoming of an emergent occasion. Where symbolic reference illuminates the intrarelatedness of minds and worlds and selves and societies, prehension illuminates the intrarelatedness of actual occasions, the final facts of reality.

It is helpful to keep holography in mind in turning to a discussion of Whitehead's concept of God. For if symbolic reference is a vector of perception and prehension a vector of feeling, God for Whitehead functions as a vector of possibility and novelty. In discussing this, I want to emphasize two points up front. The first point is that Whitehead's concept of God is functional and aesthetic. As a mathematician, the concept of "function" has a particular meaning for Whitehead, as a solution to a problem.[89] In particular, Whitehead's concept of God functions as an aesthetic hypothesis intended to solve the problem of how his cosmology can hang together in a way that is also productive of novelty. A second and related point is that the relation between Whitehead's concept of God and his cosmology is chiastic and transpositional. By this I mean that

Whitehead's concepts of God and cosmos are related to each other through crosswise inversions of origination and polarity. Through these inversions Whitehead's ultimate category of creativity crosses traditional theism's bifurcation of God and world. In place of this God-world bifurcation and the exceptionalist logic it instantiates and reproduces, Whitehead integrates the differences between God and world into an aesthetic logic of mutually enriching contrasts. As Whitehead describes this, "God and the world are the contrasted opposites in terms of which Creativity achieves its supreme task of transforming disjointed multiplicity, with its diversities in opposition, into concrescent unity, with its diversities in contrast."[90] Whitehead's God is an aesthetic medium of cosmic creativity rather than a Creator who creates the cosmos ex nihilo.[91]

Whitehead describes God as the only actual entity that is not also an actual occasion. God's actuality is a nontemporal actuality that, Whitehead insists, eminently exemplifies, rather than stands as an exception to, the processes of creativity. Like all other actual entities, God is dipolar. Whitehead describes this dipolarity in terms of God's primordial and consequent aspects. Primordially, God is the conceptually felt realization of infinite potential or cosmic possibility. But if this were all that God was, God would be monopolar and deficiently actual. Full actuality is dipolar and entails the integration of physical and conceptual feelings. As the abode of conceptually felt cosmic possibility and the eternal objects that provide actual entities with their initial aims, God's primordial aspect lures the world into its own becoming. The primordial aspect of God is God dreaming cosmic possibility, which Whitehead describes as divine eros. In mutually enriching contrast to this, the consequent aspect of God is divine pathos, God's feeling for cosmic actuality.

As stated earlier, Whitehead conceives of God as an exemplification of the processes of creativity, but in reverse order. Although God is dipolar like other actual entities, the ontological structure of God's polarities is transposed. While other entities originate through physical feelings for actual others and concresce by integrating conceptually felt eternal objects that originate from God, God originates as the conceptual feeling of all possibility and continues to become through the process of physically feeling the world's perpetually perishing actuality. As Whitehead describes this transposition, "An actual [occasion] in the temporal world is to be conceived as originated by physical experience with its process of completion motivated by consequent, conceptual experience initially derived from God. God is to be conceived as originated by conceptual experience with his process of completion motivated by consequent, physical experience, initially derived from the temporal world."[92] Thus imagined, God functions as the link between actuality and possibility, the catalytic source of cosmic novelties, and the sympathetic host to perishing actualities.

One of the central problems Whitehead's concept of God is intended to resolve is the problem of novelty. Novelty is a problem for Whitehead insofar as his most basic ontological principle states that everything that exists must exist somewhere, and every somewhere is always an actual entity. Recall that Whitehead asserts that actual entities are the finally real things in the universe; there is nothing behind them. So if there is possibility or potential for novelty in the universe, then it must exist in some actual entity. Novelty does not come from beyond what is actual but is immanent within it. God for Whitehead is the actual entity that provides an ontological location for this potential for novelty. More specifically, the potential for novelty is located within the eternal objects envisaged within God's primordial aspect. Insofar as eternal objects constitute the possible ideals or aims that shape the subjective form of any entity that comes to be, they are the hinge of novelty in the universe. But there is more to the God-world relation than this. While divinely envisaged possibilities lure the cosmos, cosmically manifest novelties enliven God. After all, given Whitehead's account of the affectual and aesthetic depths of the intrarelatedness of actual entities (or occasions), if God and the world are ontologically intrarelated, then they feelingly give form to each other. As God is enlivened by God's feeling for the perpetual perishing of the novelties of the world, from quantum occasions to ecological systems to human civilizations, so also are the things of the world enlivened by the lure of their feeling for the possibilities envisaged for them by God. As Whitehead describes this, "the consequent nature [of God] is the weaving of God's physical feelings [for cosmic actuality] upon his primordial concepts [cosmic possibility]."[93] God is enlivened insofar as the contrast within God between the consequent feeling of the cosmic past and the primordial conceiving of cosmic possibility is more intensively integrated. The world is enlivened insofar as the intensification of the aesthetic contrast within God lures the cosmos toward the actualization of its own possibilities.

Whitehead's chiastic God is an aesthetic, moral, and metaphysical hypothesis. It is constructed to solve the problem of how cosmic actuality and potentiality can hang together in a way that both conserves value and is generative of novelty. While this functionally immanent concept of God is not the ontologically exceptional, metaphysically transcendent God of traditional theistic faith, it is a concept of God that can become a basis for ongoing "leaps of the imagination," as Isabelle Stengers has evocatively argued.[94] For this very reason, wonder about Whitehead's God remains, as he would be the first to acknowledge and encourage. Among these wonderings are the questions of whether Whitehead's concept of God actually is an ontological exception, despite his insistence to the contrary, and whether it is a solution to a problem that does not need to exist.

Although Whitehead conceives of God as an actual entity, God is very much unlike other actual entities in at least two respects.[95] First, God is constantly concrescing, is never satisfied, and is nonperishing. All other actual entities concresce into a state of final satisfaction and then perish. Second, insofar as God is the source of every entity's initial aim, God is directly intrarelated to all entities. No other entity is directly intrarelated to all other entities. In both of these respects, God seems to be an ontological exception to other actual entities, rather than their chief exemplification.

It is also possible to argue that a stronger case for novelty is available by understanding it as contingent, emergent, distributed, and temporal. According to this view, instead of existing antecedently in the nontemporal form of eternal objects and ingressing into individual actual entities, novelty emerges through the becoming and perishing of complex relational combinations of things. In other words, the potential for novelty is ontologically distributed through the cosmos rather than concentrated within God's primordial aspect. Rather than solving the problem of where to locate ontologically the potential for novelty, God becomes a problem by becoming ontologically redundant. Why monopolize the potential for novelty? To the extent that everything else in Whitehead's system militates against monopolies, his concept of God seems to stand out as an exception.

Rather than proceeding to interpret and evaluate the diverse responses to these and other critiques of Whitehead's God, which would entail writing another book, suffice it to say that the jury is hung and the verdict is likely to remain out, for reasons articulated succinctly by George Allan:

> A special reality, a God of some sort, a *deus ex machina*, can be introduced into Whitehead's metaphysics in order to provide the novel aims and the novel aspects of the valuations, reversions, and transmutations involved in the creative advance of our complexly balanced dynamic universe. For those *who on other than metaphysical grounds believe in such a God, such a move is appropriate*. However, I see no metaphysical justification for doing so, since the principle of Creativity and the categoreal conditions it entails provide all that is needed to explain the world as we find it. And we should never multiply metaphysical entities beyond necessity.[96]

I am strongly inclined toward Allan's wisdom here, but for more than parsimonious reasons. Instead of staking out a position by ferreting out the subtleties of Whitehead's metaphysics, I would like to question Whitehead's God through appeal to his less speculative, earlier work *Religion in the Making*. Rather than asking about the metaphysical necessity of Whitehead's concept of God, I would like to question its pragmatic religious sufficiency.

In one of the most frequently quoted phrases from *Religion in the Making*, Whitehead defines the religious sensibility as "the art and the theory of the internal life of man," as "what the individual does with his own solitariness."[97] But Whitehead presents his fuller interpretation of religion in much more relational and "worldly" terms. With respect to the solitary individual, Whitehead writes that the religious sensibility arises out of the "concurrence of three allied concepts in one moment of self-consciousness."[98] These concern the value of the individual for itself, the value of individuals for one another, and the value of the world, which undergirds and interconnects the values of the lives of the multiplicity of individuals and their relation to one another. In other words, although the religious questions may emerge through solitary evaluative self-questioning, the problem of one's own value cannot be resolved in solitude because it leads one into relational questions concerning others' value and the value of the world.

Contrary to first appearances, then, Whitehead's point about the "internal" and "solitary" is not that this is the end or purpose of religion. Rather, the solitary self alone *is* the problem that provokes religious sensibility. Whitehead writes that, as a solitary individual, the self asks, "What, in the way of value, is the attainment of life?" He immediately adds that the individual "can find no such value till it has merged its individual claim with that of the objective universe."[99] While the question of one's own value may emerge out of the immediate and idiosyncratic particularities of one's individual experience of the world, it is resolved through the recognition that individual value is not only intrarelated to but also contingent upon the value of a multitude of others in the larger world of experience. Thus the art and theory of internal life lead outward to the idea and practice of religion as solidary "world-loyalty."[100]

Whitehead's argument for the religious significance of the world's and others' value, in combination with his accounts of the cosmic distribution of creativity, experience, and agency, leads me to the position that, aside from the question of its metaphysical necessity, Whitehead's concept of God mystifies a fuller, more vital, religiously world-loyal appreciation for the creative processes of reality. Whitehead writes that the purpose of religion is to help us to recognize that "our existence is more than a succession of bare facts." It is to help us to see, and feel, that we "live in a common world of adjustment, of intelligible relations, of valuations, of zest after purposes, of joy and grief, of interest concentrated on self, of interest directed beyond self, of short-time and long-time failures or successes, of different layers of feeling, of life-weariness and life-zest." If this is so, then for those who are willing fully to feel the brute finality of the world's perishing as integral to its beauty and value, then this religious purpose is arguably more fully realized without God.[101]

Nancy Frankenberry expresses this view of Whitehead without God with a luminosity that deserves to be quoted at length:

Now that we no longer view the world of nature as the manifestation of inevitable necessity, as in Greek metaphysics, or as the gratuitous gift of a creator God, as in the biblical myth, we can affirm the ephemeral and transitory quality of the prehensive tissues by which we hang together, agreeing with the poet Wallace Stevens that "death is the mother of beauty." . . . Regarded as infinite and inexhaustible, nature's possibilities inspire awe and commitment. No eschatological "time" need be envisaged in which all possibilities are completely exhausted or fully actualized; the very assumption that temporal process is without beginning or absolute end serves to intensify the sense of contingency. . . . As a felt quality of life itself, contingency gives rise to a sense of the poignancy of perpetual perishing, the fleetingness of all things. We see life's groundless, brief, gratuitous, and complete contingency, and we are stirred by a sense of its once- for-allness, its irrevocableness, and the solemn finality of our freedom. . . . The spirituality that goes along with the new understanding we have of the creating universe . . . is beyond belief and unbelief. Vividly, in the midst of life, creating is going on all around us, in the miraculous birthing of a child from the mother's womb, in the exquisite fingers of the concert violinist, in the lofted soaring jump of an Olympic skier . . . and in the ancient wonder of the rising moon and the myriad stars. All of these are congeries of events, complex patterns, configurations of the continual mattering of energy, bursting forth from the unlikely harmony of hydrogen, and hanging—unsupported, frameless, free—in the blackness of space and the wormhole of time, a cascade of sparks in the night.[102]

Perhaps this wondrously wild world of more-than-human creativity and experience is more than enough to provoke the deeply religious experience of world-loyalty.

———— ∞ ————

In 1935, at the conclusion of an early analysis of Whitehead's *Process and Reality*, the philosopher Charles Hartshorne posed the question of the social and ethical relevance of Whitehead's philosophy. He wondered whether it was sufficient to "aid humanity in its struggle against the incompetence, greed, and inertia which now threaten [the] very existence [of humanity] in civilized form?"[103] For Hartshorne, this struggle was "a race with catastrophe" that could be averted "not merely by improving upon [our] stock of general ideas but also by bringing more fully to bear those which [we] already [have]."[104] The idea Hartshorne believed needed to be more fully brought to bear was the idea of democracy. Writing amid the Great Depression, he was critical in particular of the contradiction of a society that was democratic in governmental form but profoundly undemocratic in economic substance. Hartshorne was thus asking, in essence, of the relevance of Whitehead's process cosmology to the contradictions of American democracy.

My motivating concern in this book is an amplified version of Hartshorne's. Thanks to the last few decades of the neoliberal form of the redeemer symbolic, economic inequality in the United States has soared. Furthermore, due to the increasing financialization of politics, economic inequality and political inequality now more intensively reinforce each other and compound persistent racial injustice. The ecological crises and climate wickedness now amplify these inequalities and injustices. In other words, the contradiction that concerned Hartshorne is deeper and wider than ever before and now has planetary implications. For these reasons, the Anthropocene paradox constitutes what Whitehead refers to as a "new element in life," a disruption so elemental that it calls into question many of the most entrenched instincts, habits, and prejudices of modern Western thought.

While this disruption enfolds a multitude of crises, I also believe that there is creative potential within it. If we view the Anthropocene as a "new element in life" through the lens of Whitehead's cosmology, it is possible to see its natal aspect as well as its dangers: by bringing an end to the idea of the human as set apart from the rest of nature, it can also bring life to an ecological view of the human. The Anthropocene paradox both demands and makes possible a new frame, ethos, and aim for the theopolitical. Similarly, to the extent that the moral phenomenology of climate wickedness brings an end to certainty, it can also bring life to a way of knowing that is more attuned to the creative potential of ambiguity. Since the immanental aspects of Whitehead's, Dewey's, and James's philosophies prefigure these possibilities, I am more confident than Hartshorne was of their contemporary relevance to both the contradictions of American democracy and the larger paradox of the Anthropocene.

As I suggested earlier, to develop this relevance more fully it is important to expand on the pragmatic naturalist idea that by resisting the false security of certainty we can more creatively engage the moral gravity of the crises we face. The melioristic, hypothetic, conjunctive, and prospective character of pragmatic naturalism is appropriate to the nonlinear, contextually uneven nature of moral and political problems such as climate wickedness. Furthermore, by breaking through the binaries of theory and practice and fact and value, pragmatic naturalism can remind us that the way we conceptualize and engage moral problems can be as morally significant as the effects of our interventions. For the pragmatic naturalist, if humans are a part of nature, if we are *terra bēstiae*, then human knowing and valuing are aspects of nature naturing. Pragmatic naturalism thus embraces the idea that insofar as knowing and imagining are modes of doing, the work of knowing and imagining is always already moral work. In the aftermath of certainty, pragmatic naturalism affirms an ethos of inquiry, curiosity, and critique attuned to the moral depths of the thinking of immanence.

From radical empiricism and process philosophy, it is important to carry forward the moral, theological, and political significance of affective relationality, the idea that we feel and value the world and our relations before we know them. In particular, Whitehead's theory of symbolic reference supports a conceptual shift in our notions of moral and political agency: it leads to a view of moral and political actors as "emotional approximators" rather than rational calculators.[105] Leveraging this conceptual shift can lead to more strategically effective approaches to social change. Furthermore, by resisting and moving beyond the empiricism of discrete objects and subjects, the radically empirical commitment to relations-as-things and things-as-relations is attuned to the uncannily viscous and nonlocal phenomenology of hyperobjects like climate change. Process philosophy's attention to the aesthetic forms and values of our connections to a multitude of creative others reminds us that we are not alone. It illuminates our dependence on more-than-human creativity, and affirms our accountability to a vast solidarity of creatures other than ourselves. And by playing upon the chords that connect the creative tones of planetary actuality with the rhythms of cosmic possibility, it can help us to discover that every particular experience of the world is embedded within a wider world of experience that arcs backward into the depths of the past and forward into the unfurling future.

I will also build upon the implications of Whitehead's ideas with respect to questions of political power and agency, and in particular for thinking through the democratic ideal of the power of the people. As I argued earlier, Whitehead's distributed view of experience and creative agency unsettles the philosophical basis for any monopolistic concept of power. It is directly opposed to the ideal of unitary, oppositional power embedded within the dominant American political theology. In direct contrast to the ideal of unitary, oppositional power, Whitehead's understanding of power is dipolar and relational. Furthermore, power is not only about the capacity to act or to do; it is also the capacity to be acted upon and to undergo. Thus power is receptive as well as active, and there is not only vulnerability in power but power in vulnerability.

In these ways among others, the philosophies of American immanence show that human thinking, feeling, and valuing unfold in a context of relational depth and complexity that is both more-than-cognitive and more-than-human. What we do to the Earth and to the myriad of more-than-human forms of life, we do to ourselves. What we do to ourselves, we do to larger social systems. What we do with our economy does not stay in the economy. How we live and move and have our being as societies of societies impacts the societies of societies in the world to come, if we do not first of all destroy the world that is. With the moral gravity of these relationships in mind, it is now time to turn to the theological lineages of American immanence and to the outline of a planetary theology that integrates the religious significance of the claims that everything is intrarelated, that we feel and value the world and our relations before we know them, and that neither God nor humans are the center of value and experience in the universe.

4

DIVINING IMMANENCE

American Immanental Theologies

Hosanna! Not in the highest, but right here, right now, this.
—URSULA GOODENOUGH, *THE SACRED DEPTHS OF NATURE*

There have been other biologically cataclysmic mass extinctions in the history of Earth. But the one that is unfolding now is the first to be biologically caused.[1] We have become the first living creatures on this planet in relation to whom the future of life has become vulnerable. We are the first about whom it may be said not only that we prey upon other living things but that we prey upon the possibility of life itself. And although we may be made of the same stuff as every other living being on the Earth, we are the first to be consciously and empathically aware that we have brought the planet to the brink of biocide.

As I discussed in the previous chapter, the philosophies of American immanence show us that we feel the world before we know it. This feeling of the world makes it possible to come to know it in a different, more vital way. What and how we claim to know the world and others influence what and how we understand ourselves; what and how we understand ourselves influence what and how we understand our responsibilities to one another and to the many other forms of more-than-human life; and what and how we understand these things are entangled with the affectual depths of causal efficacy that interconnect the processes, patterns, and precarities of nature naturing. In light of all of this, the underlying question in this chapter is the theological question of whether or not the feeling of the mass extinction of more-than-human life, along with the knowledge of our culpability for it, is enough to lead us to a form of religious life that embraces the contingency of what we assume to be necessary, the vulnerability of what we too often view as invulnerable, and the perishability of what seems permanent. In other words, can the feeling and awareness of the precarious value of life, life within the larger cosmos, and our own human lives amid a multitude of other lives awaken us to the precious depths of immanence, to living as if this, our one and only world, matters ultimately?

It is important to underscore that this is a religious path that rejects traditional theistic understandings of God. The embargo on exceptionalism in American immanence leads to the disavowal of the idea of God as a supreme supernatural being that ontologically transcends nature and history. In keeping with the naturalistic commitments of American immanence, conscious purposiveness cannot exist apart from embodied brains. For all that we know empirically and through publicly tested scientific inquiry, conscious purposiveness is a physically emergent phenomenon—it entails a brain, and a brain entails a body. But traditionally theistic ways of symbolizing God imagine God as a disembodied intentional being or a discarnate conscious reality. God is therefore imagined as an ontological exception to the embodied contingency of consciousness. The ontological antiexceptionalism of American immanence thus rejects this traditionally theistic way of imagining God.

However, the more interesting theological possibilities of American immanence have less to do with what the embargo on exceptionalism rejects than with what it affirms—that nature is all there is and that the mysteries of the patterns, processes, and precarities of nature naturing are religiously and theologically significant. As described previously, nature within the American immanental frame is not a determinate thing. It is not the environment that surrounds human life. It is not a reality set apart from other realities. There is no outside to nature and thus nature is not a term of contrast or distinction—nature has no other. For all that we can know within the naturalistic constraints of American immanence, everything that is, is nature, without exception—what there is, has been, and will be is *natura naturans* (nature naturing) and *natura naturata* (nature natured). But to say that nature has no other is not to say that there is no difference in nature, or that nature is undifferentiated, or that nature excludes alterity.[2] Nature naturing is generative of an endless multiplicity of kinds and forms and modes of nature natured, of things and beings, creatures and persons, relations and events. In this sense, the claim that nature is all opens rather than closes the curiosity that drives theological inquiry and intensifies the mystery, wonder, and awe that fund religious experience. In contrast, the idea of a supernatural God, or God as a supreme entity existing beyond or outside of nature, artificially encloses the questions of scientific and theological inquiry and the wild-eyed wonder, mystery, and awe provoked by the unfathomable depths of immanence. The God hypothesis of traditional theism may be compatible with a quest for certainty, often camouflaged in the language of faith, but the quest for certainty is incompatible with the frame of American immanence. So rather than arresting thought or stifling religious feeling, the American immanental tradition emancipates radical theological wonder, mystery, and inquiry from arbitrary enclosure.

And yet the disavowal of traditionally theistic accounts of God does not necessarily entail the rejection of all ways of symbolizing God, the sacred, or the divine. To have meaning within an immanental theological frame, such symbolizations can reflect the finally mysterious and morally ambiguous patterns, processes, and precarities of nature naturing, select aspects of nature naturing, such as the creativity that gives birth to the novelty in the universe, to the idea of nature beyond God, or of God as or within nature. I refer to nature naturing as "finally mysterious and morally ambiguous" for the reason that an immanental frame of thought, as articulated in the previous chapter, entails epistemic constraints that challenge any determinate, absolute claims about the totality of what exists. To make such claims would be to presume that one's own account of the world is an exception to the limiting epistemic conditions of embodiment, historical and culture contingencies, and social location. Such claims presume that one's tradition, revelation, methodology, or episteme is an exception to the contexts and conditions that constrain all other systems of knowledge. This does not invalidate speculative philosophy, but it does mean that speculative generalizations, as exemplified by Whitehead, should be understood as hypothetic and empirically accountable. In order not to violate the embargo on ontological and epistemic exceptions, then, nature naturing in an immanental frame is the indeterminate that is, the unfurling creative matrix of being and becoming, knowing and valuing. This indeterminacy functions simultaneously as a lure and a limit to speculation.

Within the frame of American immanence, the symbol of God can function as a religious symbol that integrates human life around phenomenologically transcendent meanings, values, and ideals that have emerged from within nature and history. As Dewey presents this in *A Common Faith*, God can be usefully, even reverently, interpreted, as a focal symbol of socially and existentially powerful ideals.[3] Although constructed by human minds and historically transmitted through human culture, these ideals, perhaps especially when integrated within a unitive symbol like God, can orient human individual and communal life in ways that morally transcend the particularities of our own historical, cultural, and personal interests. In other words, God can function as a symbol that connects us to, and inspires us to realize, a good beyond ourselves, a common good. Or, as we have seen with Whitehead, God can be understood as an aesthetic hypothesis that holds together the fecund matrix of novelty in the universe, a symbolic "poet of the world" that exemplifies and is affected by the creativity that pulses through the cosmos.

My claim from the beginning of this book has been that the overlapping and mutually amplifying climate changes of the Anthropocene paradox simultaneously provoke the need and create the conditions of possibility for reimagining and enacting a new kind of political theology. In a time in which it has become empirically and scientifically impossible to think about the human apart from nature, not to mention morally and politically irresponsible, we need more than ever to rethink our concepts of power, value, and common life in an ecological context that takes seriously the internal relatedness of human and more-than-human life. A bifocal theopolitics that combines a politics of, by, and for the people with an immanental theology of, by, and for the planet seeks to accomplish this.

With all of this in mind the purpose of this chapter is to articulate an immanental theological frame for such a political theology. I will first offer a conceptual map of American theologies influenced by the philosophical themes articulated in the previous chapter. I will then articulate a philosophy of religion that integrates elements of the American immanental tradition, insights from select African American and feminist philosophers of religion, and the discourse of vulnerability and resilience.

I will then articulate a theology of immanence that correlates an account of religious experience to what I will describe as a "prismatic" theory of value.

DIVINING THE GOOD AND BEAUTIFUL: AXIOLOGICAL AND AESTHETIC THEOLOGIES OF IMMANENCE

American philosophers of religion have interpreted and developed American theologies of immanence under various headings and with diverse thematic emphases.[4] William Dean, for example, identifies what he refers to as "American religious empiricism" as a tradition organized around the ideas that experience is the ground and test of knowledge and religious belief, and that the scope of experience includes affectional, aesthetic, moral, and spiritual as well as sensory experience.[5] Dean sees variations of these commitments throughout the history of American religious thought—in diverse Native American ways of honoring, interpreting, and valuing nature; in Puritan understandings of history as the theater of Divine Providence; in Jonathan Edwards's understanding of the "sense of the heart" as a channel of religious experience; and in the introspective nature spirituality of Transcendentalism.

An important distinction between earlier and later expressions of American religious empiricism is the recognition that if the scope of experience includes subjective and culturally conditioned affectional, aesthetic, moral, and spiritual dimensions, then the meanings and values of religious experience are historically dynamic and demand constant reinterpretation and revision. Furthermore, the reinterpretive imperative of multidimensional experience is an additive process, a hermeneutical spiral that deepens and complicates the religiously relevant contexts and objects of experience. Neither religious traditions nor their symbols, practices, and texts are static—they are in a constant process of development and reinvention. A second critical distinction between earlier and later expressions of American religious empiricism is the eschewal of any sort of supernaturalism. While prototypical expressions of American religious empiricism tended to be metaphysically dualistic and attributed conscious purposiveness to God, later expressions were naturalistic—nature is all, and it is more than enough.[6] Accordingly, the historicity of human cultural systems, including religious systems, should be interpreted within the evolutionary contexts of natural history. A full embrace of these historicist and naturalistic commitments leads not merely to relativizing the meanings and values of the histories, texts, rituals, and institutions of religious traditions, but also to the critical interrogation of objects of religious devotion, including the idea of God.

The integration of these historicist and naturalist ideas, and their implications for the study of religion and theology, led to the emergence of what has come to be called the "Chicago School" of theology. In 1904, William James was the first to identify what was going on at the University of Chicago as a "school."[7] The importance of this is not that James was the first to notice, but that he identified some of Dewey's core ideas as the school's "common core." As James described Dewey's ideas, "There is nothing real, whether being or relation between beings, which is not [a] direct matter of experience. There is no Unknowable or Absolute behind or around the finite world. . . . [There is nothing] eternally constant; no term is static, but everything is process and change."[8] Within Dewey's pragmatic naturalism, every situation or experience comprises the mutually influential relation between an organism and environment—as the organism interprets and responds to the environment the environment changes, which entails that in every situation or experience, both the environment and organism are "reconstructing" each other. Though Dewey soon left Chicago for Columbia University, his pragmatic naturalist and radically empirical appreciation for the world-in-process continued to influence Chicago for several decades, especially at the Divinity School.

The Chicago School of theology extended, roughly, from the late nineteenth century to the late twentieth.[9] Its early, sociohistorical phase was represented by thinkers such as Shirley Jackson Case and Shailer Mathews, who were especially concerned with the use of social and historical criticism to illuminate the developmental nature of religious traditions, doctrines, and dogmas. Drawing upon the evolutionary and instrumentalist impulses of Dewey's pragmatic naturalism, these thinkers were more concerned with the way religious ideas and symbols functioned in social and historical environments than with questions of absolute or eternal truths. Influenced by the organism-environment dialectic at the core of Dewey's thought, the functionalist orientation of these thinkers led them to interpret change and development in religious traditions in terms of social adaptation and adjustment. Well before Whitehead's concept of "actual occasions" entered into the lexicon of the Chicago School, thinkers such as Mathews interpreted the social history of Christianity in terms that foreshadowed Whitehead's metaphysical account of the prehensive dynamics of creativity. For Mathews, Christian thinkers and institutions adapted their symbols and practices to their environments by selectively carrying forward aspects of their inherited past. As a result, adaptation not only altered the trajectory of the tradition, but also affected the social and cultural environments in relation to which future iterations of the tradition would eventually adapt. As organisms and environments dynamically change one another through processes of reciprocal adaptation, so also do religious traditions and their social and historical contexts mutually condition and cocreate one another. Organisms and environments, and traditions and histories, are internally related to one another. While these sociohistorical dynamics may be taken for granted nowadays, in the first decades of the twentieth century, they were quite radical ideas, especially when applied to the study of religion and theology.

The early Chicago School's concern with social and historical processes eventually took a cosmological and metaphysical turn. The later phase, constituted in large part by the work of Henry Nelson Wieman, Bernard Meland, and Bernard Loomer, developed and elaborated the theological implications of Whitehead's process philosophy. Wieman, who had been invited to the Divinity School to give an interpretive lecture on Whitehead in 1927, was more centrally focused than his sociohistorical predecessors on the question of the reality of God and the object of religious devotion. For Wieman, the dynamic social meanings and historical values of Christianity could not be sufficiently interpreted apart from the question of the ultimate object of Christian religious commitment. Wieman granted that the symbols, practices, and textual interpretations of religious traditions change through time and that these changes could be interpreted as developmental or adaptive processes. Dynamic change is intrinsic to the very idea of religious experience for Wieman, but the more interesting questions for him were how and why these changes hang together through time. As he states, "There can be no questions about the fact of religious experience. . . . The only questions are: What sort of object is experienced? And second: What is the significance for human living in such experience?"[10] Wieman did not view these questions as an abandonment of the empirical, pragmatic, and naturalistic "community of temper" associated with the Chicago School. Rather, he held that the intellectual standing of theology and the study of religion as empirical enterprises depended on specifying and defining the religious object, the "whence" that gives rise to the social and historical forms of religious experience.

Over the span of his career Wieman came to imagine the religious object as that which "operates in human life with such character and power that it will transform man as he cannot transform himself."[11] The object of religious devotion, the "whence" that accounts for the continuity of religious experience and thought, is not the whole of nature's processes, but is a particular moral pattern within it—it is the pattern of creative good, or the creative event through which good increases amid the processes of nature. He writes, "When good increases, a process of reorganization is going on, generating new meanings, integrating them with the old, endowing each event as it occurs with a wider range of reference, molding the life of a man into a more deeply united totality of meaning."[12] As the pattern within nature and history through which good increases, meanings expand, and experience is enriched, the creative event represents an organic and axiological account of the divine. It is a more-than-human but fully immanent good-in-utero.

The creative event is a precarious pattern within the processes of nature naturing. It is a natal ultimate, the birthing of value within and through nature. It is neither identical to the whole of nature's processes nor reducible to human metrics of moral value. According to Wieman, although it "is always and absolutely good . . . in the sense of creating value," it "must often destroy value already created in order to achieve the best possible under the conditions prevailing."[13] In other words, while creative good always and absolutely creates good, the good it creates, including human moral good, is always and absolutely precarious. The precarity of created goods, or their ontological vulnerability, is intrinsic to the axiological pattern of the creative event. The creative good within the process of nature naturing creates precarious goods, which are integrated, destroyed, or reorganized into the pattern of creative good. Wieman's immanental divine, the creative event, is superhuman but not supernatural. The creative event works within and through human life but is irreducible to human life; it is a nonanthropocentric, more-than-human axiological ultimate.

In light of this, according to Wieman, the human moral task "is to shape human conduct and other conditions so that the creative event can be released to produce maximum good. . . . [This task consists of the effort] to remove obstacles and provide sustaining conditions which release the power of creative good to produce value."[14] Human life can affect the conditions through which the creative event unfolds, by impeding or aiding its creative advance, but human life does not create good, at least not in the ultimate sense that defines the creative event. However, one problem with this ethical aspect of Wieman's project is that if the creative event is irreducible to human moral metrics, and if human goods are intrinsically vulnerable and subject not only to reorganization but even to destruction by creative advance, then it would seem that the human moral task is flying blind. After all, how are we to discern whether or not we are removing or creating obstacles, sustaining or impeding the creation of good, if the nonanthropocentricity of the creative event is irreducible to, even potentially in contradiction with, the anthropogenic form and anthropocentric biases of our human moral metrics?

Partly in response to questions such as these, Bernard Loomer developed an alternative immanental theology. Although he was deeply influenced by Wieman, along with Whitehead, James, and Dewey, Loomer's argument is distinct in two important and intrarelated respects. First, he held that if the object of religious devotion is ultimate—that is, if the religious object is a reality, value, or truth that relativizes and contextualizes all other realities, values, and truths, then it should not be minimized to a mere aspect or pattern within nature naturing, as presented by Wieman. Second, Loomer articulated an aesthetic rather than an axiological account of the divine, and an aesthetic rather than a moral account of the human religious task. In short, Loomer developed his immanental theology in an aesthetic key in response to Wieman's axiological immanental theology, and he did so by correlating the concept of God, and human religious experience, to the aesthetic whole of nature's processes rather than to one of its precarious moral patterns.

In an essay curiously titled "The Size of God," which is arguably Loomer's most developed theological statement, he identifies his continuity with the Chicago School by claiming a process-relational mode and radically empirical method of philosophical naturalism. He states up front that "if the one world, the experienceable world with its possibilities, is all the reality accessible to us, then one conclusion seems inevitable: God is to be identified with either a part or with the totality of the concrete, actual world."[15] His essay develops the case, as already indicated, that "God should be identified with the totality of the world, with whatever unity the totality possesses."[16] If identifying some totality entails identifying some kind of unity—otherwise there is only the flux of indeterminacy—then the theological issue for Loomer is how to discern and name the unity of things. He approaches the task as a radical empiricist and a process-relational thinker. As a radical empiricist, he holds not only that concepts and ideas are derivative abstractions from sensory physical experiences, but also that sensory experiences themselves are derivative abstractions from our feeling, or affective experience, of the concrete actual world. Taking this radically empirical sensibility to its philosophical and theological conclusion, Loomer claims that "The unremovable, intellectual arbitrariness of the premises of meaning that undergird our systems of explanation symbolizes the immanence of the mystery of existence that absorbs not only our questions but also our deep-rooted criteria of value and intelligibility."[17] Importantly, Loomer's point is not only that the premises of our systems of explanation and meaning are "intellectually arbitrary," but that they are "unremovable." Thus Loomer affirms that we cannot help but to abstract, generalize, and speculate, and that our abstractions, generalizations, and speculations are always fallible, open to question, and revisable.

This affirmation can legitimately lead in two very different directions. On the one hand, it can lead to the relentless critique of concepts and categories and the deconstruction of explanatory and interpretive systems. On the other hand, it can lead to the experimental construction of new, but always revisable, flights of thought.[18] Loomer takes this second, Whiteheadian path, and develops a speculative empirical theology. He identifies the foundationless premises of meaning as a sign pointing to "the immanence of the mystery of existence." For Loomer, then, the instability of thought, the fragility and vulnerability of concepts and categories, beckons rather than blocks theological inquiry. Thus the theological insight of Loomer's radical empiricism is not only that the finally irreducible quality of affective experience "enshrouds the unfathomable or inexhaustible mystery inherent within the factuality of the world."[19] The more radical insight is that this mystery encompasses all questions, exceeds all answers, and even absorbs the criteria we develop to navigate between questions and to evaluate among answers. This liberates theology into radically constructive possibilities, allowing theology to become a kind of aesthetic project, a playful making of something new, a theopoietic divining of immanence.

So what does this leave us with? Is the unity possessed by the totality of things a mystery? Yes, this is an important aspect of Loomer's claim. And yet is evoking mystery saying anything determinative? No, and this is also an important aspect of Loomer's claim. The unity possessed by the totality of things is a mystery, and this mystery, as mystery, is indeterminate. Any determinate name for this indeterminacy is an abstraction that artificially encloses mystery. To evoke the idea of an indeterminate unity in an open way that reflexively acknowledges the abstractness of all such ideas, Loomer articulates the concept of "the interconnected web of existence."[20] The concept of "web" conveys Loomer's commitment to a Whiteheadian metaphysics of becoming and relational ontology, and, importantly, it does so in a way that prioritizes aesthetic interdependence over rational order. A web, for example, a spider's web, has order, but it is an emergent order that is precariously contingent upon the more fundamental interdependence of its threads. The concept of a "web" therefore aesthetically integrates the abstract and concrete. It is a concept that conveys two important ideas: while the totality of things can be said to possess a unity, this is always a vulnerable unity that emerges out of what is more fundamental—the mystery of concretely actual interconnections among things. Order is a consequence, or an effect of how the world is the way it is, rather than, as classical arguments from design would have it, an antecedent causal reality that explains why the world came to be the way that it is.

Loomer goes further, however, in arguing that this concept of "web" can be deified and imagined through the symbol of God. Recall that, for Loomer, concepts of ultimacy should symbolize the unity of the totality of things, rather than merely a part of things. God is a symbol that can and has functioned in this way. God is a concept of ultimacy that, Loomer argues, symbolizes the "interconnected web of existence," or the mystery that immanently pervades and indeterminately unifies the totality of things. God is a unitive symbol that—partly as a result of the unendingly contested indeterminateness inherent to it as a concept of ultimacy—refers to the indeterminate mystery that ultimately unites and is immanent within the totality of things. And yet, why is the symbol of God necessary here, and how is it useful? Is not God functioning here as a mere cipher for the "interconnected web," the mystery that immanently pervades and indeterminately unites the totality of things? Why signify the webbed indeterminacy of mystery with a sign that, in traditionally theistic usages, tends to refer to something ontologically determinate? Why not just refer to the "interconnected web" itself?

Loomer offers two rationales for deifying the web, ontological and pragmatic. Ontologically, God has historically functioned as a symbol of ultimacy, and since Loomer takes the webbed world to be ultimate, God is therefore an appropriate symbol. But this rationale problematically neglects to resolve the contradiction between traditionally supernatural and entitative concepts of divine ultimacy and the naturalistic, immanental, process-relational reality that Loomer takes to be ultimate. Be that as it may, Loomer's pragmatic rationale is more compelling. He argues that using the concept of God to symbolize the interconnected web can animate a style or mode of living that increases the "stature," "size," and "potential richness" of life. It is the ambiguity within the symbol of God itself that can lead to a way of living within, rather than a quest to overcome, the ambiguous indeterminacy of the interconnected web of existence. The symbol of an ambiguous God, as he puts it, "conjoins the sense of ultimacy in meaning and the immediacy of experienceable actuality."[21] By conjoining ultimacy and immediacy, the symbol of God can evoke an "attachment to life" that integrates the "heights and depths of existence, including the qualities of profound religious encounters and the resources for living an abundantly meaningful life" with the "concrete realities of this world," including "all the evil, waste, destructiveness, regressions, ugliness, horror, disorder, complacency, dullness, and meaninglessness, as well as their opposites."[22]

In light of these ideas, the human religious task for Loomer is closer to aesthetic integration than moral discernment. It is about the enrichment of experience that can come from holding together, and deeply feeling, the intense contrasts in life—the highs and lows, the good and the bad, the surprising and the mundane. If, as Loomer's and Wieman's colleague Bernard Meland once put this, "we live more deeply than we think," then an important element of the religious task is to think and feel into those depths, the depths of immanence.[23] The point of that task is not to finally come to know what is ultimately true or absolutely good. Rather, the aim is to enrich and enliven human experience of the webbed interconnectedness of the world in a way that enriches and enlivens others' experience as well, and to live out more fully an "attachment to life" that gives reverent witness to what Whitehead referred to as "world-loyalty."

Through thinkers such as Wieman and Loomer, the Chicago School of theology developed important and wide-ranging expressions of American immanental theology. In recent decades, contemporary theologians and philosophers of religion have extended and innovated, revised and redeveloped the pragmatic naturalist, radically empirical, and process-relational "community of temper" in a myriad of ways. These thinkers include, among others, Christian process theologians such as John Cobb, David Griffin, and Marjorie Suchocki; Christian theistic naturalists such as Charlie Hardwick and Karl Peters; the feminist philosopher of religion Nancy Frankenberry, who works with radical empiricism, classical and neopragmatism, and analytic philosophy; religious naturalists such as Donald Crosby, Loyal Rue, and Jerome Stone, who work on philosophical, historical, comparative, and religious ethical issues; the philosophical theologian Robert Corrington, who has developed ecstatic and aesthetic forms of naturalism influenced by ordinal metaphysics, semiotics, and psychoanalytic theory; pragmatic naturalist philosophers of religion including Victor Anderson and William D. Hart, who have each contributed significantly to expanding the canons of both African American religious studies and the philosophy of religion more broadly; the prolific philosophical theologian Robert Neville, whose wide-ranging, systematic philosophy of religion works across west and east Asian religious traditions and draws especially from the semiotic pragmatism of Charles Sanders Peirce; the philosopher of religion Wesley Wildman, who works across the fields of philosophical theology, religious studies, and the sciences; the Womanist theologian Monica Coleman, who works with process theology to cross boundaries in African American religious studies and queer and disability theology; the theopoeticist Catherine

Keller, who blends process, ecological, and feminist theologies with continental philosophy of religion; and the philosopher of religion Carol White, who works in feminist philosophy of religion and has recently developed an African American religious naturalism.

As prolific as these scholars are and as varied as their projects and interventions have been, they would all agree that there is important ongoing work to do in the way of developing new connections between the pragmatic naturalist, radically empirical, and process-relational lineages of American immanence and other contemporary discourses. And the purpose of this ongoing developmental work is of course not simply to extend the tradition for its own sake, but to innovate the tradition in ways that continue to address contemporary challenges and opportunities. If there is a "community of temper" that holds these disparate thinkers and projects together, it is similar to the one that John Randall suggested held together the diverse projects of mid-twentieth-century American philosophical naturalism. The thinkers who today continue to innovate this tradition, such as those just mentioned, reflect this temperament of inquiry in their willingness to think without foundations, to think against philosophical and theological absolutes, and to think across disciplinary divides. In these ways, this tradition continues to divine the relevance of the immanence of the divine to the problems, possibilities, and paradoxes of the present.

AN IMMANENTAL PHILOSOPHY OF RELIGION

It is now time to articulate the immanental philosophy of religion and theology that will frame the theopolitical work in the next chapter. I will make the case that a systems-theoretic interpretation of vulnerability and resilience helps to mobilize the pragmatic naturalist, radically empirical, and process-relational temper of American immanence for the critical and constructive tasks of political theology. I will then articulate a theology of religious experience in planetary perspective. The aim is to develop a theology of immanence that resists the bifurcation of natural and human life and spans the boundaries between the cosmic and the planetary. This is needed in order to open an imaginary space of reason and desire through which to negotiate the questions of power, value, and common life provoked by the paradox of the Anthropocene. It should go without saying that, in keeping with the experimental spirit of American immanence, what I offer is suggestive rather than final, a revisable set of concepts, ideas, and hypotheses that inevitably require further testing and development.

At the outset it is important to recall that by the Anthropocene paradox I refer to the condition of living as ecological creatures in a human age for the Earth—in making the Earth *homo imago*, we have discovered ourselves as *terra bēstiae*. The cultural anthropologist Roy Rappaport captures this paradox well when he writes that "The nature of humanity . . . is that of a species that lives and can only live, in terms of meanings it itself must fabricate in a world devoid of intrinsic meaning but subject to physical laws. We face now the maturing of the contradiction, inherent in that nature from its very beginnings, but which modern conditions or the conditions of modernity allow, or even encourage, to become acute."[24] The maturing of the contradiction described by Rappaport is close to what John Dewey understood as the epistemically and culturally revolutionary implications of affirming both that nature is all and that nature is in process. My gloss on Dewey is that his pragmatic naturalism not only turns a spectator approach to philosophical reflection on the world into a process of instrumentally engaged inquiry within the world, but transforms inquiry into a mode of moral responsibility. Insofar as human inquiry is an expression of nature's processes, it is an element within the unfurling of nature naturing. If human inquiry and behavior are embedded within and emerge out of nature's processes, and if these processes are evaluative in the deep sense that Whitehead has described them, then human inquiry and behavior not only are causally effective within but also morally impinge upon nature. Rappaport acknowledges this moral dimension of inquiry as well. He writes that it is not just that "humanity's conventional foundations . . . [are] fabrications," but also that our fabrications can "so misconstrue the world's physical nature as to lead to actions that will damage it, possibly irreparably."[25] What and how we claim to know the world, and the images and stories we fabricate within it, are morally consequential, for good and for ill.

The American immanental tradition provides a way to critique the "fabricated" modern Western bifurcation of nature and to repair the damage it has caused to human and more-than-human life. The philosophies and theologies of American immanence show that this bifurcation grounds and enables the opposition of mind and world, thinking and feeling, fact and value, human and animal, culture and nature, and God and world. By bridging this bifurcation in various ways, the philosophical and theological lineages of American immanence transform these oppositions into contrasts and show that conscious human experience of the world is but the bare surface of a deeper, wider world of experience. They show that the world is felt before it is known, that valuation is a dynamic aspect in the coming-to-be of all things, and that there are diverse ways of divining immanence that move beyond the question of the life or death of God.

In these ways among others, the American immanental tradition provides a philosophical and theological imaginary that resists the dualisms, binaries, and oppositions that, as I argued in chapters 1 and 2, sustain and sanction the theopolitical logic that drives climate wickedness and has led to the Anthropocene. Insofar as the concepts of vulnerability and resilience, as I will define them, cross these bifurcations and span the conceptual chasm between social, cultural, and ecological systems, they can be usefully integrated into a countersymbolic that moves American immanence into a theopolitical register.

One reason for working with these concepts is related to the importance of dialectical thinking and the idea of contradiction in the theopolitical work ahead. Although I will discuss this at more length in the next chapter, it is important to say now that by "contradiction" I refer to a tension or conflict within a system that is simultaneously intrinsic to its functionality and yet also a potential source of its dysfunction and collapse. By "system" I mean any functionally organized set of things, or a set of things integrated around a purpose. Such systems can be physical, mechanical, economic, cultural, or religious, and they can be simple or complex. For example, a disassembled bicycle is only a set of physical things, a latent mechanical system at best. An assembled bicycle, however, is a manifest system, a set of things functionally organized. When an intelligent rider is added to the simple system of the assembled bicycle, it becomes a complex adaptive system, or a system that can learn through dialectically iterated cycles of experience.

Contradictions in systems do not inexorably lead to collapse. It depends on the internal state of the system, the nature of the contradiction, and the behavior of the surrounding and interconnected systems. One hypothesis informing my work in what follows is that contradictions in dialectical systems are functionally analogous to vulnerabilities in complex adaptive systems. Identifying contradictions and analyzing vulnerabilities in systems are thus a critical interpretive task that can help us to understand how systems function. And understanding system functionality is a necessary step in the moral and political work of discerning where, how, and when to intervene in systems in order to change them. In other words, dialectical contradictions and complex systemic vulnerabilities can be "catagenic"—system breakdown can be leveraged for system change.[26] Thought of in this way, vulnerabilities and contradictions are significant sites of critical learning and system change as well as potential sources of system breakdown.

Vulnerability and resilience can be defined in many ways for different contexts. For my purposes at this point, I interpret them as metadisciplinary analytic concepts referring to the behavioral habits of systems in response to the inevitability of change in a processive world. Systems can be more and less vulnerable, more and less resilient. Degrees of vulnerability and resilience vary according to the components, structures, and processes that internally constitute a system, on the one hand, and the exposure of a system to external threats and risks, on the other. The degree to which a system can anticipate, identify, integrate, resist, or adaptively learn from change is the degree to which it is vulnerable or resilient. Resilient systems are characterized by internal diversity, redundancy, agility, cohesion, and responsivity. Conversely, vulnerable systems are relatively homogenous, inflexible, internally disconnected, and unresponsive. Instead of adaptively "bouncing back" from disturbance or resisting, mitigating or being strengthened by change, vulnerable systems decompose and are prone to collapse.

Thus defined, vulnerability and resilience are nonmoral attributes of system functioning. They are not in themselves morally or politically charged. So the question of whether a system is good or bad or just or unjust is categorically different from the question of whether it is resilient or vulnerable.[27] But these concepts have analytic power relevant to the critical and constructive tasks of political theology. In particular, as I will illustrate in the next chapter, they provide a powerful set of concepts useful to the hermeneutic task of interpreting the cultural depths and the multilayered dynamics of socioecological and socioeconomic systems. They can also be used to identify weaknesses and strengths in systems in order to strategically intervene within them, whether to critically interrupt them and accelerate their demise, or to creatively leverage change in order to build up their resilience. Thus the analytic and strategic utility of these concepts corresponds not only to the constructive and critical tasks of political theology, as formally defined in my introduction, but also to the theoretic and practical dimensions of resilient democracy, as I will show in the next chapter.

To the extent that vulnerability and resilience productively perform these analytic functions, they illuminate some important insights. The first and most basic is that in a world of overlapping and interpenetrating systems, some cooperative and some countervailing, vulnerability and risk are ontologically basic—*esse qua esse vulnerabilis est*. To be a system in a world of systems is to be vulnerable. Though many systems are resilient, some more than others, all systems are vulnerable to some degree and at some point. The second truth is that human systems—from individual selves to cultural and social systems and economies—are structurally embedded within, functionally dependent upon, and interconnected with all of the other systems of nature. The human habitat is socioecological. This interconnectedness means that systems mutually influence one another in diverse ways, positively and negatively. The third truth is that systems are dynamic, and the more complex they are, the more nonlinear and unpredictable their behavior will be.

The discourse of vulnerability and resilience illumines the world as a multilayered nest of systems and interpenetrating feedback loops, of chance and randomness, of surprise and uncertainty, of incremental changes cumulatively leading to tipping points, of cascading phase shifts, of the emergence of novelty, and of the possibility of renewal through breakdown. The world seen as a system of systems is a scene of uncertainty, creativity, and risk—a world of wicked problems in the aftermath of certainty, a vulnerable world that includes within it opportunities for critical learning and the possibility of more resiliently democratic expressions of social and ecological justice. With this brief summary of these concepts, and a hint at their relevance to the critical and constructive tasks of political theology, I will now integrate these concepts into a philosophy of religion and an immanental theology.

I would like to draw together several different ways of thinking about religion, beginning with the idea that religion is about the more-than-cognitive expression of what ultimately orients human life. I refer here to the theory of the African American philosopher of religion Charles Long, who argued that religion refers to "orientation in the ultimate sense, that is, how one comes to terms with the ultimate significance of one's place in the world."[28] By exploring the diverse cultural contexts of religious expression, and particularly the diversity of African American religion, he elaborates that religion is "more than a structure of thought; it is experience, expression, motivations, intentions, behaviors, styles and rhythms. Its first and fundamental expression is not on the level of thought."[29] Religion for Long is neither merely belief, nor merely feeling, nor merely action, nor merely devotion or worship. It is all of these things and more insofar as it embodies a person's or a community's sense of the ultimate significance of life.

Long's view of religion resonates with a radically empirical philosophy of religion. Consider the Chicago theologian Bernard Meland's evocative claim, referenced earlier, that "we live more deeply than we think." Meland's expression is an apt, compressed summary of radical empiricism. It reflects the radically empirical deflation of intentional consciousness, which, as previously described, is one of the sharpest contrasts between radical and classical empiricism. By deflating the epistemic function of intentional consciousness, radical empiricism inflates the epistemic function of affect and feeling. It prioritizes the affectively felt, aesthetic depths of immanence over abstract cognitive propositions or beliefs about the world. Similarly, by interpreting religion through concrete "experience, expression, motivations, intentions, behaviors, styles and rhythms," Long resists the tendency to reduce religion to matters of mere belief. As radical empiricism affirms the epistemic significance of the affective and perceptual over the cognitive and the sensory, Long's understanding of religion highlights the aesthetic forms and styles of religious life.

Along with Long's aesthetically embodied account of religion, aspects of Grace Jantzen's feminist philosophy of religion also inform this immanental philosophy of religion. For Jantzen, a philosophy of religion attuned to contemporary cultural conditions and injustices should "work towards a new religious symbolic focused on natality and flourishing rather than death."[30] In keeping with this natal symbolic, Jantzen conceives of the sacred as "a horizon of becoming, a process of divinity ever new, just as natality is the possibility of new beginnings."[31] This account of the natal becoming of the sacred resonates with a process ontology of the divine as well as the axioaesthetic theological visions of Wieman and Loomer.

Integrating Jantzen's and Long's insights with the systems concepts of vulnerability and resilience offers a way of imagining "religion" as a constellation of symbols, rituals, values, aesthetic practices, and institutions that is oriented around the natal potency of some transcendent ideal. The transcendent ideal has natal potency insofar as it gives life to meanings, purposes, and desires that empower and sustain resilience in human lives and communities. It is transcendent functionally and phenomenologically, rather than metaphysically or ontologically, insofar as it provides a critical standard that relativizes and orders other ideals. Within this immanental philosophy of religion, "the religious" can be interpreted as the qualitative experience of being sensitized to, and reverent before, the existentially, socially, and morally orienting presence of phenomenologically transcendent ideals as they are manifest in the diverse registers of life. In keeping with Dewey's philosophy of religion, the "religious" is not a special type of experience monopolized by religion, but is a quality of experience that exists potentially within and across diverse registers of human life—intellectual, aesthetic, moral, political. In these ways, and in resonance with Whitehead, religion and the religious express the solidary and solitary aspects of living amid the vulnerabilities of life in an aleatory, processive world.

Integrated into a broader theoretical hypothesis, this immanental philosophy of religion informs a view of diverse religious traditions as historically extended, cultural systems of symbols, rituals, and beliefs that transform vulnerable groups of humans into resilient human communities by binding them together with common identity, meanings, and purposes. Through story and ritual religions establish, justify, and regulate the moral norms, behavioral conventions, and social hierarchies necessary to ordering large-scale human groups. They console, inspire, pacify, and provoke. Religions have done great good and great harm. They have joined together and they have divided. But in the end, as the religious naturalist Loyal Rue has wittily put this, religion is not about

God.[32] Instead, religions are about us. They are historically adaptive cultural projects that transform humans who merely happen to be grouped together in space and time into human communities bound together with identities and purposes that transcend space and time. They reinforce norms of reciprocity, fairness, and sanctity that simultaneously integrate their adherents socially and set them apart from others. Through mutually reinforcing networks of ritual practices, stories, values, transcendent ideals, and social institutions, religions orient individuals and communities through the blessings and burdens of life's vulnerabilities.

This broader theoretical hypothesis is useful for comparison across traditions, for interpretations of their internal diversity, and also for analyses of the religious aspects of traditionally nonreligious phenomena. For example, one could say that, for Christians, the transcendent ideal is salvation and that vulnerability can be understood as a cognate of sin, or alienation from God, self, and others. For Buddhists, the transcendent ideal is nirvana, the bliss of the extinction of ego, while the vulnerabilities of delusion, greed, and hatred are both cause and effect of dukkha and of egocentric attachment to the impermanence of things. For Hindus, the transcendent ideal may be moksha, or karmic release, while vulnerability is related to the future-constitutive karmic weight of the moral past on the moral present. For Muslims, the transcendent ideal is imagined as the paradise of Allah, while vulnerability is caused by disobedience to Allah. In Judaism, as well as Christianity, vulnerability is a primary condition of all created things—to be human is to be a finite dust creature, a creature made of earth (adamah), a creature of the dirt who will return to the dirt. The story of Jacob wrestling the angel in search of the name of God, and receiving a wound along with his own name in return, can be read as a figure of the enlivening embrace of human vulnerability that comes through spiritual quest. In the New Testament God's own vulnerability is expressed by images of the natality of Jesus, his bastard birth in a barn, and his suffering of scorn and crucifixion, and the thorn in the flesh of Paul can also be interpreted as a figure of vulnerability. Differences within traditions can be interpreted as internally diverse ways of calibrating the symbols, rituals, and institutions that orient adherents to their transcendent ideals. For example, Roman Catholics and Protestant Evangelicals have different ideas about the proper calibration of salvation, symbol, ritual, and institution, just as Theravada and Mahayana Buddhists present different ideas about how to achieve nirvana, and so on. My point, which is merely suggestive, is that different religious traditions signify vulnerability as a fundamental ontological condition in diverse ways, and that various ways of dealing with this vulnerability are central to their historical meaning as religious traditions.

But vulnerability is not only a theme across religious traditions; it is also a central theme in the modern sciences. In biology, all living things and living systems are dynamic and perishable. To live is to be subject to decay and interdependent. Vulnerability is the essence of bios—organic life is intractably perilous, to live is to walk the metabolic razor's edge between consuming and being consumed. And in physics, the hardest of the hard sciences, the vulnerability of our theories about the physical world are apparent to the extent that regularities have taken the place of laws and probabilities and relativities have replaced certainties and absolutes. Beyond science and religion, vulnerability is also a prominent literary trope. The pathos of ancient Greek tragedy, for example, pivots around the interplay of human and divine vulnerability. Sophocles's Antigone illustrates moral vulnerability in a world of competing goods and duties, while the Oedipus cycle illustrates the limitations of human insight and the vulnerability of the present and future to the past. All of these traditions seem to point to vulnerability as fundamental to reality and human existence. Human being, doing, and knowing are a venture in vulnerability. Vulnerability is an ontological, existential, and epistemic condition. To be vulnerable, as the Latin roots *vulnus* and *vulnerare* indicate, is to be liable to wounding, in both senses of the word—to being wounded, and to being a potential cause of others' wounding.

This immanental philosophy of religion holds promise as a way to span boundaries and dissolve dualisms—between reason and faith, understanding and explanation, nature and culture—that have alienated humans from one another and from the planet as a whole. It outlines a way to hold together an interpretation of the religious significance of nature with a naturalistic interpretation of religion. It affirms that nothing human, and thus nothing cultural, can be fully understood apart from its evolutionary biological context. This is not to say that evolutionary theory, in itself, provides a sufficient understanding of all things human and cultural. More modestly, it is saying that evolutionary theory is a necessary element in understanding what humans are and what humans do. In addition to this, it affirms that the quest to understand more about ourselves as a bio-cultural species can be experienced religiously, even when the quest is driven by a naturalistic, empirical, evolutionary perspective. Rather than viewing an evolutionary account of religion as an impediment to religious life and experience, this philosophy of religion opens the way to a religious experience of our cosmic and planetary contexts. By demystifying religion this philosophy of religion creates new spaces for the religious experience of mystery, as I will now show.

AN IMMANENTAL THEOLOGY

The ideas about religion, the religions, and religious traditions discussed earlier have significant theological implications. If there is no essential outside of the "religious," if it is not monopolized by religion, and if it is a potential quality of experience that crosses diverse contexts of feeling, acting, thinking, and being, then theology is less a particular form of thinking about given religious meanings and values than it is the work of giving form to religious meanings and values. Theology is a religio-poietic enterprise rather than a set of truth propositions about the nature of ultimate reality.[33] It is the process of forming, critiquing, and transforming the religious meanings, purposes, and desires through which human communities negotiate the hazards and graces of vulnerable life in an ambiguous world.

Committed to the idea that nature is all, that it is in process, and that this idea is religiously and morally significant, an immanental theology provokes a life of contemplation, inquiry, and moral practice devoted to the beauty and creativity of nature naturing. By taking nature naturing as the context for the discernment of meaning, value, and what orients us ultimately, and by understanding human cultures as aspects of nature natured, an immanental theology is inquisitively open to the wisdom of diverse human cultures and forms of religiosity. In other words, by affirming that nature is all, an immanental theology affirms, as William David Hart puts this, that the various "conceptual, factual, and value distinctions that" we make as a species, "such as is/ought, good and evil, animals, humans, and God(s)," are "contingencies of our bio-cultural evolution." In an important sense, then, not only do "we create God and the gods," but we are ourselves "gods who shit: transcendent animals."[34] The sacred text of this immanental theology is the epic that arcs from the genesis of the Universe with the Big Bang and the swirling of the earliest cosmic elements, to the birth pangs of stars and planets and the constellation of galaxies, an epic that includes everything from the Sun's gestation of our solar system to the emergence of life on Earth, from the stunning ubiquity of bacteria to the biospheric tipping point that our own species has precipitated. An immanental theology presents a humble religious path that decentralizes the human species within the infinitely broader metaphysical and aesthetic rhythms of the Universe. Rather than questing for certainty or resting in faith, it is an appreciative search for the value of things. As an appreciative search, it adds value into the universe by noticing and revering the depth of the value that is already here. It seeks wisdom from wherever it may come: from the symbols, myths, and rituals of the world's diverse religious traditions, from literature and the arts, from the intricate splendors of indigenous knowledges to the mind-bending ways of the modern sciences. In this immanental theological frame, there is no "outside" of revelation—the whole of the cosmos rings with it, from the subatomic to the interstellar, from the unicellular to the civilizational.

But the most potent affirmation within this immanental theology is the claim that nature is processive and unfurling. In addressing the question of how this affirmation can orient life religiously, it is important to briefly situate it in relation to the multiplicity of meanings assigned to the concept of "nature" throughout Western intellectual history. This is important because the concept of "nature" has had many meanings. Indeed, as the American philosopher Justus Buchler wryly observed, "Nature has been distinguished from man, from art, from mind, from chance, from purpose, from history, from eternity, from irregularity, from society, from civilization, from God, from evil, from good—to name some of the best known historical contrasts. Yet with respect to every one of these same ideas, nature has also been made inclusive of it or synonymous with it or continuous with it."[35] Through Western intellectual history the many meanings assigned to the idea nature—and the way this idea has been used to interpret observed contrasts in nature between order and disorder, stasis and change, and identity and difference—have often conflicted and sometimes even contradicted one another.[36]

Ancient Greek philosophy, for example, tended to think of nature as analogous to an intelligent organism. Nature was imagined as a vital, dynamic reality, internally ordered by a rational principle, knowable through human reason. By contrast, Renaissance ideas about nature, as reflected in the work of Nicolaus Copernicus, Francis Bacon, Galileo Gallilei, and Isaac Newton, were dominated by mechanistic, aesthetic, and theological analogies. By comparing nature to a machine, or a work of art, Renaissance notions of nature rejected the idea that nature possessed its own internal rationality. Whereas the ancient Greeks attributed nature's orderliness to the internal reasonableness of its patterns and processes, the Renaissance attributed this order to external laws imposed by an intelligent and powerful divine creator.

With the moderns, a different emphasis appears, as we have seen with respect to the American immanental tradition. Instead of being concerned primarily with the problem of order in nature, modern thinkers focused on the problem of change. And rather than assuming a correlation between orderliness and antecedent rationality, they looked to change itself for an explanation of why things are the way they are. Interpreting nature as historically dynamic, rather than as a static contrast to human history, made it possible to interpret nature's changing character as a key rather than an obstacle to understanding it.

Charles Darwin's theory of evolution illustrates this especially well. For Darwin, change and orderliness in nature are the cumulative effects of the mutual influence of organisms and their environments on one another over long periods of time. As a result, no species is the way it has always been and no species will remain the way it is forever. This undermines the logical concept of the species as a fixed and independent category and elevates the interpretive significance of contingency, history, and context. In contrast to Renaissance and Greek analogies to external and internal reason, moderns imagined nature in terms of a historical dialectic, a process that can be rationally and purposively studied but that has no extrinsically rational, all-inclusive purpose.

It is important to note here, since I will return to this point shortly, that although the Darwinian theory of evolution posits that the evolutionary process is nonteleological, and thus that it has no overarching purpose, this does not entail that there is no purposiveness within evolution. In other words, although the Darwinian theory of evolution does not affirm that *natura naturans* has a final cause or overall purpose or aim, it does affirm that purposes and aims are present within *natura naturata*. This is an important distinction. Although evolutionary theory can evoke a sense of the scope and indifference of nature, it provides a way to interpret purposiveness and value as emerging out of the processes of nature, even as expressions of nature's own internally potent self-transcending character. To say that nature is all is in no way to say that the meanings of nature are settled.

Within an immanental theological frame, nature is more than any of its names. And yet if it is all, then there is no "outside" of nature, and nature has no "other." If there is no "outside" of nature, then nature has no circumference, no particular shape, no boundaries, and no edge. Nature is not a container that contains. Nor is it an object or entity that can be quantified or a place from which one can come and go—nature is unbounded. If there are no boundaries or edges to nature, then nature has no center. The implications of this are profound, and perhaps profoundly unsettling. In relation to the infinite geometry of nature, all that we know and hold most dear is quite unremarkable. We're but one species among millions of others on a single planet hitched to a middle-sized star, just one among billions and billions of others in a galaxy that is itself only one among trillions of others—in the observable universe alone.[37]

The unimaginable scale of the Universe and its acentric indeterminacy call into question the persistence of human-centered moral thinking. It even calls into question fundamental aspects of moral thinking itself, insofar as the idea of "center" is instrumental to the way we think about moral value. Essential to common meanings of moral value is the idea that something has, or signifies, more or less of some property deemed to be valuable. Value's meaning has everything to do with "more and less." Why is this morally important? Just imagine trying to live if everything had equivalent value. Every choice would be tragic, requiring the arbitrary sacrifice of one valuable thing or option for another of equal value. But we don't live this way. We rank our values. We treat some as higher and others as lower, some as more important and others as less, some as intrinsic and others as instrumental. We don't all do this in the same way, using the same evaluative criteria, but these are pervasive patterns in moral thinking. We rank our values, and that ranking is contingent on some central value, or cluster of values, that relativizes others. In short, the ordering of values is necessary to the ordering of human moral life: getting through the kind of life that humans live requires making choices at every turn to do one thing rather than another, opting for one possible future over another, aiming for certain objectives rather than others.

To affirm that nature is all, that it is infinite and inexhaustible, and therefore that it is without a center takes us a long way from the exceptionalism and moral anthropocentrism of the dominant American political theology. But what does the acentricity of nature mean within an immanental theological frame? It means that a concept that has been integral to being morally oriented in a human experience of the world has no objective grounding in the larger world of experience. It is a humanly constructed concept. This does not mean it is not an important concept or that it does not serve a purpose. But it does mean that its meaning and purpose are relative.

Recall from earlier the idea that it is possible to affirm simultaneously that nature itself has no purpose and yet that nature is inclusive of purposes. This is merely an empirically descriptive claim rather than a moral or evaluative assertion. That there are entities in nature, such as humans, that have purposes does not imply anything necessarily about whether those purposes are good or right in relation to the broader world of experience and nature. Given the immanental embargo on epistemic exceptionalism, which follows from the idea that we are part of nature, there is no possible standpoint from which we could empirically access nature as a whole in order to determine, unambiguously, whether or not it has an all-inclusive general purpose. And yet we do empirically observe purposes in nature wherever and whenever we observe behaviors and motivations such as desire, fear, curiosity, hunger, and intentionality. For an organism to intend some thing or another, whether or not that intention is mentally represented, means that it has a purpose or an interest, of some kind. And the satisfaction of that interest or the realization of that purpose is a value for that organism. For example, a dog walking to his food bowl behaviorally displays the intention to eat for the purpose of satisfying his hunger, and the satisfaction of his hunger is a value to him, whether or not it is a value consciously held in view.

It can even be argued that purposes and intentions, and thus values, are present wherever there is metabolism.[38] Metabolism is a life-sustaining transfer of energy between an organism and its environment. Though no organism consciously controls its metabolism, its metabolic processes express themselves in behavioral intentions to secure from its environment what it needs to go on living. These intentions indicate purposes and values. And so, while a naturalistic empirical standpoint will never allow us to know if nature as a whole has a central purpose, it is nonetheless the case empirically that the purposive behavior of living things is value-oriented.

The organismic centrality of purposes and values is in keeping with Whitehead's organic cosmology. Recall the ontology at the core of his metaphysics. The most concretely actual things or entities in the universe are occasions of internally related energy-events. The particularity of these concrete occasions, or the qualitative aspect of their concreteness, is constituted by "decisions" to follow certain relational paths, or to creatively advance by integrating certain relations rather than others (that is, Whitehead's "feelings" and "prehensions"). These "decisions" are evaluative, which means that in Whitehead's vision, there is an evaluative process intrinsic within the coming-to-be of all things. Value is inherent, relational, and emergent. Thus Whitehead's relational ontology not only transforms the opposition between subjects and objects into a dense network of dynamically contrasting modes of experience, but also leads to the rejection of the fact/value dichotomy, which has segregated modern Western moral philosophy from other forms of inquiry. Just as there are not some kinds of things that are subjects and some kinds of things that are objects, neither are there some kinds of things that are facts and some kinds of things, or properties of things, that are values. Subjectivity and objectivity, facticity and value are relationally dynamic aspects of each thing, occasion, or entity, at different moments in their unfolding as events in relation to other events.

In Whitehead's metaphysics, value indwells reality; it is intrinsic to the affective and aesthetic dynamic of nature naturing. This makes it possible to affirm that to exist is to become through affective evaluation; where there is affective evaluation, and thus a form of becoming, there is aesthetic value; where there is personally ordered aesthetic value, or a living form of becoming with identity, there is the potential for vital awareness; where there is vital awareness, there are purposes and values; and where there is a consciousness of value, including the values central to other forms of becoming, there is moral value and moral responsibility. The idea that nature is all and that it is in process, that it is unbounded, does not subvert the possibility or reality of values as such. Valuation is a constitutive process within the becoming of things. As centers of value, things, entities, occasions, and organisms do not precede valuation, but are effects of valuation.

All of this compels the need to rethink common human assumptions about meaning and value within the "frame" (without borders) of an impossibly vast, imponderably complex cosmos that, although it may have no center or inclusive purpose, is inclusive of centers of value and purposes. Among the other assumptions it unsettles, this immanental theological frame throws a wrench into the view that we should assent to meanings and commit ourselves to values only if those meanings and values are absolute rather than relative. One concern driving this assumption is that the structure of moral thinking and the ordering of social systems will be undermined if meanings and values are merely circumstantial, contingent, and relative. However, this concern is based on the fallacy that if meanings and values are relative, then they are merely subjectively projected preferences and prejudices of particular moral individuals or groups. Against that assumption, this immanental theology affirms simultaneously that meanings and values are relative rather than absolute, and yet that they are also objective rather than subjective. Meanings and values can be objectively grounded in the nature of things even when they are relative to different forms of life.

This leads to a prismatic theory of meaning and value. On this theory, every consciously held meaning and value becomes a portal through which others' meanings and values, whether consciously held or not, can be seen, felt, and affirmed, or not. For example, insofar as the idea that nature is all includes humans, and the ideal of human flourishing is objectively valuable to us as a species, then the value of human flourishing has objective status in the universe, even though it is a species-relative value. Keeping this in mind, let us say that human flourishing includes, and yet transcends, the satisfaction of basic human needs. Human flourishing also entails exercising higher-level cognitive, emotional, and imaginative capacities, among others, that are typical of our species. Exercising these capacities entails that we have both the freedom and the resources to do so. As a social species, we need others to help us to meet our basic needs and to secure the resources necessary to freely exercise our various human capacities. Minimally, then, a flourishing human life is (1) a relationally enriched and enriching life in which (2) basic needs are met and (3) the capabilities to exercise the cognitive, affective, and imaginative capacities typical of our species are secured.

The objective goodness of human flourishing is not an anthropocentric prejudice. It is not a form of species exceptionalism that assumes that the goodness of human flourishing is or should be the metric of value for all other goods. To the contrary, if nature is in process and the entities and creatures of nature are internally related, then human flourishing is interdependent with the flourishing of other forms of life and the ecological systems that make and sustain life's very possibility. The claim that human flourishing is objectively good not only doesn't exclude the objective value of other things, beings, and systems in the world; it is emphatically dependent upon them. Human flourishing is relationally complex; it is objectively good and yet relative, rather than absolute.

The objective relativity of the good of human flourishing opens human moral experience into a prism through which the luminous plurality of other objectively relative values in nature can be seen, felt, and affirmed. As Carol Wayne White eloquently expresses this, "Each human birth is a glorious event, and the starting point of yet another spectacular phenomenon that helps transform the enigmatic cosmos into an even more vital, dramatic" world of experience. This is not to say that "the knowable universe is enlivened only through human activity," but that "humans are individual and collective destinies engaging an appreciable world."[39] Instead of taking the human as the measure of all value in the world, human moral experience and imagination become prismatic vectors of the radiance of more-than-human values. The more-than-human world of experience appreciates—is enriched, enlarged, and enlivened—through human valuation. Paradoxically, then, it is precisely insofar as the meanings and values that orient human life are relative that they can claim to have robust objective grounding; and precisely insofar as they can claim to have robust objective grounding, the values and meanings of the rest of nature can be registered more fully and vibrantly.

Within the frame of this immanental theology, nature has neither a singular center nor an overarching purpose, and yet there are nonetheless purposes and centers of value in nature. Although the claim that nature is all and that it is in process undermines absolutist assumptions about values, purposes, and meanings, the undermining of absolutism does not lead to nihilism. One can remain devoted to and morally oriented by objectively grounded meanings, purposes, and values even if they are contingent, relative, and contextual. What is more, this contingency, relativity, and contextuality signify the fundamental precarity of what we hold most dear—from the goodness and beauty of friendship and family to democracy and the ideals of justice. And through the precarious significations of what we hold most dear, we come to witness and deeply feel the vulnerability of the planetary conditions of human and more-than-human life.

Recall my suggestion earlier that within an immanental theological perspective, mystification is inimical to religious experience. By this I mean that religious experience in this frame is revealing rather than concealing. One way to consider this is to look briefly at the two Latin roots of the word *religion*: *religare* and *relegere*. Though philologists may doubt the derivation of *religion* from *relegere*, a suggestion that comes from Cicero, it illuminates a way of thinking about religious experience in an immanental frame. Whereas *religare* conveys the ideas of binding back, rebinding, or reconnecting, *relegere* indicates reading again, rereading, or seeing anew. The semantic range of *religare* resonates with familiar religious tropes such as being lost and then found, broken and then healed, disconnected and reconnected. Religious experience through these tropes has to do with the integration of what was fragmented, the remembrance of what was forgotten, and the reunion of the separated. On the other hand, *relegere* is conveyed by tropes of insight and second sight. It is anthropomorphized by seers and by blind people regaining their sight, by enlightened ones. Religious experience according to these metaphors has to do with seeing the world again or seeing it in a new way, seeing it deeply and carefully. Though *religare* and *relegere* are resonant with mystery, they are emphatically demystifying. On the contrary, they seem to suggest experiences of revelation, enlightenment, discovery, insight, and heightened awareness. Although historic religious traditions may have their origins in experiences such as these (for example, the Buddha under the Bo tree, Mohammed in the cave, Moses on the mount, Jesus in the Jordan), and although their symbols, rituals, and texts memorialize those experiences and can provoke them anew, they do not have a monopoly on them.

Religious experiences within an immanental theological frame provoke questions about the meanings and values that ultimately orient life—they are interrogative rather than declarative. They are events, encounters, insights, relationships, undergoings, and overcomings that throw life into suspense, stripping away the pretense of the givenness and permanency of things. Experiences such as these rend the veil of the ordinary; they can interrupt and can sometimes transform one's life. Along with Henry Nelson Wieman, immanental religious experience is about the widening of the "bounds of awareness" or a "diffusive state of awareness, where habitual systems of response are resolved into an undirected, unselective aliveness for the total organism to the total event then ensuing."[40] Experienced at times as the "undefined awareness of the total passage of nature," it is provoked by the feeling of contact with "a far larger portion of that totality of immediate experience which constantly flows over one."[41] Experiences such as these contour an immanental theological frame into a form of religious life and thought.

Since we humans are embedded in nature and since, like every other thing that exists, we are unplanned creatures of an exquisite latticework of natural processes that originated in mystery about 13.7 billion years ago, the answer to the question of why the Universe exists or why there is something rather than nothing is likely to remain infinitely out of reach of our human comprehension. But we know that we are creatures of the stars. We know that if the rate of acceleration of the elements out of the Big Bang varied even in the slightest, the Universe would not have unfolded the way that it has. We know that even a slight adjustment of the Earth's coordinates in relation to the Sun would have made life impossible. We know that life first emerged on our planet about 3.5 billion years ago. We know that since then life has been in the midst of relentless transformation. We know that since modern humans have only been around for about three hundred thousand years we are latecomers to the Universe.[42] We know that we have purposes and values. And what is more, we are consciously and empathically aware that other living creatures also have purposes and values—if our eyes and ears are open, we have no choice but to witness them.

TOWARD A THEOPOLITICS OF
RESILIENT DEMOCRACY

The alchemy of consciousness, empathy, and agency yields moral responsibility. This responsibility emerges out of our awareness that human life is inextricably interwoven with the rest of life, that other lives besides our own have purposes and values, that life as such seems to be rare in the Universe, and that we as a species have far more power than any other living thing to manipulate the conditions upon which life depends. By becoming a massive planetary force, we humans have also become nature's custodians of value. Perhaps becoming more fully human and more fully realizing our nature as *terra bēstiae* have something to do with summoning the courage to face this burden of responsibility and even to embrace it as a blessing, an invitation to come more fully alive by recovering our relations with more-than-human life.

Though we are newborns on this far-flung planet, swirling amid the fathomless geometry of a Universe without edges, we have crossed a threshold that no other living thing on Earth has ever crossed. No living species other than our own has ever become a cause of the mass extinction of other living things.

In his evocatively titled essay "The Outcry of Mute Things," the Jewish philosopher Hans Jonas expressed the religious significance of this with unmatched pathos:

> It was once religion which told us that we are all sinners, because of original sin. It is now the ecology of our planet which pronounces us all to be sinners because of the excessive exploits of human inventiveness. It was once religion which threatened us with a last judgment at the end of days. It is now our tortured planet which predicts the arrival of such a day without any heavenly intervention. The latest revelation—from no Mount Sinai, from no Mount of the Sermon, from no Bo (tree of Buddha)—is the outcry of mute things themselves that we must heed by curbing our powers over creation, lest we perish together on a wasteland of what was creation.[43]

What will it take for us to hear this revelation, to feel this loss of creatural vitality? Might the hearing of this outcry and feeling of this loss be the event, encounter, insight, and undergoing that will lead us to feel the contingency of what we assume to be necessary, the vulnerability of what we too often view as invulnerable, the perishability of what seems permanent? If anything might rend the ordinary meanings and values that orient our lives, and thus count as religious experience, shouldn't this?

This theology of planetary life, rooted in the theological and philosophical lineages of American immanence, offers an imaginal frame for the ethos and aims of a theopolitics of resilient democracy. It is committed to the practical and provisional nature of knowledge and values, to pluralism as a creative condition of religious and moral life, to the sacred precarities of *natura naturata* and the sacred profundities of *natura naturans*. It takes nature to be all, without center or periphery. It interprets every creatural center of value as "all window," as a vector of objectively relative value through which the radiance of other centers of values can be felt and honored. It provides an ideal context for the enrichment, revision, and enlargement of the life-orienting meanings, purposes, and values of religious life amid the revelatory demystifications of the Anthropocene paradox.

5

TOWARD A THEOPOLITICS OF
RESILIENT DEMOCRACY

OF REBELLION AND REVOLUTION

I had the good fortune to meet Grace Lee Boggs, the Chinese American philosopher and activist, about a year before she died at the age of one hundred. She and her husband, James Boggs, were active in the Black Power movement and worked as social and environmental justice leaders for many decades. Early in their collaborations they developed a pragmatic discipline of moving from action to reflection and back, of testing, revising, and innovating theory in the laboratory of practical political engagement. Over time they evolved a highly transformative approach to radical politics that was place-based and communal, spiritually pluralistic, coalitional, and committed to the inevitability of ongoing democratic struggle. Grace Lee and Jimmy Boggs lived their commitments and now they live on in the lives and communities they helped to empower.

One of the many nuggets of wisdom that Grace Lee Boggs shared on the day I met her was about the importance of distinguishing between rebellion and revolution. As she describes this in one of her books, rebellion is important because it "represents the massive uprisings and protests of the oppressed" and "throws into question the legitimacy and supposed permanence of existing institutions."[1] Rebellion is a morally cathartic, politically catalytic collective decision to resist the way things are. Through a decisive interruption of the status quo, rebellion foments a crisis and creates the opportunity for systemic change.

However, a rebellion is not a revolution. Rebellion is a potent but isolated event in time whereas revolution is the extended process of transforming time. Where rebellion is largely about resistance, Boggs held that "a revolution requires that a people go beyond struggling against oppressive institutions. . . . A revolution involves making an evolutionary/revolutionary leap toward becoming more socially responsible and more self-critical human beings. In order to transform the world, we must transform ourselves."[2] It is a way of giving life to a new world and new life to ourselves: "Unlike rebellions, which are here today and gone tomorrow, revolutions require a patient and protracted process that transforms and empowers us as individuals as we struggle to change the world around us."[3] Revolution is about innovation, making something new; its logic is natal.

Another way to say this is that while rebellion is about resistance, the work of revolution entails resilience. An analogy will help to explain what I mean by this. Boggs's distinction between rebellion and revolution is similar to Whitehead's distinction between individual actual occasions and societies of occasions. Like rebellions, occasions emerge out of a relational decision to resist certain things within a proximate spatiohistorical context and to integrate and advance others. This decision interrupts the historical flow of experience and creates a crisis, both for the occasion itself and for its relational context. The decision is critical to the subjective shape and trajectory of the occasion, but once the occasion has fully concresced, achieved satisfaction, and realized its subjective form, it immediately fades back into the objective flow of experience. Yet things are not the same. Something new has entered into the life of the cosmos—the many became one and were increased by one. By interrupting and redirecting the cosmic flow of creativity, however modestly, the occasion enacts a microrebellion. This microrebellion does not transform the cosmos, but the coming-to-be and perishing of the occasion interject a ripple of new possibilities into it. The occasion enacts a quantum insurrection.

In contrast, Whiteheadian societies can achieve a different degree of creative impact: societies are to revolutions what occasions are to rebellions. Recall that societies are constituted by a multiplicity of occasions. When they are personally ordered, this multiplicity is held together serially through time as well as formally in space. Given this structure, the creative efficacy of societies is both irreducible to and contingent upon the creative efficacy of the constitutive occasions. In other words, societal creativity is emergent—it is "something more" than the occasions it comprises even as it comprises "nothing but" those occasions.[4] As emergently creative and collectively structured, societies can provoke and sustain revolutionary waves of new possibility. When conjoined with others, the cosmic ripple caused by the bubbling concrescence of an occasion can crest into a wave. If the occasion enacts a quantum insurrection, societies can coalesce and cascade into resonant revolutions.

Boggs's distinction between rebellion and revolution, as I interpret it, is a distinction not of ontological kinds, but of contrasting degrees of system complexity and creative efficacy. As societies are more complex than the occasions that constitute them, revolutions are more systemically complex, and therefore also more difficult to sustain, than rebellions. The critique and resistance of rebellion are necessary but insufficient to the complex creativity of revolutions. As Boggs put this, when it comes to revolution, "We have to shift what unifies [us] from just rejection to projection, from just denunciation to annunciation."[5] While rebellion entails a critique of the way things are, revolution seeks to turn things around. Where rebellion is about resisting what is and has been, revolution is about realizing what could and should be. And realizing the world that could and should be requires that it be deeply and vividly imagined.

My argument in this book has been that the Anthropocene paradox opens a space for this imaginative work. I suggested previously that as a cultural condition the Anthropocene is an example of what Whitehead described in his philosophy of symbolism as a "new element of life." As such, it demystifies and disrupts the instinctive emotions, habits, and prejudices of entrenched religious and political imaginaries, such as the dominant American theopolitical tradition. Like Whitehead's occasions, it provokes a crisis in the historical life of this tradition—it is a rejection of the logic of extraction, externalization, and exception. But precisely insofar as it rejects this logic, it also has creative potential. As mortally threatening as it is, the Anthropocene also has a natal aspect: the beginning of the human age for the Earth is also the ending of the idea of humans as separate from the rest of nature. The death of this idea could bring life to more "world-loyal" ways of being human in a more-than-human world.

According to some observers, something like this is indeed what is happening. In response to the diverse crises and injustices enfolded within the Anthropocene paradox, the concrescent ripples of rebellious critique around the world are coalescing into waves of revolutionary creativity. As Paul Hawken has boldly declared, "We are in the midst of the largest social movement in all of human history," comprising tens of millions of people committed to diverse forms of environmental activism and social justice.[6] This revolution is embodied by countless grassroots groups, religious communities, families, and individuals around the globe who aspire to live by principles of interdependence, equity, diversity, and ecological responsibility. This is evident, for example, in the creative convergence of social justice, environmental, and indigenous people's movements as they resist the antidemocratic forces of climate injustice,[7] in the resonances of the economic and racial justice agendas in the radically democratic structures of the Occupy and Black Lives Matter movements, in the increasingly sophisticated experiments with economic and ecological democracy in the commons movement,[8] and even in the business world through the renegade work of B-corporations and "social entrepreneurs" as they strive to create a new business "honor code" committed to the social and ecological benefits of stakeholders as well as shareholder financial benefits.[9]

However, since there is no center to the revolution, since its creative efficacy is distributed rather than concentrated, it can be difficult to see. And yet whether one can see the revolution or not, many more of us feel the emergency provoking it. We feel the emergency collectively through the hyperpolarity of party politics, the breathless drama of cable news and social media, the hair-trigger volatility of financial markets, and the frenzy of fear toward sexual, ethnic, and religious others fostered by the far right. From a radically empirical perspective, in which we feel the world before we know it, it is no surprise that the emergency is broadly and deeply registered. The danger in this, as I discussed in chapter 1, is that emergency can provoke the temptation to suspend democracy, and sometimes an exception is claimed to justify that suspension. But the temptation can be resisted and the exception denied. The revolution described by Paul Hawken appears to be a case in point. It is emerging through the efforts of many communities who have taken it upon themselves to deepen democracy rather than to denigrate it. They witness to the possibility of a more resilient democracy emerging through the experience of shared vulnerability, in direct contrast to the exceptions to democracy claimed by sovereign power.

Of course, more fully realizing a revolutionary transition such as this is no easy task. There is a great deal of inertia to overcome. As Whitehead wrote, "In every age of well-marked transition there is the pattern of habitual dumb practice and emotion which is passing, and there is oncoming of a new complex of habit. Between the two lies a zone of anarchy, either a passing danger or a prolonged welter involving misery of decay and zest of young life."[10] To live in the crisis of the Anthropocene paradox is to live in such a zone of anarchy. It is a time of risk, of great possibility and great danger.

A theopolitics of resilient democracy is one way to live through this risk that resists the antidemocratic voices of emergency and prefigures an alternative. It is a theopolitics for an uncertain world. I do not present this as the only or the best way, but as a hypothesis to test in the communities we inhabit. Resilient democracy affirms Sheldon S. Wolin's idea of democracy as a "fugitive" and "anti-totality" politics: "The power of a democratic politics lies in the multiplicity of modest sites dispersed among local governments and institutions under local control . . . and in the ingenuity of ordinary people in inventing temporary forms to meet their needs."[11] Engaged in medias res, amid the uncertainties and urgencies of human life in a more-than-human world, resilient democracy is a grassroots theopolitics committed to the practices of democracy as a way of life. Although it is certainly not a solution to our global political and planetary ecological crises, it emerges out of a deep sense of the complexity and urgency of those crises. As a bifocal theopolitics that can help us to see more clearly how the planetary and the local and the ultimate and the intimate are immanent within one another, resilient democracy seeks to catalyze the more empathic, emancipatory, and equitable forms of common life our crises call us to create.

Resilient democracy is rooted in the idea that, as Wolin puts this, "ordinary individuals are capable of creating new cultural patterns of commonality at any moment," but it also understands that "a range of problems and atrocities exists that a locally confined democracy cannot solve."[12] This is part of the "wickedness" of wicked problems. As described earlier, the complexity, nonlinearity, and urgency of wicked problems simultaneously resist and provoke simplistic solutions. While their systemic nature entails macrolevel policy and legislative interventions, a theopolitics of resilient democracy leverages change from the ground up and the middle out by amplifying the countervailing democratic resonances of ecologically attuned and socially just associations, communities, and solidarities. This is in keeping with my view, articulated previously, that one of the important tasks of political theology is to theorize the complex forms of political and religious community that will incubate multiple, diverse responses to systemic problems. On this view, political theology does not seek so much to answer questions or solve problems as to coalesce and catalyze the forms of common life in which ultimate questions and wicked problems can be more creatively engaged. Informed by the American immanental tradition, the theopolitical aim is to build melioristic capacity through new democratic fusions of religious and political life.

With this aim in mind, this chapter is divided into three sections. In what immediately follows, I will return to a discussion of resilience and vulnerability, focusing on the concept of "panarchy," a theoretical hypothesis about the adaptive cycles of complex systems. By calibrating Whitehead's metaphysics to the level of socioecological systems, panarchy provides a critical hermeneutical category for thinking across cosmic and creatural contexts, as well as for thinking through the contradictions of capitalism. I turn in the second section to an interpretation of the vulnerability of power and the power of vulnerability. In the third section, I articulate the theory and practice of resilient democracy as an associational ethos of vulnerable life, and in the concluding section I discuss the relevance of Whitehead's concept of beauty to the shaping of justice.

PANARCHY AND THE CONTRADICTIONS OF CAPITALISM

One of the central commitments within the American immanental tradition is to an ontology of internal relatedness—all things and beings exist in degrees of mutually constitutive relationship to one another. To affirm the ontology of internal relatedness is to reject the idea that any entity, subatomic or cosmic, human, animal, vegetable, or mineral, is what it is independently of other things and relations. Things are what they are

in their concreteness by way of their relations, and apart from their constitutive web of relations, they are abstractions. No thing or relation stands
fully apart from all other things, or fully outside of all other relations.

This idea has profound political and theological implications. As I
suggested earlier, the denial of ontological exceptionalism brings into
relief the historical, cultural, and sociopolitical contingency of all other
kinds of exceptionalism, whether species-based, racial, theological, nationalist, or otherwise.[13] It also illuminates the dangerous fallacy of all other
kinds of externalization—it means that there is no pure "outside" to anything. Overcoming ontological exceptionalism is important therefore
not only to deconstructing the bifurcation of nature but also to the critique
of separatist and supremacist political, religious, and economic systems.

Social systems live and die by the symbols that orient them. They are
sustained and sanctioned by symbolically mediated ideas about power
and value that become deeply entrenched in the historical flow of experience and reinforced by the systems of institutional power through which
dominant social groups maintain their influence. But as I quoted Whitehead saying earlier, "societies which cannot combine reverence to their
symbols with freedom of revision must ultimately decay either from
anarchy, or from the slow atrophy of a life stifled by useless shadows."[14]
Although everything is perpetually perishing, sometimes it becomes
important to help the process along. The theopolitical work of deconstructing and reconstructing symbols is pivotal to the work of disrupting, intervening within, and transforming social systems.

The theory of panarchy provides a powerful hermeneutical bridge for
crossing over from symbols to social systems. Panarchy is an emerging
multidisciplinary theoretical hypothesis used to interpret the dialectical
patterns of vulnerability and resilience in interconnected complex adaptive systems. Relevant from the level of cells to civilizations, it is an
example of a metaphysical scheme in the style of Whitehead—it names
an observationally grounded, imaginatively generalized set of speculative
hypotheses intended to illumine how systems work, revisable in light of
their adequacy to further empirical engagement with the world. Panarchy also shares a holographic element with Whitehead's philosophy, but
where the ontological root of Whitehead's system is the relational pro-
cessing of actual occasions, with panarchy it is the adaptive cycling of
complex systems.

As a way to picture panarchy, consider a three-dimensional image of the infinity symbol. As three-dimensional, it appears as a pair of entangled "S-curves"—a front curve interlooped with an inverted back curve. Now multiply these entangled S-curves. Imagine them overlapping, intersecting, and diversely scaled, from the infinitesimally small to the impossibly huge. Now imagine that time is cycling through them, at different rates. Some are cycling so quickly as to blur, others so slowly that they seem to be standing still. Thus imagined, panarchy is a theoretic representation of "how things in the broadest possible sense of the term hang together in the broadest possible sense of the term," as Wilfred Sellars described such things.[15] It theorizes the world as a complex system of relations, of flows and processes and cycles within cycles, a nested world of nests of nested systems.

The systems ecologist C. S. "Buzz" Holling formulated the theory after decades of close observation of the multilayered and multiscaled adaptive cycles in forest ecosystems. As he explains it, "Panarchy [refers to] the hierarchical structure in which systems of nature . . . and [systems of] humans . . . as well as combined human-nature systems . . . are interlinked in never-ending adaptive cycles of growth, accumulation, restructuring, and renewal. These transformational cycles take place in nested sets at scales ranging from a leaf to the biosphere over periods from days to geologic epochs, and from the scales of a family to a socio-political region over periods from years to centuries."[16] Holling identifies the four intrarelated phases within these transformational cycles as growth, accumulation, release, and restructuring. The growth phase is characterized by high diversity, high potentiality, and low connectivity. This is the phase of system experimentation and exploitation. Young, diverse forest ecosystems or bazaars and open markets in emerging capitalist societies are examples of systems in this phase. They respond to change and disturbances with agility, but they are decentralized and inefficient. The growth phase shifts into the accumulation phase when exploitation and experimentation lead to consolidation. The accumulation phase is characterized by higher connectivity, lower diversity, and increased efficiency. Systems in this phase have "locked in" on a particular value or task or purpose. The price of increased efficiency is diminished agility. Systems in this phase are accidents waiting to happen—think of monocultural agrosystems. When a system at the height of its accumulation phase is disturbed or disrupted, for instance, by a drought or flooding, it is prone to release and collapse. The shock to the system can be relatively minor, but because the system has become fragile as a result of sacrificing diversity for the sake of efficiency, system collapse can occur quickly. If the collapse is not total, the elements of the system released by the disruption begin to experiment anew, and the system enters into a phase of restructuring and renewal.

In keeping with the immanental "law" of association and the ontology of internal relatedness, the theory of panarchy assumes that no complex system exists independently of others—instead, they are nested within one another at higher and lower levels and larger and smaller scales and they move through their adaptive cycles at different rates. As the Canadian systems thinker Thomas Homer-Dixon explains, in relation to a forest system:

> The higher and slower-moving cycles [for example, the regional ecosystem, the global biogeochemical system] provide stability and resources that buffer the forest for shocks and help it recover from collapse. A forest may be hit by wildfire, for example, but as long as the climate pattern across the larger region that encompasses the forest remains constant and the rainfall adequate, the forest should regenerate. Meanwhile, the lower and faster-moving cycles [for example, from particular niches in the forest ecosystem down to soil bacteria] are a source of novelty, experimentation, and information.
>
> Together, the higher and lower cycles help keep the forest's collapse from being truly catastrophic. But for this healthy arrangement to work, these various adaptive cycles . . . mustn't all peak at the top of their growth phases simultaneously. If they do, if they are "aligned at the same phase of vulnerability," to use Holling's phrase—they will together produce a much more devastating collapse [for example, a forest fire coinciding with a regional drought].[17]

So panarchy is an integrated theoretical hypothesis that seeks to illumine the dialectic of vulnerability and resilience in the adaptive cycles of diverse kinds and scales of interconnected complex systems. To provide another example, consider the global financial system, the supranational network of borrowers, lenders, investors, governmental and intergovernmental financial entities, international trade organizations, and multilateral treaties operating on a global scale. Over the past few decades, as a result of globalized deregulatory, privatizing, and free trade policies, the financial system, once a subsystem embedded within and constrained by other economic, social, and ecological systems, has morphed into the metasystem that now interconnects all the others. Why and how has this happened? The economist Roger Boyd applies panarchy theory to offer an explanation. He writes that "the actions of governments and central banks to forestall crashes during the period from the early 1980's to the present day have allowed the financial system to grow to a scale and complexity well beyond what would have been possible without the repeated forestalling of collapse."[18] In other words, governmental and central bank interventions have paradoxically allowed the financial system to expand to become a driver of other systems and also to have become less resilient. It has become bigger, faster, and more volatile all at the same time. Its diminished resilience is evidenced by the hypersensitivity of capital markets to social and political events and by the hyperactivity of monetary policy seeking to prevent collapse.

In becoming a simultaneously less resilient system and a more powerful influence on local and regional economic, social, and ecological systems, the magnitude of the financial system's potential collapse will be much more pronounced than if it had been allowed to cycle beyond the accumulation phase into release and reorganization. That it has been prevented from cycling through these phases as a result of state interventions at national and international levels is one of the great hypocrisies of neoliberal free market ideology. Given the global interconnectedness of economic, social, and ecological systems to a now highly combustible financial system, disruptions to or within any one of them could lead, through interconnected and mutually amplifying feedback loops, to a dominoes- or pancake-type multisystem collapse.

By bringing the interconnections among these systems into view, panarchy also exposes the intrarelatedness of their contradictions. The idea of contradiction in dialectical thinking refers to a tension in a system that is simultaneously constitutive of it and also a source of its potential demise. A primary contradiction in Marx's critique of capitalism is the social contradiction in the relations of production. This is intrinsic to Marx's labor theory of value, in which capital accumulation depends on the extraction of surplus value from labor. Capital accumulates as owners of the means of production keep labor wages lower than commodity value, make production as efficient as possible, and expand markets. The labor theory of value is intrinsic to the Marxian account of the logic of capital accumulation. But it yields a contradiction insofar as the combined effects of production's increased efficiency and labor's diminishing consumer power leads to overproduction. According to the Marxian critique, these constitutive tensions within the dynamics of capital accumulation drive class conflict and the cyclical phases of boom and bust that characterize free market systems.

This social contradiction in the relations of production between labor and capital is one of the constitutive contradictions of capitalism as theorized by Marx. But there is also an ecological contradiction within the conditions of production.[19] Just as the imperative of capital accumulation exploits workers, it exploits the natural environment; and just as the exploitation of workers manifests in an untenable social contradiction within the relations of production, the exploitation of the natural environment manifests as an untenable ecological contradiction within the conditions of production. John Bellamy Foster describes this as the "metabolic rift" in capitalism between humans and the rest of nature.[20] In Whiteheadian terms, capitalism's "metabolic rift" can be interpreted as the historical materialization of the bifurcation of nature.

In the nineteenth century, this rift was evident in the depleted soil fertility that resulted from intensive agricultural industrialization and the mass migration of people from rural farming to urban manufacturing environments. The need for fertilizer was so desperate that England and the United States colonized territories to gain access to guano. For example, in 1856 in the United States there was even an act of Congress, the Guano Islands Act, which reads, verbatim from the US Code of Law, title 48, chapter 8: "Whenever any citizen of the United States discovers a deposit of guano on any island, rock, or key, not within the lawful jurisdiction of any other government, and not occupied by the citizens of any other government, and takes peaceable possession thereof, and occupies the same, such island, rock, or key may, at the discretion of the President, be considered as appertaining to the United States."[21]

In this classic colonial example, capitalism's metabolic rift led to the imperial extraction of natural resources from the peripheries of capitalism's industrial centers. But the rift also appears in neocolonial and carbon-colonial forms. The neocolonial form emerges through the harvesting of low-wage labor and commodities markets and emerging consumer bases in the postcolonial and developing world. The carbon-colonial rift links the classical and neocolonial examples and is caused by the exploitation of the atmospheric commons by the fossil-fueled economies of the developed, industrialized, wealthy nations of the global North.

While wealthy nations account for less than one-fourth of the world's population, they account for more than two-thirds of cumulative historical GHG emissions. Between 1800 and 2010 a wealthy minority of nations (Annex I countries in the language of the UN Framework Convention on Climate Change [UNFCC]) emitted a cumulative total of roughly 900 to 950 metric tons of CO_2. The rest of the world, including rapidly developing countries such as China, India, Brazil, and Mexico, emitted a cumulative total of roughly four hundred metric tons. Although the emissions of wealthy nations began to escalate rapidly around 1860, the rest of the world's emissions didn't begin to escalate until after World War II. While the total annual emissions in developing countries like China and India surpassed the developed countries in the early 2000s, their per capita and cumulative historical emissions remain much lower. Furthermore, the increased emissions in developing nations over the past couple of decades coincides with the rise of global neoliberalism and is due in no small part to the global North's outsourcing of carbon-intensive production and manufacturing to the global South. In concert with the logic of exception, extraction, and externalization, emissions from production are assigned to developing nations while most of the profit and consumption occur in rich nations.[22]

As wickedly unjust as the climate crisis is, might the convergence of the social and ecological contradictions of capitalism also present an opportunity for revolutionary social change? Might it precipitate new forms of political power and a new democratic ethos? Could the aligning of the vulnerability phases of the social, economic, and ecological systems of the capitalist panarchy lead to a moment of breakthrough and democratic renewal? James O'Connor argues along these lines that the two contradictions of capitalism can be correlated to different kinds of social movements: class-based, labor movements through the contradiction in the relations of production, and social justice and environmental movements through the contradiction in the conditions of production.[23] As

Foster has said of this analysis, it leads naturally to the possibility of "an alliance between the two types of movements based on the combined force of the two contradictions."[24] Though there has historically been a significant and sometimes raging divide between the class and labor movements of the "old left" and the environmental and multicultural movements of the "new left," the coalescence and emergence of something new out of these movements are no mere theoretical speculation.

According to the theory of panarchy, the conditions for such a possibility should be expected. When subsystem weaknesses or vulnerabilities align at the same time, the coincidence of their breaking points catalyzes the breakdown of the larger system, and systemic breakdown seeds and fertilizes the emergence of a new system. In the example being discussed here, it is being posited not only that the social and ecological contradictions of capitalism are coinciding with each other, but also that this coincidence could lead to the revolutionary coalescence of emergent social and environmental movements. To return to the discussion of Grace Lee Boggs, if the rebellious energy of the movements can coalesce around something beyond critique, if they can announce, amplify, and unite around a revolutionary common purpose, then a transformative restructuring of larger economic, social, and ecological systems may become possible. But let us not forget that for Boggs, revolutions must begin from wherever we are, in medias res. Organic systemic change emerges from the bottom up and middle out and the theopolitics of resilient democracy provides a way to frame this work and to cultivate the ethos needed to sustain it.

VULNERABLE POWER AND THE POWER OF VULNERABILITY

To make the foregoing ideas more concrete, it will be helpful to narrow in from the theory of panarchy to a discussion of risk and vulnerability. The work of the sociologists Anthony Giddens and Ulrich Beck is important in this regard. Giddens, for example, helpfully distinguishes two types of risk, external and manufactured. "External risk," he writes, is "risk experienced as coming from the outside, from the fixities of tradition or nature."[25] Until recently in the history of our species, we experienced risk in mainly this sense. Manufactured risk, on the other hand, is "risk created by the very impact of our developing knowledge upon the world."[26] There is an ironic link between the increase of manufactured risk and the attempt to decrease external risk—in an age of increasingly powerful technologies, every effort to control external risk and manage our vulnerability seems to lead to the production of new kinds of risks. But it is not only that we are generating new kinds of risk and vulnerability. It is also that the risks we face are riskier than ever before. Along this line, Ulrich Beck writes that "contemporary nuclear, chemical, ecological, and biological [risks] are . . . not limitable, either socially or temporally,. . . not accountable according to the prevailing rules of causality, guilt, and liability; and [are] . . . neither compensable nor insurable."[27] For these reasons, he continues, "the regulating system for the 'rational' control of industrial devastation is about as effective as a bicycle brake on a jetliner."[28]

Beck's and Giddens's theories of risk can help us to grasp the significance of the moral threshold we've crossed as a species. They also help to name an important element of wicked problems, the fact that sometimes our solutions to one problem create another kind of problem. A case in point is the unintended effects of the success of the Montreal Protocol. The Montreal Protocol came out of a collective international effort to do something about the hole in the ozone layer caused by the heavy use of chlorofluorocarbons (CFCs) in aerosols, solvents, and refrigerants. The use of CFCs was gradually phased out according to the terms of the treaty. But recent research has found that the compounds used to replace them, hydrofluorocarbons (HFCs), are extremely potent greenhouse gases, in some cases over one thousand times more potent than carbon dioxide (CO_2).[29] Eliminating HFCs has thus become a critical task in the larger effort to mitigate some of the worst effect of the climate crisis.[30]

While risk theory illuminates aspects of the nature of wicked problems, it is also important to address disparities of exposure to risk. In order to address this issue better, the unevenness of vulnerability and the types of vulnerability need to be taken into account.[31] The most important distinction morally and politically is between what I refer to as creatural and contingent vulnerability. Creatural vulnerability is an ontological condition of life—it is universal, given, inherent. To be a living creature, to be a person, is to be woundable, able to cause and to suffer wounds, to harm and to be harmed, to eat and to be eaten. Contingent vulnerability, on the other hand, names the kind of vulnerability that disproportionately afflicts some of us more than others. Contingent vulnerability is determined by any number of factors, such as where and when we are born, the bodies and minds we are born into, the social and class locations we inhabit, and proximity to environmental hazards.

Unlike creatural vulnerability, which is universal, given, and inherent, contingent vulnerability is uneven, constructed, and systemic. For example, some kinds of bodies are more vulnerable than others. Gender, skin color, and sexual orientation all influence a human body's vulnerability. And this is not because being female or transgender or gay or brown- or black-skinned is inherently more vulnerable than being male or cis gendered or straight or light- or white-skinned. It is because social norms and cultural values confer advantages and disadvantages related to gender, race, ethnicity, and sexuality, and these advantages and disadvantages are systemically transmitted, institutionally reinforced, and historically cumulative. By accident of genealogy and geography some of us have been born into contexts of advantage and have consciously and unconsciously consented to systems that reinforce, justify, and exacerbate our disproportionate and unearned advantages. People and groups who are advantaged in these ways suffer all the "slings and arrows" of creatural vulnerability and natural risk.

But people and groups who, through accident of genealogy and geography, have been born into socially, economically, and ecologically disadvantageous contexts are contingently vulnerable. The contingently vulnerable are of course creaturally vulnerable as well, but they are disproportionately exposed to manufactured risks such as climate wickedness.

In response to the injustices of diverse forms of contingent vulnerability, socioeconomic, ethnoracial, environmental, and climatic, people and communities around the world are harnessing their political and moral agency for new expressions of revolutionary democratic power.[32] In a time of manufactured risk and ecological emergency, these communities are becoming the emergently powerful base of a more resilient democratic ethos. Living at the ruptured edges of the increasingly visible social and ecological contradictions of neoliberal capitalism, they are the most exposed to the multisystem risks produced by the aligning of the vulnerability phases of global social and economic systems and planetary dynamics.

Vulnerable power, the power of people who recognize and rage against the injustices of contingent vulnerability, is coalescing all around us. But as Paul Hawken has observed, there is no center to this movement. As contingent vulnerability is uneven, constructed, and systemic, the political agency and movement power of the contingently vulnerable are diverse and dispersed rather than unitary and concentrated. On the one hand, diversity and dispersed power are ingredients of resilient systems, contributing to their agility and responsiveness to change. On the other hand, if insufficiently coordinated, diversity and dispersed power can lead to system dissipation. The political efficacy of vulnerable power depends on the building up of systemic resilience, systemic resilience depends on systemic connectivity, and connectivity in a movement as dispersed and diverse as this requires the forging of common purposes across different identities and cultural contexts.

To more democratically address wicked problems such as the climate crisis, we must learn more creatively to work across our cultural, ethnoracial, sexual, and even political differences. Diverse skills, experiences, and perspectives are necessary to the work of cultivating new approaches to wicked problems. We need to build cross-difference coalitions in order more fully to bring to life the experimental communities, polities, and economies upon which genuine innovation depends. But our differences often polarize and paralyze us. To a significant degree, dissent, debate, and division are to be expected, and even encouraged, as aspects of a vital democracy.[33] But there is also a collaborative spirit—a spirit of epistemic, moral, and social generosity—necessary to the pragmatics of democracy.[34] This collaborative spirit is manifest in humility toward our own convictions, curiosity about others' experiences and points of view, a willingness to learn from others, readiness to revise our own perspectives in light of ongoing experience and dialogue, and commitment to a common life larger than our own self-interest. The spirit of collaboration necessary to functional democracy requires recognition of the fallibility of our own standpoints and generous regard for the potential wisdom of others.

Although our differences often polarize and paralyze us, difference itself is not the problem. From within the immanental frame outlined in previous chapters, the deeper problem is the concept of power that underlies our ideas about difference and shapes the way we live in community. This concept of power is rooted in the deep philosophical and theological assumption that power is functionally oppositional and unitary. It is oppositional because it is scarce—there is only so much to go around; it is unitary because so long as there are others who have power, one's own power is thought to be diminished. As the Chicago theologian Bernard Loomer argued, "it follows factually as well as logically," given these assumptions about power, "that the gain in power by the other is experienced as a loss of one's own power and therefore of one's status and sense of worth. At the human level, at least, and possibly with respect to nature itself, the other is often experienced as a threat or a potential threat to our ability to realize our purposes."[35]

Our idealities of power affect the way we understand our own agency, the agency of others, and the purposes and values of common life, and the way we understand these things has a profound bearing on questions of democracy and justice. The assumption that power is oppositional, unitary, and scarce breeds a competitive antagonism into our politics and fuels the mechanics of injustice. It provides the deep infrastructure for the manufacturing of inequality and the hierarchical structuring of social difference. While inequality is in some respects a fact of human existence— we are naturally unequal, for example, in terms of aesthetic, athletic, and mechanical aptitudes, in terms of height, in our genetic predispositions— inequality becomes a matter of justice when it is manufactured by concentrations of power in systems of privilege and when constructed differences of class, gender, sexual orientation, and race become politically naturalized.

The manufacturing of inequalities and social hierarchies is a necessary effect within any society governed by a scarcity concept of power, and this concept of power is a legacy of classical theism and the metaphysics of being. This is not surprising, since behind every working concept of power there is an operative ideal of power. And in the West, the historically dominant ideal of power has long been the omnipotent God of classical theism. The metaphysics of being undergirds and reinforces this construction of divine power. From the premises that humans and the divine share the attribute of being (that is, both humans and God exist, where existent being is understood within the logic of substance), and that God is that which is highest, classical theism reasons analogically (*analogia entis*) from the limitations of human power to the conclusion that divine power must be unlimited and absolute. If it is absolute, then it must be undivided; if it were divided, say, between a good and an evil power, then divine power could not be absolute, for the divisions would qualify and relativize each other. Thus the oneness of the God of classical theism is sealed by the absoluteness of divine power, and the absoluteness of divine power is consolidated by the oneness of God.

The immanental tradition offers a different construction of power, and thus also different ways of engaging difference and enacting democracy. Recall my previous discussion of Whitehead's understanding of power. In contrast to the ideal of power as unitary and oppositional, power for Whitehead is dipolar and relational. It names the capacity not only to act, but also to be acted upon; it is receptive as well as active. With this concept of power in mind, one can affirm that power is vulnerable, and that vulnerability can be a form of power. Both these ideas, the power of vulnerability and the vulnerability of power, are critical to the theory and practice of resilient democracy.

What if instead of externalizing vulnerability we embraced its shared experience as the precondition of more empathic, emancipatory, and equitable democratic practices? What if instead of answering creatural insecurity with the quest for certainty we found the courage to build uncertainty into our ways of knowing and our social, religious, moral, and political habits? What if rather than seeking to redeem or to be redeemed we sought to build more resilient democratic communities, ones whose constitutive differences enriched their common purposes and whose sympathies were expanded by the common vulnerabilities they share? Let us now turn to a discussion of how the theopolitics of resilient democracy seeks to embody these possibilities.

RESILIENT DEMOCRACY

We are living through a time in which democracy is idealized almost everywhere and yet realized almost nowhere, even where it is thought most fully to be actualized.[36] Although democracy has had many suitors, democracy remains, as C. Douglas Lummis has put this, "a virginal political idea,. . . a promise yet to be fulfilled."[37] But isn't this as it must be? Isn't it intrinsic to the nature of democracy, literally intrinsic to the organic conditions of the "power of the people," that it can never be realized fully, at least not in any final form. One reason for this, as Paulina Ochoa Espejo has recently argued, is that "the people" are always changing, "the people" are not a static thing but a process.[38] But it is also the case that the idea of democracy itself is a process rather than a form, one that is never finally achieved but is always in a state of becoming. The ideal of democracy, as the power (in the broadest sense of the term) of the people (in the broadest sense of the term), entails that the struggle for democracy be conducted democratically, which is to say, by people empowered. But it is not only the people—as embodied and embedded, as gendered and racialized, as bio-cultural animals—who are constantly changing. So are the conditions of their empowerment and the threats to those conditions.

Thus one of the great paradoxes of democracy is that it is most faithfully idealized when it is embraced as unfinalizable, and yet it is most fully actualized when its unfinalizability activates continuous democratic struggle—in all spheres of life. As Dewey expressed this point, "*The fundamental principle of democracy is that the ends of freedom and individuality for all can be attained only by means that accord with those ends. . . . The end of democracy is a radical end. For it is an end that has not been adequately realized in any country at any time.* It is radical because it requires great change in existing social institutions, economic, legal and cultural. . . . There is, moreover, nothing more radical than insistence upon democratic methods as the means by which radical social changes be effected."[39] The work of empowering the people, which is simultaneously the ground, context, and aim of democracy, is continuous.

This democratic paradox is the vital and life-giving matrix of resilient democracy, for it reveals the fundamental vulnerability of democracy: the power of the people is vulnerable power. This revelation provokes the basic questions of how to build the resilient communities and practices needed to sustain the unfinalizable struggle for democracy in face of the many powerful countervailing forces opposed to democracy. Building more resilient democratic communities to sustain democratic struggle depends on embracing democracy's vulnerability, and embracing democracy's vulnerability entails rejecting every claim to democracy's fulfillment. Resilient democracy accepts that the struggle for democracy is unending and that there is no transcendent reality that is "democracy achieved."

Embracing democracy as an *imminent* ideal, as a perpetual possibility, is critical to the emancipative task of an *immanental* theopolitics.[40] The imminence of democracy is a critical and emancipatory ideal insofar as it can lead us to turn away from some of the more fixed ideas about politics and religion that dominate our world—for example, the unimaginative idea that there is no alternative to the way things are, the patronizing idea that the way things are is the way they should be, the belittling idea that the way things are, whether we like it or not, is of secondary importance to higher spiritual concerns, and the insane idea that existing institutional forms of the state and market are the only vectors for radical change.

In contrast to these ideas, resilient democracy understands democracy as an associational ethos of vulnerable life grounded in the collective experience of uncertainty and animated by the living desire to bring about a more beautiful world. The idea of democracy as an associational ethos is drawn in part from John Dewey's philosophy of democracy. It is well understood that for Dewey democracy is irreducible to any particular institutionalized form of government. "The idea of democracy," Dewey writes, "is a wider and fuller idea" than any particular governmental form, even the most allegedly democratic, can ever exemplify: commitment to democracy as a social idea, rather than a political form, should "affect all modes of human association, the family, the school, industry, religion."[41] But it is no more accurate to conflate Dewey's conception of democracy with a particular form of life, either. The relevant contrast for Dewey is not between democracy as a form of government and as a form of life, but between fixed forms and everything else. As I explained previously, the philosophical implications of evolutionary theory entail, for Dewey, that "the fixed structure, the separate form, the isolated element, is henceforth at best a mere stepping-stone to knowledge of process."[42] Politically extrapolated, this leads to the idea of democracy as a fundamentally formless phenomenon—what Dewey refers to as a "way of life."[43]

The institutional deformation of democracy opens a clearing in which to reimagine democracy as a set of practices and processes and thereby to reclaim the ethos of democracy from its formal governmental and corporate enclosures.[44] Though it is only a clearing, it brings the essential question into focus—granting that democracy has no fixed form, what makes an associational ethos democratic? After all, there is nothing intrinsically democratic about association. As Dewey puts this, in language resonant with the influence of Whitehead and James:

Association in the sense of connection and combination is a "law" of everything known to exist. Singular things act, but they act together. Nothing has been discovered which acts in entire isolation. The action of everything is along with the action of other things. The "along with" is of such a kind that the behavior of each is modified by its connection with others. There are trees which can grow only in a forest. Seeds of many plants can successfully germinate and develop only under conditions furnished by the presence of other plants. . . . The life history of an animal cell is conditioned upon connection with what other cells are doing. Electrons, atoms and molecules exemplify the omnipresence of conjoint behavior. . . . There is no sense in asking how individuals come to be associated. They exist and operate in association. If there is any mystery about the matter, it is the mystery that the universe is the kind of universe it is.[45]

While nature and the things of nature are inherently associative and associations are inherently relational, it is not the case that the relational ethos in every association is inherently democratic. What then makes for a democratic associational ethos? Following Dewey, such an ethos entails, at the level of individuals, "having a responsible share according to capacity in forming and directing the activities of the groups to which one belongs" and "participating according to need in the values which the groups sustain." And at the level of the group, it entails "liberation of the potentialities of members of the group in harmony with the interests and goods which are common."[46] A democratic ethos encourages people to actively participate in defining a community's purposes and values and strives to ensure that the goods and benefits of the community are equitably enjoyed.

As I define it, then, an ethos of associational life is democratic when it is empathic, emancipatory, and equitable—it entails identifying and liberating human gifts and talents in ways that mutually enrich individual and social life. It presumes, first, that all individuals have something to contribute to one another and to the whole of the larger community; second, that each member and the community can be enriched by every other member's active participation; third, that the empathic work of identifying and emancipating individual capacities is a communal responsibility; and, fourth, that the coordination and equitable enjoyment of the "interests and goods" of common life are an ongoing struggle, and a blessing.

What does any of this have to do with "vulnerable life"? I argued earlier that democracy is an imminent ideal, a fundamentally formless, emergent, and natal phenomenon. Insofar as the power of the people is never finally formed or fully secure, democratic power is intrinsically vulnerable. If one embraces a dipolar, relational concept of power, then the vulnerability of democratic power is both unexceptional and integrally related to its creativity. All power, understood as dipolar and relational, is vulnerable. To register, see, and feel the vulnerability of democratic power can lead us to value it in creative new ways. Embracing its natality, for example, can compel us to nourish it, to seek its well-being, to support its flourishing. To commit to democracy as an imminent ideal, to feel its vulnerability as well as intellectually affirming it, can and should move us to protect and care for it.

Judith Butler's ideas about vulnerability and grief illuminate what I am talking about here. Butler interprets vulnerability, as I do, as both an embodied and a relational reality. She writes, "The body implies mortality, vulnerability, agency: the skin and the flesh expose us to the gaze of others, but also to touch, and to violence, and bodies put us at risk of becoming the agency and instrument of all these as well."[47] As I suggested earlier in relation to creatural vulnerability, we are vulnerable, capable of wounding and causing wounds, because we are bodies and minds intra-related to other bodies and minds. In light of this, Butler argues that loss and grief are intrinsic to human vulnerability: "Loss and vulnerability seem to follow from our being socially constituted bodies, attached to others, at risk of losing those attachments."[48] We can be wounded by the wounds of others. When someone we love is injured, becomes ill, dies, or is killed, we grieve the loss of their wholeness, their health, their life.

By correlating vulnerability and loss, Butler argues that grief is both ontologically and political disclosive. As she eloquently describes this:

Loss has made a tenuous "we" of us all. . . . But maybe when we undergo what we do, something about who we are is revealed, something that delineates the ties we have to others, that shows us that these ties constitute what we are, ties or bonds that compose us. It is not as if an "I" exists independently over here and then simply loses a "you" over there, especially if the attachment to "you" is part of what composes who "I" am. . . . Let's face it. We're undone by each other. And if we're not, we're missing something.[49]

Grief is a political emotion—it tells us something about our nature as political creatures. It reveals that we are connected to others, that those connections are constitutive of who and what we are, that we can suffer when those connections are severed. In other words, grief is an affective, moral, and political manifestation of the human embodiment of the ontology of internal relatedness.

Butler's reflections on the relation between vulnerability, loss, and grief are profound, but to make my point, I would like to think about them "at a slant" (Emily Dickenson). By defining democracy as an associational ethos of vulnerable life, and thereby acknowledging the vulnerability of the power of the people, I am defining democracy as a relationally embodied, creatural politics. The power of, by, and for the people is creatural power, embodied, relational, and vulnerable. The importance of this is that it underscores the obvious but easily forgotten idea that democracy can be lost. Affirming that democracy, like our bodies, is vulnerable can remind us not to take democracy for granted. Democracy can be wounded, it can take ill, it can be injured, it can be killed.

The significance of this became especially vivid to me during a trip to Berlin in summer 2016. I was with a group of other scholars on a tour at the Reichstag, the German parliament. Our guide, a Green party delegate, showed us through all the old and the new parts of the building and made a point of interpreting some of the art installations. One of them was sculpted out of hundreds of tin mailboxes used by German parliamentarians since the founding of the Reichstag in 1871. Stacked in two rows from floor to ceiling and extending in length about ten meters, the mailboxes were sculpted into an artificial hallway so that one had to enter into the sculpture to experience it. The names of parliamentarians were etched into the mailboxes. Although people had attempted to scratch it out, Hitler's name was also on one of the boxes. I will never forget what our guide said when we observed the gap in the years between 1933 and 1949, the years of the Third Reich. He said that as a German observing the American political scene, and especially the rise of resentment and hate fueled by the (at the time) presidential candidacy of Donald Trump, his great fear was that Americans might not know, as Germans have had to painfully and violently learn, that democracy can be lost, a little at a time, and then all at once.

The idea that democracy is vulnerable, that it has and can be lost, should awaken us from our political slumber.[50] Affirming the vulnerability of democracy becomes creatively efficacious when our grief for what has been and could be lost leads us to deepen the democracy that remains, to extend and enliven it by practicing it more fully, to commit anew to struggling for it as an imminent ideal, and thereby to contribute to a more resilient democracy.

However, there is also a risk in affirming the vulnerability of democracy. For the experience of vulnerability can trigger the creatural quest for security, which itself can trigger and intensify the quest for certainty. But democracy and certainty are antithetical. As Claude Lefort has famously argued, "Democracy is instituted and sustained by the *dissolution of the markers of certainty*. It inaugurates a history in which people experience a fundamental indeterminacy as to the basis of power, law, and knowledge, and as to the basis of relations between self and other."[51] Along these same lines, Benjamin Barber writes that democracy begins "where certainty ends."[52]

As a politics of uncertainty, democracy is an antifoundational politics. Foundationalism is problematic for democracy for intrarelated epistemic and political reasons. Epistemically, foundationalist reasoning assumes that "there exists a knowable independent ground—an incorrigible first premise or 'antecedent immutable reality'—from which the concepts, values, standards, and ends of political life can be derived by deduction."[53] The problem with this assumption is not the idea of "starting points" or "first premises" as such. After all, whenever and wherever and however one begins to inquire and reason, one cannot help but to begin from somewhere, in medias res. Foundationalist reasoning is the epistemic incarnation of the ex nihilo mythos. It also enables Whitehead's bifurcation of nature and reinforces Dewey's chain of dualisms. As Barber contends, it cuts off the knower from the known, isolates epistemology from ontology, differentiates thought from action, and identifies fact and value as "residents of hostile universes."[54] The problem with this, as Whitehead, James, and Dewey would agree, is that these oppositions contradict our experience, and therefore also, as Barber rightly adds, are contrary to "political reality."[55] A foundationalist epistemology is insufficient to our experience as embodied and relational, to our creatural and contingent vulnerability, and to the systemically entangled nature of our political realities.

Rather than asking the foundationalist question of what epistemology is needed to ground or justify democracy, the pragmatist asks what epistemology democracy entails. What "way of knowing" follows from, or is appropriate to, democracy as an associational ethos of vulnerable life? Barber argues for an "epistemology of process" in which "truth [is] a product of certain modes of common living rather than the foundation of common life."[56] Such an epistemology would seek to articulate "enabling norms developed amidst concrete problems"; it would replace "absolute certainty" with "relative conviction," "philosophical incorrigibility" with "practical agreement," and "ultimate knowledge" with "shared ends, common values, community standards, and public goods."[57]

Barber's "epistemology of process" obviously shares a great deal in common with my account of pragmatic naturalism as a mode of immanental thinking. This is not surprising, given that Dewey is a primary source for both of us. For pragmatic naturalism, knowledge claims are always provisional, hypothetic, and revisable. And as an epistemology of process proceeds from rather than precedes his account of democracy, pragmatic naturalism follows from the experience of the self and the world in process. Pragmatic naturalism is a mode of immanental thinking appropriate to the imminent ideal of democracy. But the question at hand is more than epistemological.

If the epistemic problem with foundationalism is its exceptionalist neglect of the uncertainties and the embeddedness of thought, the political problem is its externalization of difference. By treating starting points and first premises as indubitable, absolute, true for all time, all places, and all people, foundationalist reasoning externalizes the differences of historical context, social location, and embodiment. But insofar as democracy is a continuous struggle to widen the circle of empathy, to extend the reach of emancipation, and to deepen equality, as I suggested earlier, democratic deliberation and democratic community must include these and other kinds of difference. Foundationalist political reasoning argues deductively from antecedently held political ideals to the ideal ordering of political life. In contrast, the assumptions of democracy as an associational ethos of vulnerable life are, first, that we don't already know how best to order our common life and, second, that we don't know what the abstract ideals of empathy, emancipation, and equity entail in the concrete.

While uncertainty can foment feelings of fear and dread, uncertainty is also the birthplace of possibility. We need democracy not only because we are uncertain about how to order our common life, but also because life and the world are fundamentally uncertain. The point is not merely that democracy is an antifoundational politics. It is that democracy is a politics of and for the uncertainty of life. If democracy begins where certainty ends, then, from within an immanental theopolitical frame, democracy is always beginning. Democracy is a politics calibrated for a world in process because a world in process is a world of uncertainty, of infinite possibilities, of undetermined futures—in a world that is always coming to life, the future is natal. This is what it means to describe uncertainty as the birthplace of possibility. In the insufficiently democratized, gendered idiom of his time, Dewey expressed the relation between uncertainty and democracy as follows: "A philosophy animated . . . by the strivings of men to achieve democracy will construe liberty as meaning a universe in which there is real uncertainty and contingency, a world which is not all in, and never will be, a world which in some respect is incomplete and in the making."[58] The unfinalizability of the struggle to cultivate a more empathic, emancipatory, and equitable democratic ethos is a political struggle attuned to the uncertainty of life in an undecided and unfinished cosmos of infinite possibilities.

In the uncertainty of life in a world-in-process, the need for democracy is pervasive. Fortunately, the potential for democracy is as pervasive as the need. For it can be argued that democracy exists as an imminent possibility in any political context, no matter how undemocratic that context may be. Democracy is the prepolitical precedent of every other political possibility. As C. Douglas Lummis argues, even the autocratic rule of a monarch is contingent on subjects who implicitly consent to be so ruled.[59] This implicit consent is most in evidence when it is collectively withdrawn—when, through insurrection and rebellion, through a refusal to be governed, through civil and uncivil disobedience, the monarch's rule is jeopardized. In other words, the prepolitical democratic moment becomes visibly political when implicit consent is explicitly taken back. For Lummis, the ideal of radical democracy builds out from this idea and is based on a claim of fact and a claim of value. The claim of fact is that "all power is generated by the people," or that "political power is generated not by the rulers but by the ruled."

The claim of value is that "people who generate the power ought also to have it."[60] Following Lummis, one can say that the fact of democracy is that it is always ready to begin. As the seed of every other political possibility, it is not only an imminent political ideal but also an immanent political potency.

Democracy is a vulnerable politics for vulnerable creatures in a vulnerable world in a cosmos without a center. And since the prospects of our common life have been made more uncertain by climate wickedness and the Anthropocene paradox, the need for democracy is as urgent as it has ever been. This combination of uncertainty and urgency is the mark of the crisis we face. We are at a crossroads. The ending of the human difference from the rest of nature could simply signify the beginning of a human age for the Earth in which climate wickedness continues to spiral out of control, the sixth extinction accelerates, and the planetary boundaries that sustain human life as we have known it are compromised beyond the point of return. Or it could mark the beginning of a more ecological conception of common life.

THE SOLIDARY AIM FOR BEAUTY

But how can a theopolitics of resilient democracy help to catalyze this possibility? I am persuaded by Grace Lee Boggs's argument that revolutions can only begin from wherever we are, and that in fact to begin from where we are is the most radical thing we can do. With this in mind, I have been slowly making a case for the theopolitics of resilient democracy as a grassroots theopolitics for the here and now, a theopolitical hypothesis responsive to the liminality of our present "zone of anarchy." To this point I have interpreted and made a case for the relevance of the philosophical and theological lineages of the American immanental tradition for such a theopolitics. I have articulated an immanental theological frame that brings to view the objectively relative goodness of human flourishing in a more-than-human world and an acentric cosmos. I have argued that far from being anthropocentric, this construal of human flourishing is organized around a prismatic axiology that can enable us to see, feel, and honor the aesthetic and moral value of more-than-human life. In this chapter I have made a case for panarchy as a hermeneutic category useful to critiquing the vulnerabilities and contradictions in systems and to advancing their potential for reorganization and renewal. I have discussed the vulnerability of power and the power of vulnerability in relation to the paradox of democracy. I have articulated the idea of resilient democracy as an associational ethos of vulnerable life oriented by the ideals of empathy, emancipation, and equity, as an imminent political possibility that begins where certainty ends.

No doubt many questions remain, which is how it is with hypotheses. Rather than attempting to close my case in these final pages, I would like to open it anew to further experimental inquiry by returning to Grace Lee Boggs's point that revolutions require a shift from "rejection to projection, from just denunciation to annunciation." As I discussed earlier, this is an especially important challenge in light of the dispersed and decentralized nature of contemporary social, environmental, and climate justice movements. On the one hand, the distributed power of these diverse movements is intrinsic to their democratic nature and their political agility and creativity. On the other hand, the democratic resilience necessary to long-term movement efficacy requires the development of system connectivity. And the most important element of a resilient system, democratic or otherwise, is a unitive purpose, aim, or telos that collectively integrates the system.

Earlier in this chapter I made a point of defining democracy as a formless phenomenon. I described it instead as an ethos or a way of living characterized by certain aims that can never be fulfilled in any final way but must be struggled for continuously. I identified these as the aims for empathy, emancipation, and equity. I argued that for an associational ethos to be democratic it needs to be an ethos that struggles always more fully (but never finally) to realize these aims. But instead of presenting these aims as foundational principles necessary to justifying democracy, I articulated them as normative aims internal to the meaning of democracy. Furthermore, I suggested that the concrete meanings of these ideals would need to be democratically discerned in context. Precisely what an empathic, emancipatory, equitable associational ethos of vulnerable life looks like and entails cannot be set out in advance, but must emerge through democratic process. Although this position is consistent with both a pragmatic naturalist mode of immanental thinking and a "presumptively generous" commitment to pluralism, it poses a significant challenge in relation to Boggs's argument that revolutions demand a unifying vision (and my own argument that complex system resilience is contingent on an integrative system purpose).

So, is there a way through or around this dilemma? My hypothesis is that a way can be found by following a path from justice to beauty. Recall my discussion earlier in this chapter about how different idealities of power format alternative approaches to difference: where a unitary ideal of power foments opposition, a dipolar ideal is inherently relational. That discussion is important insofar as the reconciliation of power and pluralism is at the heart of the revolutionary challenges of life in the Anthropocene. The work of social, environmental, and climate justice depends upon the realization of more empathic democratic practices and institutions. This is because justice cannot be realized in the abstract, but *must be lived*. A theopolitics of resilient democracy isn't rooted in an a priori principle of justice. It is agnostic on principles, for political as well as epistemic reasons. It isn't premised upon foundationalist theological or political reasoning. It is resistant to finalities and absolutes of all kinds, theological and otherwise, out of religious reverence for the unfolding adventure of life and the emergent creativity of the cosmos.

Living justice is impossible apart from the willingness and the ability of people with diverse life experiences to empathically cross over to the experiences of others. Justice in this sense is not so much a moral principle or political ideal as an aspirational form of relationship—a form of relationship upon which the flourishing of individuals and communities, social and ecological, depends. Just relationships are ones in which the power to act and to decide, to be and to do and to know, is shared rather than concentrated, in which the good of each and the good of the whole mutually enrich each other. The possibility of mutually enriching individual and communal flourishing depends upon the emancipation of the human functions of being, doing, and knowing; the full emancipation of these functions requires that the capacities or capabilities to enact them are equitably distributed; and the equitable distribution of the capabilities conducive to flourishing both depends upon and is brought about through the communal embodiment of just relationships—relationships of shared power and mutual enrichment bound by commitments to the good of a common life larger than one's own.

The work of living justice depends on the embrace of the creative potential of uncertainty, empathic response to the creatural vulnerabilities that we all share, and the prophetic critique and dismantling of the contingent vulnerabilities that disproportionately afflict some of us. A theopolitics of resilient democracy understands these tasks of living justice as sacred work, as an expression of reverence for the nature of reality-in-process, humility in face of the finitude of human being and knowing, and deep respect for the priceless perishability of all things. To embrace this sacred work is to broaden the bounds of empathy; the broadening of empathy is necessary to spanning diverse communities; spanning diverse communities is integral to the work of building solidarities of difference; and solidarities of difference are the gardens in which to cultivate resilient democracy.

Solidarities may be necessary, but the ubiquitous interest in "community" in our time signals an important human desire for belonging and stability in a changing world. However, a fixation on communal belonging, especially insofar as it tends to privilege shared identity, can be politically limiting. Communities of identity tend to divide us by our differences when what we most need to learn in a time of pluralism and moral urgency is how to collaborate across them. Communities tend to reinforce a politics of special interest when what we most need is a politics of common purpose. Thus, while the lure of community makes sense in a splintering, fracturing, polarizing world, the privileging of shared identity within community can reinforce those splinters, fractures, and polarities. We may need community, but the complexity of the challenges we face demands more than communities.

In response to this challenge, the sociologist David Hollinger recently claimed, echoing W. E. B. DuBois, that "The problem of solidarity is shaping up as the problem of the twenty-first century."[61] As he interprets it, the problem of solidarity arises when a group or community is capable of asking who they are as a "we." As he defines the concept, "community" is commonly used as a way "to classify people, to denote a group defined by one or more characteristics shared by its members—whether or not those members are disposed to act together."[62] In contrast to communities, solidarities are performative; they are constituted by a "special claim . . . that individuals have on each other's energies, compassion, and resources."[63] As Hollinger argues, "We will miss the character and scope of the problem of solidarity if we conflate solidarity with the mere possession of a set of traits or antecedents or confinements. On the other hand, the problem of solidarity is real when there is at least some opportunity for choice, when people can exercise some influence over just what 'we' they help to constitute."[64]

Solidarities, then, are a special kind of association, an association that performatively answers the question of who they are as a "we." While communities tend to define themselves as a "we" in terms of common identity, racial or cultural or otherwise, solidarities comprise diverse individuals or communities organized around common purposes. Though the question of "we" is of course not a uniquely twenty-first-century question, it is a question that has arguably become especially acute in the "anarchical zone" of the Anthropocene paradox. The uncertainty of life in a zone such as this simultaneously increases the demand for solidarities of purpose and drives many people to dive more deeply into the comforting confines of communities of identity.

The problem of solidarity emerges out of the challenge of justice in a pluralistic world and is an instance of the larger challenge of sustaining the systemically complex work of long-term revolution. What is the role of beauty in relation to the problem of solidarity and sustaining revolution? The theopolitics of resilient democracy engages the problem of solidarity and foments revolutionary possibilities in the here and now by *aiming for beauty*. More precisely, rather than being oriented by a prespecified principle of justice, or by a preexisting concept of the good, a theopolitics of resilient democracy is normatively oriented by Whitehead's dipolar concept of beauty as the harmonization of contrast and the intensification of experience. Oriented by this concept of beauty, resilient democratic solidarities are associations of maximally diversified unity—not harmonized unities, but experientially enriching unities of contrast. These solidarities may be diverse in any number of the nearly numberless respects in which we humans differ from one another—age, gender, ethnicity, nationality, sexual orientation, religiosity, temperament, physical ability, moral purposes, and so on. But insofar as they compose a "we" by way of a common purpose rather than a shared identity, and insofar as they strive for resilience, there must be some aim, some willed or chosen purpose, that unites them. While solidarities can be unified by any number of chosen purposes, resiliently democratic solidarities are unified by a common aim for "the more beautiful world our hearts know is possible."[65]

A living desire for a more beautiful world is the phenomenologically transcendent ideal whose natal potency binds and sustains resiliently democratic solidarities. The degree to which a resiliently democratic solidarity compositionally approximates the aim for beauty is the degree to which its constitutive internal differences mutually enrich their experience of one another and the world they share in common and, through this mutual enrichment, add value to (literally appreciate) the broader world of more-than-human experience. To say this is to say something not only about the structuring (always in process, never finalized) of such solidarities, but also about the nature of the desire that animates them. It is not insignificant that where Whitehead offers his most careful analysis of beauty he also turns to the erotic in his discussion of the primordial aspect of God. Whitehead refers to the primordial aspect of God as the eros of the universe and beauty as the telos of the universe. By intrarelating God, desire, and beauty, Whitehead is simultaneously appealing to the classical Western association of beauty and the erotic—that which is longed for cannot fully be possessed—and recasting it theologically. This is consistent with the metaphor of God as fellow-sufferer, insofar as erotic experience, understood as insatiable longing, is also a form of suffering. In naming beauty as the telos of the universe and relating it to the divine eros, Whitehead implies that running through the whole and each intrarelated part of what is and what may be, within every process, occasion, and relation, are the restlessness, the agitation, the grief, the vulnerable sting of longing for the beautiful. As Whitehead famously writes, "the teleology of the Universe is directed toward the production of Beauty. . . . [And beauty is] the one aim which by its very nature is self-justifying."[66] As telos of the universe, beauty is potential rather than actual, ideal rather than real. It is precisely as potential, as unrealized possibility, that the aim for a more beautiful world has the generative, natal power of a religiously transformative transcendent ideal and the unitive power necessary to sustain political revolution.

What we aim for is what holds us together, and what holds us together is what we aim for—the more beautiful world whose possibility we feel more deeply than we know. Is this naïve? Does it sufficiently account for the recalcitrance of human self-interest, the inward curvature of human pride, the centrifugal, entrenched powers of anger, greed, and delusion? If the mark of taking such realities into account is a prohibition against risk, then yes, perhaps so. But might it also be that aversion to risk is itself naïve, a stultifying symptom of the quest for certainty in an uncertain world?

The theopolitics of resilient democracy embodies risk as pious hope, hope for the more beautiful world that may be. As Whitehead wrote, "The ideals cherished in the souls of men enter into the character of their actions. The inter-actions within society modify the social laws by modifying the occasions to which those laws apply. Impracticable ideals are a program for reform. Such a program is not to be criticized by immediate possibilities. Progress consists in modifying the laws of nature so that the Republic on Earth may conform to that Society to be discerned ideally by the divination of Wisdom."[67] In this light, then, risk is revered as part of our adventure with the universe toward the making of a more beautiful world. Within this present zone of anarchy, and consistent with the temper of the tradition of American immanence, a theopolitics of resilient democracy embraces the creative potential of ambiguity, the finitude of human being and knowing, and the priceless perishability of all things as expressions of the sacred work of *natura naturans*.

NOTES

INTRODUCTION

1. Robert Bellah, *The Broken Covenant: American Civil Religion in a Time of Trial* (New York: Seabury, 1975), 1.

2. By *posttruth* what is meant is an emergent political style that appeals primarily to emotions, neglects policy details, and normalizes falsehoods and conspiracy theories through communicative repetition. Of course, the appeal to emotion is neither new nor problematic. What is new is that this appeal is combined with a rabid suspicion of facts and evidence. This is enabled by, among other things, the rise of new forms of social media, the proliferation of for-profit "fake news," and the long-standing conservative campaign against the traditional journalistic standards of "mainstream media." In 2016, the Oxford dictionaries named *posttruth* as their "Word of the Year."

3. Although these traditions have been explored and expanded by many scholars, and although there has been a great deal of work in process theology through the decades, this book is unique in its effort to constructively develop the *theopolitical* significance of their *immanental* aspects. The process theologian John Cobb's *Process Theology as Political Theology* (Philadelphia: Westminster, 1982), for example, is more probative than constructive. It is also written from a Christian theological framework and excludes pragmatism from its purview. Of course, John Cobb is a prolific scholar and has published many other works, but none of them is an explicitly theopolitical work. It will also become clear in the chapters ahead that I am interested in a less theistic and more radically empirical and pragmatic version of process thought than Cobb. In comparison to Cobb, the philosopher James L. Marsh's *Process, Praxis and Transcendence* (Albany: State University of New York, 1999) is more constructive but its process perspective is developed from a Christian existentialist standpoint. The political philosopher and social ethicist Douglas Sturm's *Solidarity and Suffering* (Albany: State

University of New York, 1988) applies process-relational thinking to an array of important political questions, but doesn't develop a theopolitical standpoint. While Catherine Keller's work is radically innovative, philosophically eclectic, ecologically attuned, politically significant, and inimitably theopoetic, it does not engage the American philosophical or theological traditions that are my focus here. See, for example, Keller's most recent book, *Cloud of the Impossible: Negative Theology and Planetary Entanglement*, Insurrections: Critical Studies in Religion, Politics, and Culture (New York: Columbia University Press, 2014).

4.   The theology of immanence I will develop thus fits squarely into the broad tradition of "religious naturalism" as Wesley Wildman describes this in "Religious Naturalism: What It Can Be, and What It Need Not Be," *Philosophy, Theology, and the Sciences* 1, no. 1 (2014): 36–58. For an excellent historical survey of the modern American variants of this tradition, see Jerome A. Stone, *Religious Naturalism Today: The Rebirth of a Forgotten Alternative* (Albany: State University of New York, 2008).

5.   William David Hart, "Neville's Metaphysics," *American Journal of Theology and Philosophy* 37, no. 3 (September 2016): 255.

6.   Spinoza famously put these distinctions to work in his *Ethics* to contrast between the infinite and finite aspects of "God, or Nature" (*Deus, sive Natura*). *Natura naturans* refers to that aspect of God/Nature that is infinitely creative or always creating, whereas *natura naturata* refers to the finitude of singular things (that is, particular entities or beings) and their modes (that is, physical or mental) created by *natura naturans*. See *A Spinoza Reader: The Ethics, and Other Works*, ed. and trans. Edwin Curley (Princeton: Princeton University Press, 1994). Although I do not intend to invoke the particularities of Spinoza's system, the other terms I use to mark contrast and difference in nature approximate the general distinction: *processes* approximates the meaning of *natura naturans* and *patterns* and *precarities* approximate the meaning of *natura naturata*. The prominent American philosophers of religion Robert S. Corrington and Donald L. Crosby have also used these concepts in especially distinctive and creative ways. For example, by arguing that nature's "inexorable processes of change" are more fundamental than its "present patterns," Crosby's philosophy of nature emphasizes the dynamic ambiguity of *natura naturans* over the relative stabilities of *natura naturata*. See Donald L. Crosby, *A Religion of Nature* (Albany: State University of New York, 2002), 41. See also Crosby, *Living with Ambiguity: Religious Naturalism and the Menace of Evil* (Albany: State University of New York, 2009). For Corrington, the alterity of these aspects of nature in their relation to one another is what is most creatively significant. As he writes, "Within the one nature that there is lies the fundamental process of fissuring, a process that gives rise to the most primal distinction in thought—namely, that between nature naturing and nature natured. This natural difference represents the complex 'how' of nature as it both arises *and* shapes the orders of the world." See Robert S. Corrington, *Deep Pantheism: Toward a New Transcendentalism* (New York: Lexington, 2016), 1. See also Corrington, *Nature and Spirit: An Essay in Ecstatic Naturalism* (New York: Fordham University Press, 1992); Corrington, *Ecstatic Naturalism: Signs of the World* (Bloomington: Indiana University Press, 1994); Corrington, *Nature's*

Religion (Lanham, MD: Rowman and Littlefield, 1997); and Corrington, *A Semiotic Theory of Theology and Philosophy* (New York: Cambridge University Press, 2004); and Corrington, *Nature's Sublime: An Essay in Aesthetic Naturalism* (New York: Lexington, 2013). Rather than following Crosby or Corrington on this, I use the terms in a general way to emphasize four fundamental points: (1) that nature is all; (2) that nature is differentiated; (3) that nature is in process; (4) that the things and relations of nature are vulnerable and precarious. And rather than drawing directly from Spinoza, I develop these positions in relation to James, Whitehead, and Dewey.

7. William E. Connolly, *The Terms of Political Discourse*, 2nd ed. (Princeton: Princeton University Press, 1983); Raymond Williams, *Keywords: A Vocabulary of Culture and Society*, rev. ed. (New York: Oxford University Press, 1983).

8. Connolly, *Terms of Political Discourse*, 14.

9. Williams, *Keywords*, 15.

10. William Connolly's work has significantly influenced my critique of the dominant American political theology, especially his analyses of the coupling of socially conservative Christian evangelicalism and free-market fundamentalism, which he refers to as the American "evangelical-capitalist resonance machine." While this might seem an odd coupling, Connolly astutely observes that they embody faith positions that mutually amplify each other. Where evangelical spiritual commitments to a future second coming deflate care for "this" world, secular capitalist faith in the sovereign market leads to the casting of any position other than the ideal of a purely free market as heretical. Connolly argues that the politically powerful fusion of market fundamentalist faith in the purifying powers of deregulatory privatization and otherworldly evangelical spirituality has led to increasing economic inequality, "self-defeating" consumptive practices, and both the fueling and the denial of global warming. See Connolly, *Christianity and Capitalism, American Style* (Durham: Duke University Press, 2008); and Connolly, *A World of Becoming* (Durham: Duke University Press, 2011), esp. 87–88. While Connolly's argument has significantly influenced my critique, I explore an extended historical arc. I also organize my critique around the interplay of American exceptionalism and what I refer to as the "redeemer symbolic," demonstrating how this interplay legitimates the extraction of diverse forms of value and the externalization of diverse forms of cost. All of this will be addressed in chapter 1.

11. It's a telling sign when new "guides," "companions," and "readers" begin to be published, such as Elizabeth Phillips, *Political Theology: A Guide for the Perplexed* (New York: T and T Clark, 2012); Peter Scott and William T. Cavanaugh, eds., *Blackwell Companion to Political Theology* (Oxford: Blackwell, 2004); and Craig Hovey, Jeffrey Bailey, and William Cavanaugh, eds., *An Eerdmans Reader in Contemporary Political Theology* (Grand Rapids, Michigan: Eerdmans, 2012). And of course, Jeffrey Robbins and Clayton Crockett, two of the editors of the Insurrections series, in which this book appears, have made several important recent contributions in political theology. See, for example, Jeffrey W. Robbins, *Radical Democracy and Political Theology* (New York: Columbia University Press, 2013); Clayton Crockett, *Radical Political Theology: Religion and Politics After Liberalism* (New York: Columbia University Press, 2013); and Crockett and

Robbins, *Religion, Politics, and the Earth: The New Materialism* (New York: Palgrave, 2012).

12. See, for example, Charles Taylor, *A Secular Age* (Cambridge: Harvard University Press, 2007); Daniele Hervieu-Léger, *Religion as a Chain of Memory* (New Brunswick, NJ: Rutgers University Press, 2000). I discuss some of these ideas at more length in Hogue, *The Promise of Religious Naturalism* (Lanham, MD: Rowman and Littlefield, 2010).

13. The literature on these questions is vast. Some exemplary contributions include Talal Asad, *Genealogies of Religion: Discipline and Reasons of Power in Christianity and Islam* (Baltimore: Johns Hopkins University Press, 1993); Daniele Dubuisson, *The Western Construction of Religion: Myths, Knowledge, and Ideology*, trans. William Sayers (Baltimore: Johns Hopkins University Press, 2003); Tomoku Masuzawa, *The Invention of World Religions: Or, How European Universalism Was Preserved in the Language of Pluralism* (Chicago: University of Chicago Press, 2005); Brent Nongbri, *Before Religion: A History of a Modern Concept* (New Haven: Yale University Press, 2013).

14. Clayton Crockett, "The Conception of Insurrections," Columbia University Press Blog, March 25, 2013, www.cupblog.org/?p=9760.

15. With the term *externalization* I refer to a broadened account of the economic concept of a *negative externality*. A *negative externality* is a discounted cost of production that is displaced onto and negatively impacts a third party that is not directly involved with the producer-consumer transaction. For example, many costly environmental and human health impacts of industrial air or water pollution are suffered at public expense, such as taxpayer funded ecological remediation, or increased healthcare costs. By externalizing costs such these, the producer profits more and the consumer pays less than if the cost were internalized. By *extraction* I refer in general to the possessing, procuring, or claiming of something of value, such as the extraction of fossil fuels. I use these terms in a way that includes but extends beyond an economic frame of reference, including cultural, social, and ecological forms of extraction and externalization. My argument in chapter 1 is that extraction and externalization are often correlated by some form of exception and that the "redeemer symbolic" has historically justified such correlations throughout US history.

1. AMERICAN EXCEPTIONALISM AND THE REDEEMER SYMBOLIC

1. Siddhartha Roy, "Lead Testing Results from Two Worst Case Homes in Flint (Before and After Water Switch)," Flint Water Study Updates, December 11, 2015, http://flint-waterstudy.org/2015/12/lead-testing-results-from-two-worst-case-homes-in-flint-before-and-after-water-switch/.

2. Timothy Cama, "$220 Million Flint Aid Package Included in Water Bill," *Hill*, April 26, 2016, http://thehill.com/policy/energy-environment/277664–220-million-flint-aid-package-included-in-water-bill.

3. Carl Schmitt, *Political Theology: Four Chapters on the Concept of Sovereignty*, trans. George Schwab (Chicago: University of Chicago Press, 1985), 36. Originally published

as *Politische Theologie: Vier Kapitel zur Lehre von der Souveranitat* (Berlin: Duncker und Humblot, 1922).

4. "Dan Wyant Group Executive of DEQ, DNR and Agriculture and Rural Development," *Farm Progress*, December 2, 2010, http://farmprogress.com/story-dan-wyant-group -executive-of-deq-dnr-and- agriculture-rural-development-9–44349.

5. "Snyder Splits DEQ, DNR," *CBS Detroit*, November 30, 2010, http://detroit.cbslocal .com/2010/11/30/snyder-splits-deq-dnr/.

6. Chad Halcom, "Dan Wyant's Foundation Work an Asset as He Joins Gov.-Elect Sny-der's Team," *Crain's Detroit Business*, December 8, 2010, www.crainsdetroit.com/arti-cle/20101208/SUB01/312089996/dan-wyants-foundation-work-an-asset-as-he - joins-gov-elect-snyders.

7. "Why Are CAFO's Bad?," Sierra Club—Michigan Chapter, www.sierraclub.org/michi-gan/cafo-facts.

8. Dave Dempsey, "Snyder Appointments: Better Lock the Henhouse," *Lansing City Pulse*, December 8, 2010, http://lansingcitypulse.com/search-articles-better+lock+the+hen house.html.

9. Zoe Clark, "In First Executive Order, Snyder Splits Up the State Department of Natural Resources and Environment," *Michigan Radio*, January 5, 2011, http://michiganradio.org /post/first-executive-order- snyder-splits-state-department-natural-resources-and-envi ronment#stream/0.

10. "Comparing the New Emergency Manager Law with the One Repealed by Voters," *Michigan Radio*, March 28, 2013, http://michiganradio.org/post/comparing-new-emer gency-manager-law-one-repealed-voters#stream/0.

11. Michigan Legislature, *Local Financial Stability and Choice Act*, Act 436 of 2012, www .legislature.mi.gov/(S(af3qncmzllaneqgnylc1mlqe))/mileg.aspx?page=GetObject&obj ectname=mcl-act- 436-of-2012.

12. Ron Fonger, "General Motors Shutting Off Flint River at Engine Plant Due to Corro-sion Worries," January 17, 2015, *MLive*, http://www.mlive.com/news/flint/index.ssf /2014/10/general_motors_wont_use_flint.html.

13. Paul Egan, "Amid Denials, State Workers in Flint Got Clean Water," *Detroit Free Press*, January 29, 2016, www.freep.com/story/news/local/michigan/flint-water-crisis/2016/01 /28/amid-denials-state- workers-flint-got-clean-water/79470650/.

14. Amy Goodman and Denis Moynihan, "The Terror of Flint's Poisoned Water," *Democracy Now*, February 4, 2016, www.democracynow.org/2016/2/4/the_terror_of_flint_s _poisoned.

15. Flint Water Advisor Task Force (FWATF), "Flint Water Advisor Task Force: Final Report," March 2016, 5, http://mediad.publicbroadcasting.net/p/michigan/files/201603 /taskforce_report.pdf?_ga=1.147700144.60903321 3.1458749402. See also David A. Gra-ham, "Who Is to Blame for Flint's Lead Crisis," *Atlantic*, March 24, 2016, www.the atlantic.com/politics/archive/2016/03/flint-task-force-rick-snyder-blame/475182/.

16. FWATF, "Final Report," 1.

17. Ibid., 6.

18. Ibid.

19. Ibid., 1.

20.   Ibid., "Appendix 2: Letters to Governor Snyder, December 29, 2015," 2. For the evidence and history of environmental injustice in the modern United States, see Robert D. Bullard, Paul Mohai, Robin Sana, and Beverly Wright, *Toxic Wastes and Race at Twenty, 1987–2007: A Report Prepared for the United Church of Christ Justice and Witness Ministries* (Cleveland: United Church of Christ, 2007); and Robert D. Bullard, *Dumping in Dixie: Race, Class, and Environmental Quality* (Boulder: Westview, 2000). For a broader historical treatment that correlates environmental racism to the racial coding of hygiene, see the recently published book Carl A. Zimring, *Clean and White: A History of Environmental Racism in the United States* (New York: New York University Press, 2015).

21.   FWATF, "Final Report," 54. The Flint case is in fact a definitional case of environmental injustice, insofar as the two principles of environmental justice are equal protection from environmental hazards and meaningful participation in decisions that influence development, implementation, and enforcement of environmental law, policy, and regulation. See, for example, US Environmental Protection Agency, www.epa.gov/environmentaljustice.

22.   See Catherine Keller's critique of American "messianic imperialism" in *God and Power: Counter-Apocalpytic Journeys* (Minneapolis: Fortress, 2005).

23.   Godfrey Hodgson, *The Myth of American Exceptionalism* (New Haven: Yale University Press, 2009).

24.   Several recent studies document the strong correlations in the United States between conservative politics, fossil-fuel interests and corporate funding, and varieties of climate denialism. Conservative and libertarian "think tanks" such as the Heartland Institute, the American Enterprise Institute, the Heritage Foundation, and the Cato Institute have been especially prominent in rejecting the global scientific consensus regarding anthropogenic climate change. Part of the reason for this, as Jean-Daniel Collumb argues, is that "Global warming poses a philosophical challenge to libertarians and small-government conservatives: their world view is premised on the idea that government power should always be held in check lest it destroy individual freedom while the world is faced with a crisis of global proportions that could only be averted by a strong and prolonged government action." See, for example, Jean-Daniel Collomb, "The Ideology of Climate Change Denial in the United States," *European Journal of American Studies* 9, no. 1 (Spring 2014): 12, doi:10.4000/ejas.10305; and A. McCright and R. Dunlap, "The Politicization of Climate Change and Polarization in the American Public's Views of Global Warming, 2001–2010," *Sociological Quarterly* 52 (2011): 155–194. For a study of the funding of climate denial, see Justin Farrell, "Network Structure and Influence of the Climate Change Counter-Movement," *Nature Climate Change* 6 (2016): 370–374, doi:10.1038/nclimate2875. Interestingly, according to a recent comparative global study, climate denial is a primarily Anglo-Saxon phenomenon. See James Painter, *Poles Apart: The International Reporting of Climate Scepticism*, Reuters Institute for the Study of Journalism (Oxford: Oxford University Press, 2011). For a good, brief overview of the relation between cultural ideology and climate denialism, see Andrew J. Hoffman, *How Culture Shapes the Climate Debate* (Stanford: Stanford University

Press, 2015), 10. For an analysis of the history of corporately funded efforts to deliber-
ately confuse the public understanding of science in the United States, see Naomi
Oreskes and Erik M. Conway, *Merchants of Doubt: How a Handful of Scientists
Obscured the Truth on Issues from Tobacco Smoke to Global Warming* (London:
Bloomsbury, 2010).

25.   The scholarship on the idea of the United States as a "redeemer nation" is vast. A classic source is Ernest Lee Tuveson, *Redeemer Nation: The Idea of America's Millennial
Role* (1968; Chicago: University of Chicago Press, 1980). For a more recent, wide-ranging critique of the idea, with prominent appeal to American literature, post 9/11 politics, and a host of continental philosophers, see William V. Spanos, *Redeemer Nation
in the Interregnum: An Untimely Meditation on the American Vocation* (New York:
Fordham University Press, 2016). Though Spanos does not explicitly interpret American exceptionalism as a theopolitical tradition, he presents a genealogical analysis of
American exceptionalism as a "calling" or "vocation" and ends up defining it as "simultaneously an ontological, a moral, an economic, a racial, a gendered, and a political
phenomenon: a deeply structured *ethos* or *ethics*—a total way of life" (140). This is close
to what I have in mind by referring to American exceptionalism as the dominant
American theopolitical tradition. My argument in this chapter is unique in interpreting the redeemer symbolic in a way that connects American exceptionalism to the
culturally and ecologically destructive logic of extraction and externalization.

26.   The leading interpreters of the theological and philosophical significance of Peirce's
semiotics include Robert Corrington, Robert Cummings Neville, and Michael Raposa.
See, for example, Robert Corrington, *Introduction to C. S. Peirce: Philosopher, Semiotician, Ecstatic Naturalist* (Lanham, MD: Rowman and Littlefield, 1993); Robert
Cummings Neville, *On the Scope and Truth of Theology: Theology as Symbolic Engagement* (New York: T and T Clark, 2006); Michael Raposa, *Peirce's Philosophy of Religion*
(Bloomington: Indiana University Press, 1989).

27.   Peirce's specific formulation is as follows: "Consider what effects, which might conceiv-
ably have practical bearings, we conceive the object of our conception to have. Then
the whole of our conception of those effects is the whole of our conception of the
object." See Charles Sander Peirce, "How to Make Our Ideas Clear," in *Collected Papers
of Charles Sanders Peirce*, ed. Charles Hartshorne and Paul Weis (Cambridge: Harvard
University Press, 1935), 5:258.

28.   Under the imperative of capital accumulation, industries and corporations extract
resource value from the environment and labor value from workers, whose creative
powers transform those resources into commodities. While the profits from the sale
of commodities are internalized and capitalized, diverse ecological, social, and public
health impacts are externalized and socialized. A recent report by the International
Monetary Fund finds that the social and environmental costs of fossil-fuel externalities come to approximately $10 million per minute. This amounts to a $5.3 trillion sub-
sidy of the fossil-fuel industries by the world's governments. This figure is greater than
the total sum spent globally on healthcare. See Damian Carrington, "Fossil Fuels Subsidized by $10m a Minutes, says IMF," *Guardian*, May 18, 2015, www.theguardian.com

/environment/2015/may/18/fossil- fuel-companies-getting-10m-a-minute-in-subsidies-says-imf. For the full report, see David Coady et al., "How Large Are Global Energy Subsidies?," International Monetary Fund, Working Paper 15/105, www.imf.org/external/pubs/cat/longres.aspx?sk=42940.0.

29. Ta-Nehsi Coates, *Between the World and Me* (New York: Spiegel and Grau, 2015), 8.

30. Thomas King, *The Truth About Stories* (Toronto: House of Anansi, 2003), 112.

31. Robert Bellah, *The Broken Covenant* (New York: Seabury, 1975), 3.

32. As quoted in Richard T. Hughes, *Myths America Lives By* (Urbana: University of Illinois Press, 2004), 6.

33. John Locke, *Two Treatises of Government*, ed. Peter Laslett (Cambridge: Cambridge University Press, 1988), 99.

34. Bellah, *The Broken Covenant*, 5.

35. Francis Jennings, *The Invasion of America: Indians, Colonialism, and the Cant of Conquest* (New York: Norton, 1976), 30.

36. Quoted in Tuveson, *Redeemer Nation*, vii.

37. John Winthrop, "A Model of Christian Charity," in *The American Bible: How Our Words Unite, Divide, and Define a Nation*, ed. Stephen Prothero (New York: HarperCollins, 2012), 43.

38. Jonathan Edwards, "Some Thoughts Concerning the Present Revival of Religion in New England" (1742), quoted in Hughes, *Myths American Lives By*, 98.

39. See Tuveson, *Redeemer Nation*, viii–xi.

40. Ezra Stiles, "The United States Elevated to Glory and Honor," in *God's New Israel: Religious Interpretations of American Destiny*, ed. Conrad Cherry (Chapel Hill: University of North Carolina Press, 1998), 90.

41. Hughes, *Myths America Lives By*, 104.

42. Ibid., 105.

43. Thomas Jefferson, *Notes on the State of Virginia* (New York: Penguin, 1998), 170.

44. Ibid., 181.

45. H. Richard Niebuhr, *The Kingdom of God in America* (1937; Middletown, CT: Wesleyan University Press, 1988), 179.

46. John L. O'Sullivan, "The Great Nation of Futurity," Making of America Series, Cornell University, http://ebooks.library.cornell.edu/cgi/t/text/text-idx?c=usde;cc=;view=toc;subview=short;idno=usde0006–4; originally published in *United States Democratic Review* 6, no. 23 (November 1839).

47. John L. O'Sullivan, "Annexation," Making of America Series, Cornell University, http://ebooks.library.cornell.edu/cgi/t/text/text-idx?c=usde;cc=usde;view=toc;subview=short;idno=usde0017–1; originally published in *United States Democratic Review* 17, no. 85 (July-August 1845).

48. O'Sullivan, "Editorial," *New York Morning News*, December 27, 1845.

49. Jedediah Purdy, *After Nature: A Politics for the Anthropocene* (Cambridge: Harvard University Press, 2015), 81.

50. Hughes, *Myths America Lives By*, 109.

51. On May 28, 1830, Jackson signed into law the Indian Removal Act, which granted him the authority to negotiate with Native American tribes in the east to exchange their

lands for territories in the west then not included within the boundaries of the United States.

52. Andrew Jackson, First Annual Message to Congress, December 8, 1829, American Presidency Project, University of California Santa Barbara, www.presidency.ucsb.edu /ws/index.php?pid=29471.

53. Edward E. Baptist, *The Half Has Never Been Told: Slavery and the Making of American Capitalism* (New York: Basic, 2014), xxii.

54. Ibid., xxi.

55. Coates, *Between the World and Me*, 131–132.

56. Eugene McCarraher, "The Heavenly City of Business," in *The Short American Century*, ed. Andrew J. Bacevich (Cambridge: Harvard University Press, 2012), 189.

57. William Lawrence, "The Relation of Wealth to Morals," in Cherry, *God's New Israel*, 252.

58. US Department of State, *The National Security Strategy of the United States* (Washington, DC: US Department of State, 2002), 17, www.state.gov/documents/organization /63562.pdf.

59. Ibid.

60. "At O'Hare, President Says 'Get on Board,'" Remarks on September 27, 2001, by President Bush to Airline employees, O'Hare International Airport, Chicago, Illinois, http:// georgewbush- whitehouse.archives.gov/news/releases/2001/09/20010927–1.html.

61. "President Outlines War Effort," Remarks on October 17, 2001, by President Bush at the California Business Association Breakfast, Sacramento Memorial Auditorium, Sacramento, California, http://georgewbush- whitehouse.archives.gov/news/releases/2001 /10/20011017–15.html.

62. US Department of State, *The National Security Strategy*, 18.

63. William Finnegan, "The Economics of Empire: Notes on the Washington Consensus," *Harper's*, May 2003.

64. Hughes, *Myths American Lives By*, 136.

65. The ruling states: "Political spending is a form of protected speech under the First Amendment, and the government may not keep corporations or unions from spending money to support or denounce individual candidates in elections. While corporations or unions may not give money directly to campaigns, they may seek to persuade the voting public through other means, including ads, especially where these ads were not broadcast." See "Citizens United vs. Federal Election Commission," www.scotusblog .com/case-files/cases/citizens- united-v-federal-election-commission/.

66. Jeffrey Stout, *Democracy and Tradition* (Princeton: Princeton University Press, 2004), 23.

67. Niebuhr, *The Kingdom of God in America*, 30.

68. Ibid., 84.

69. Julian Boger, "'A Recipe for Scandal': Trump Conflicts of Interest Point to Constitutional Crisis," *Guardian*, November 27, 2016, www.theguardian.com/us-news/2016/nov /27/donald-trump-conflicts-interest- constitutional-crisis.

70. Natasha Lennard and Adrian Parr, "Our Crimes Against the Planet, and Ourselves," *New York Times*, May 18, 2016, www.nytimes.com/2016/05/18/opinion/our-crime-against -the-planet-and-ourselves.html. For more on Parr's position, see her important new

book, Parr, *The Wrath of Capital: Neoliberalism and Climate Change Politics* (New York: Columbia University Press, 2013).

71. David Harvey, *A Brief History of Neoliberalism* (Oxford: Oxford University Press, 2005), 2.

72. William Davies, "The New Neoliberalism," *New Left Review* 101 (September-October 2016): 128.

73. Ibid., 130.

74. Ibid., 126.

75. Ibid., 127.

76. Ibid.

2. THE ANTHROPOCENE AND CLIMATE WICKEDNESS

1. Jedediah Purdy, "Anthropocene Fever," *Aeon*, March 31, 2015, https://aeon.co/essays /should-we-be-suspicious-of-the-anthropocene-idea. Purdy has also recently published a beautifully written, deeply reflective book that explores the potential political meanings of the Anthropocene: Purdy, *After Nature: A Politics for the Anthropocene* (Cambridge: Harvard University Press, 2015). A philosopher of law, Purdy situates his reflections in the context of four historical versions of the American "environmental imagination": settler/colonial, Romantic, utilitarian, and ecological. At the center of Purdy's reflections is a question quite like my own, the question of what kind of democracy is appropriate to the Anthropocene. I affirm his claim that justice in the Anthropocene demands a more deeply democratic politics, as I will show through this chapter and then develop more fully in chapter 5. Given the entanglement of humans and nature in the Anthropocene, he calls for a democracy that restrains human power, builds solidarity, and encourages moral imagination and ecological literacy. He points toward, but does not fully develop, a political anthropology that integrates aspects of liberal humanism with posthumanist insights. As similar as our questions are, and as much as we share a focus on American thought, there are two major differences between our projects. First, where he draws primarily from American political and legal sources, I look primarily to American philosophical and theological traditions. Second, Purdy's project neglects the theopolitical roots of the American environmental imagination. Though we draw from different traditions, I strongly affirm, as I will show in chapters ahead, Purdy's position that in the context of the Anthropocene, "taking responsibility for nature and taking responsibility for democracy come together" (286).

2. Bill McKibben, *The End of Nature* (New York: Random House, 1989).

3. Purdy, *After Nature*, 3.

4. Will Steffen, Jacques Ginevald, Paul Crutzen, and John McNeill, "The Anthropocene: Conceptual and Historical Perspectives," *Philosophical Transactions of the Royal Society A* (2011): 369, 843, doi:10.1098/rsta.2010.0327.

5. Ibid.

6. Simon L. Lewis and Mark A. Maslin, "Defining the Anthropocene," *Nature* 519 (March 12, 2015): 171–180, doi:10.1038/nature14258.

7. Simon L. Lewis and Mark A. Maslin, "Anthropocene Began with Species Exchange Between Old and New Worlds," *Conversation*, March 11, 2015, https://theconversation.com/anthropocene-began-with-species- exchange-between-old-and-new-worlds-38674.

8. Ibid.

9. David Biello, "Mass Deaths in Americas Start New CO2 Epoch," *Scientific American*, March 11, 2015, www.scientificamerican.com/article/mass-deaths-in-americas-start-new-co2-epoch/.

10. Ibid.

11. David E. Stannard, *American Holocaust: Columbus and the Conquest of the New World* (Oxford: Oxford University Press, 1992).

12. Alexander Saxton, *The Rise and Fall of the White Republic: Class Politics and Mass Culture in Nineteenth-Century America* (London: Verso, 1991), 153, quoted in Stannard, *American Holocaust*, xii.

13. Stannard, *American Holocaust*, xii.

14. Will Steffen et al., "The Anthropocene," 848.

15. See Will Steffen, Wendy Broadgate, Lisa Deutsch, Owen Gaffney, and Cornelia Ludwig, "The Trajectory of the Anthropocene: The Great Acceleration," *Anthropocene Review* 2, no. 1 (April 2015): 81–98; John R. McNeill and Peter Engelke, *The Great Acceleration: An Environmental History of the Anthropocene Since 1945* (Cambridge: Harvard University Press, 2014).

16. Clive Hamilton, "Getting the Anthropocene So Wrong," *Anthropocene Review* 2, no. 2 (August 2015): 101–107, doi:10.1177/2053019615590922.

17. Ibid., 101.

18. Eileen Crist, "On the Poverty of Our Nomenclature," in *Anthropocene or Capitalocene: Nature, History, and the Crisis of Capitalism*, ed. Jason W. Moore (Oakland, CA: Kairos, PM, 2016), 14. For another strong example of this line of critique, but through a queer-theoretic framework, see Whitney A. Bauman, "Climate Weirding and Queering Nature: Getting Beyond the Anthropocene," *Religions* 6, no. 2 (2015), special issue, "Religion and Ecology in the Anthropocene," ed. Michael S. Hogue, 742–754; doi:10.3390/rel6020742; Crist, "On the Poverty of Our Nomenclature," 14.

19. Crist, "On the Poverty of Our Nomenclature," 15.

20. Ibid., 16.

21. Jason Moore, *Capitalism and the Web of Life: Ecology and the Accumulation of Capital* (London: Verso, 2015).

22. Ibid., 169–192.

23. By "wealthy, developed nations," I refer to the Annex I nations in the United Nations Framework Convention on Climate Change (UNFCC). See List of Annex I Parties to the Convention, United Nations Framework Convention on Climate Change, http://unfccc.int/parties_and_observers/parties/annex_i/items/2774.php.

24. For data, see Carbon Dioxide Information Analysis Center (CDIAC) Data Base, United States Department of Energy, http://cdiac.ornl.gov/. See also Johannes Friedrich and Thomas Damassa, "The History of Carbon Dioxide Emissions," World Resources Institute Blog, May 21, 2014, www.wri.org/blog/2014/05/history-carbon-dioxide-emissions.

25. For analysis of differential impacts, see, for example, Working Group II, "Climate Change 2014: Impacts, Adaptation and Vulnerability," Assessment Report 5, Intergovernmental Panel on Climate Change (IPCC), www.ipcc.ch/report/ar5/wg2/.

26. Dipesh Chakrabarty, "The Climate of History: Four Theses," *Critical Inquiry* 35 (Winter 2009): 219.

27. Ibid.

28. Ibid., 219–220.

29. Jan Zalasiewicz, Mark Williams, Will Steffen, and Paul Crutzen, "The New World of the Anthropocene," *Environmental Science and Technology* 44, no. 7 (2010): 2229.

30. Christophe Bonneuil and Jean-Baptiste Fressoz, *The Shock of the Anthropocene*, trans. David Fernbach (London: Verso, 2016), xi.

31. One of the most perceptive analyses of the geopolitical dynamics of the Arab Spring and its aftermath, including the refugee crisis, is Scott Anderson, "Fractured Lands: How the Arab World Came Apart," *New York Times Magazine*, April 10, 2016. Based on eighteen months of embedded reporting and several decades of journalistic experience in the region, Anderson reports on the lives of six individuals from different countries in the region. The report is empathic and humanizing. The geopolitical argument, in essence, is as follows: (1) each of the disintegrated states of Iraq, Syria, and Libya was first an artificial state; (2) they were created by the West with Western interests in mind; (3) they were ruled by religious and ethnic minority dictators whose tenuous claim to rule was supported by Western backing; (4) the West created a system of geopolitical codependence: the minority dictators needed us to support and legitimate them (except when we wouldn't), and we needed them and their hardline rule to keep order in the region; (5) we benefited politically and economically from this fragile system of codependencies, alliances, and counteralliances, until after we invaded Iraq. In sum, the West created a vulnerable system of counterbalancing powers that the United States then blew apart. And now, in our present political climate, many of our national and state-level political leaders, almost exclusively Republican, scapegoat the millions of vulnerable people who suffer as a result of the chaos we precipitated. On the amplifying role of climate change in relation to the drought and agricultural crisis that immediately precipitated the civil war in Syria, see Colin P. Kelly, Shahrzad Mohtadib, Mark A. Canec, Richard Seagerc, and Yochanan Kushnirc, "Climate Change in the Fertile Crescent and Implications of the Recent Syrian Drought," *Proceedings of the National Academy of Sciences of the United States of America* 112, no. 11:3241–3246, doi: 10.1073/pnas.1421533112, www.pnas.org/content/112/11/3241.abstract?sid=2a81a88f-1087–4cf6-bd38-d797dd 8cc723. See also John Wendle, "The Ominous Story of Syria's Climate Refugees," *Scientific America*, December 17, 2015, www.scientificamerican.com/article/ominous-story-of-syria -climate- refugees/.

32. James Lovelock, *Gaia: A New Look at Life on Earth* (Oxford: Oxford University Press, 1979).

33. See the reports by Working Group II of the IPCC. For analysis of climate-induced human migratory patterns, see "New Data Brings New Answers on Climate Migration," *United Nations Climate Change Newsroom*, May 19, 2016, http://newsroom.unfccc .int/unfccc-newsroom/human-mobility-and-the-paris-agreement/.

34. Dale Jamieson, *Reason in a Dark Time: Why the Struggle Against Climate Change Failed—and What It Means for Our Future* (Oxford: Oxford University Press, 2014), 102.

35. Gilbert's acronym and theory are described in George Marshall, *Don't Even Think About It: Why Our Brains Are Wired to Ignore Climate Change* (New York: Bloomsbury, 2014), 46–47.

36. Joseph Tainter, *The Collapse of Complex Societies* (Cambridge: Cambridge University Press, 1988), 91. The basic idea here is that "Human societies and political organizations, like all living systems, are maintained by a continuous flow of energy.... At the same time, the mechanisms by which human groups acquire and distribute basic resources are conditioned by, and integrated within, sociopolitical institutions" (91).

37. More specifically, Tainter's explanation of collapse is based on four ideas: "1. Human societies are problem-solving organizations; 2. Sociopolitical systems require energy for their maintenance; 3. Increased complexity carries with it increased cost per capita; and 4. Investment in sociopolitical complexity as a problem solving response often reaches a point of declining marginal returns." Ibid., 93.

38. Ian Morris, *Foragers, Farmers and Fossil Fuels: How Human Values Evolve* (Princeton: Princeton University Press, 2015), 14.

39. I discuss Gardiner's ideas at more length in Hogue, *The Promise of Religious Naturalism* (Lanham, MD: Rowman and Littlefield, 2010).

40. Stephen M. Gardiner, *A Perfect Moral Storm: The Ethical Tragedy of Climate Change* (Oxford: Oxford University Press, 2011), xii.

41. Ibid., 7.

42. Ibid.

43. Ibid., 9. See also Naomi Oreskes and Erik M. Conway, *Merchants of Doubt: How a Handful of Scientists Obscured the Truth on Issues from Tobacco Smoking to Global Warming* (New York: Bloomsbury, 2010).

44. Timothy Morton, *Hyperobjects: Philosophy and Ecology After the End of the World* (Minnesota: University of Minnesota Press, 2013), 7.

45. Ibid., 17.

46. Ibid., 15.

47. In addition to viscosity and nonlocality, which I discuss, Morton analyzes temporal undulation, phasing, and interobjectivity as characteristics of hyperobjects. For more on these characteristics, see ibid., 55–95.

48. Ibid., 1, 20.

49. Ibid., 38.

50. Jamieson, *Reason in a Dark Time*, 61.

51. Morton, *Hyperobjects*, 17.

52. Ibid., 17–18.

3. THINKING, FEELING, AND VALUING IMMANENCE

1. John Dewey, "'Introduction,' to 1948 reprint of *Reconstruction in Philosophy*," vol. 12 of *The Middle Works of John Dewey*, ed. Jo Ann Boydston (Carbondale: Southern

Illinois University Press, 1982), 271. Hereafter, when I refer to Dewey, the first reference to a particular work will cite the title of the book or essay, and then locate it in Early Works as EW, Middle Works as MW, and Later Works as LW. I will reference volume number, page numbers, and the year the volume was published with Southern Illinois University Press. For example, this current note would appear as follows: "'Introduction' to 1948 Reprint of *Reconstruction in Philosophy*," MW 12:271 (1982). Later references to the same work will include only the volume and page numbers.

2. I will discuss this more in what follows, but in his early philosophical work *The Concept of Nature*, Whitehead concisely defines the problem as following: "What I am essentially protesting against is the bifurcation of nature into two systems of reality. . . . Thus there would be two natures, one is the conjecture and one is the dream. . . . Another way of phrasing this theory which I am arguing against is to bifurcate nature into two divisions, namely into the nature apprehended in awareness and the nature that is the cause of awareness. The nature which is in fact apprehended in awareness holds within it the greenness of the trees, the song of the birds, the warmth of the sun, the hardness of chairs, and the feel of the velvet. The nature which is the cause of awareness is the conjectured system of molecules and electrons which so affects the mind to produce the awareness of apparent nature. The meeting point of these two natures is the mind, the causal nature being influent and the apparent nature being effluent." Whitehead, *The Concept of Nature* (1920; Ann Arbor: University of Michigan Press, 1957), 30–31.

3. Alfred North Whitehead, *Adventures of Ideas* (1933; New York: Free, 1967), 14.

4. Robert Cummings Neville, *The Highroad Around Modernism* (Albany: State University of New York Press, 1992).

5. Although I focus in what follows on Dewey, recent constructive expressions of pragmatic naturalism include Victor Anderson, *Pragmatic Theology: Negotiating the Intersections of an American Philosophy of Religion and Public Theology* (Albany: State University of New York Press, 1988); S. Morris Eames, *Pragmatic Naturalism: An Introduction* (Carbondale: Southern Illinois University Press, 1977); Philip Kitcher, *Preludes to Pragmatism: Towards a Reconstruction of Philosophy* (Oxford: Oxford University Press, 2012); and John Ryder, *The Things in Heaven and Earth: An Essay in Pragmatic Naturalism* (New York: Fordham University Press, 2013).

6. John Randall, "The Nature of Naturalism," in *Naturalism and the Human Spirit*, ed. Yervant H. Krikorian (New York: Columbia University Press, 1944), 368.

7. Ibid., 356.

8. Thelma Z. Lavine, "Naturalism and the Sociological Analysis of Knowledge," in Krikorian, *Naturalism and the Human Spirit*, 183–209.

9. Dewey, "Context and Thought," LW 6:19 (1985).

10. John Dewey, *Experience and Nature*, LW 1:40 (1981).

11. Dewey, LW 1:7.

12. Dewey, "Introduction to 1948 reprint of *Reconstruction in Philosophy*," MW 12:257.

13. Dewey, MW 12:257.

14. Dewey, MW 12:260.

15. Nancy Frankenberry, "Contingency All the Way Down: Whitehead Among the Pragmatists," in *Thinking with Whitehead and the Pragmatists: Experience and Reality*, ed. Brian G. Henning, William T. Myers, and Joseph D. John (Lanham, MD: Lexington, 2015), 103.

16. Dewey, "'Consciousness' and Experience," MW 1:123 (1983).

17. Dewey, MW 1:123.

18. Dewey, MW 12:260.

19. Dewey, MW 12:271.

20. Dewey, *The Quest for Certainty*, LW 4:204 (1984).

21. Dewey, MW 12:261.

22. Dewey, MW 12:276.

23. Dewey, LW 4:7.

24. Dewey, *Experience and Nature*, LW 1:43.

25. Dewey, LW 1:43–44.

26. Dewey, LW 1:101.

27. Dewey, LW 1:98

28. Dewey, LW 1:98.

29. Dewey, LW 1:98.

30. Dewey, MW 12:113.

31. Dewey, MW 12:114.

32. Dewey, MW 12:117.

33. Dewey, MW 12:106.

34. Dewey, "The Development of American Pragmatism," LW 2:11 (1984).

35. Dewey, LW 2:11. Dewey is quoting James from "What Pragmatism Means." See William James, *Pragmatism: The Works of William James*, ed. Bruck Kuklick (Cambridge: Harvard University Press, 1975), 32.

36. Dewey, LW 2:12.

37. Dewey, LW 2:13.

38. William James, "The Chicago School," in *William James: Writings, 1902–1910*, ed. Bruce Kuklick (New York: Library of America, 1987), 1136–1137.

39. Dewey, "Pragmatic America," MW 13:308 (1983).

40. Alfred North Whitehead, *Symbolism: Its Meaning and Effect* (1927; New York: Fordham University Press, 1985), 16.

41. Nancy Frankenberry, *Religion and Radical Empiricism* (Albany: State University of New York Press, 1987), 88.

42. Ibid.

43. William James, *Essays in Radical Empiricism*, vol. 5, *The Works of William James*, ed. Fredson Bowers and Ignas K. Skrupskelis (Cambridge: Harvard University Press, 1976), 22.

44. Ibid.

45. James, *Pragmatism and The Meaning of Truth*, vol. 11, *The Works of William James* (Cambridge: Harvard University Press, 1978), 6–7.

46. Ibid.

47. Ibid.

48. James, *Essays in Radical Empiricism*, 46.

49. William James, *The Principles of Psychology*, vol. 1 (New York: Holt, 1890), 488.

50. James, *Essays in Radical Empiricism*, 43.

51. Alfred North Whitehead, *Process and Reality*, corrected ed., ed. David Ray Griffin and Donald W. Sherburne (New York: Free, 1978), 21.

52. Isabelle Stengers, *Thinking with Whitehead: A Free and Wild Creation of Concepts*, trans. Michael Chase (Cambridge: Harvard University Press, 2011), 3.

53. Whitehead, *Adventures of Ideas*, 226.

54. Specifically, Whitehead states that to meet the necessary speculative and rational criteria, a speculative philosophical scheme "should be coherent, logical, and, in respect to its interpretation, applicable and adequate. Here 'applicable' means that some items of experience are thus interpretable, and 'adequate' means that there are no items incapable of such interpretation. 'Coherence,' as here employed, means that the fundamental ideas, in terms of which the scheme is developed, presuppose each other so that in isolation they are meaningless.... The term 'logical' has its ordinary meaning, including 'logical' consistency, or lack of contradiction." Whitehead, *Process and Reality*, 3. Despite, or perhaps because of, his commitment to this rigorous architecture of speculation, Whitehead develops his philosophy in a fallibilistic spirit. As he writes, "the merest hint of dogmatic certainty as to finality of statement" in any philosophical discussion "is an exhibition of folly." Ibid., xiv. As he puts this elsewhere, although philosophy "begins in wonder," in the end, "when philosophical thought has done its best, the wonder remains." See Whitehead, *Modes of Thought* (1938; New York: Free, 1968), 168.

55. Whitehead, *Process and Reality*, 50. "Buzzing" is likely an allusion to William James's *Principles of Psychology*.

56. Whitehead's *Symbolism: Its Meaning and Effect*, is based on the Barbour-Paige lectures he gave in 1927 at the University of Virginia. The lectures were presented and published just prior to his Gifford lectures, in 1927–1928, which were later published as his opus magnum, *Process and Reality*. While the basic analyses in *Symbolism* are also present in *Process and Reality*, I refer primarily in what follows to *Symbolism* since it punctuates the social-theoretic significance of those analyses.

57. Whitehead, *Symbolism*, 68–69.

58. Ibid., 74.

59. Ibid., 68–69.

60. Ibid., 65.

61. Ibid.

62. Ibid., 69.

63. Ibid., 88.

64. Ibid., 18–19.

65. Ibid., 30.

66. Ibid., 21, 15.

67. Ibid., 21, 23.

68. Ibid., 25.

69. Ibid., 44.

70. Ibid., 58.

71. Whitehead brings this all together nicely: "The conception of the world here adopted is that of functional activity. By this I mean that every actual thing is something by reason of its activity; whereby its nature consists in its relevance to other things, and its individuality consists in its synthesis of other things so far as they are relevant to it. In enquiring about any one individual we must ask how other individuals enter 'objectively' into the unity of its own experience. This unity of its own experience is that individual existing *formally*. We must also enquire how it enters into the 'formal' existence of other things; and this entrance is that individual existing *objectively*." Whitehead, *Symbolism*, 26–27, italics original.

72. Ibid., 58.

73. Ibid., 44.

74. Ibid., 43.

75. Ibid., 44, 50.

76. The flaw in both Hume's and Kant's philosophies, as Whitehead interprets it, is the "extraordinarily naïve assumption of time as pure succession," as episodic and serial. The assumption that time is purely successive is an example of "the fallacy of misplaced concreteness," of an abstraction taken as a concrete reality. Whitehead, *Symbolism*, 34, 41. It is an abstraction that results from limiting perceptual experience to the mode of presentational immediacy, which leads to the idea that sensory perception is correlated to isolated objects sensed in discrete moments or episodes. This abstraction is what leads Hume to his skepticism about anything other than the impressions of discrete particulars—if all that we can know is by way of particular and direct experience, then belief in synthetic concepts such as "causality" is unjustified. The inadequacy of this experiential solipsism leads Kant to his transcendental argument for the categories of understanding. With Hume, the rational is foreclosed by the empirical; with Kant, the empirical is transcended by the rational. In both cases, but from opposite sides, the rational and empirical are severed—while Hume's empiricism is insufficiently vague, Kant's rationalism is insufficiently haunted.

77. Whitehead, *Symbolism*, 47.

78. Whitehead uses both terms interchangeably, but I will use the term *actual occasion*, which expresses the processual nature of these phenomena better than *entity*. Insofar as God is the chief exemplification of reality, God's nature too has the character of an actual entity. In contrast to other actual occasions, however, God is nontemporal, and with this distinction in mind, Whitehead refers to God as an actual entity, rather than actual occasion. God is the only actual entity that cannot also be described as an occasion. So while the most basic phenomena in the universe share the same basic dipolar structure as God, their relations to time are distinct. Where actual occasions emerge out of relational processes and then perish into objective immortality, God endures nontemporally and ingresses into the flow of time. As I will explain more fully soon, the polarities of God and actual occasions are reversed.

79. Whitehead, *Process and Reality*, 18.

80. Whitehead, *Religion in the Making* (New York: Macmillan, 1926), 100.

81.   Donald W. Sherburne, "Whitehead, Alfred North," in *The Cambridge Dictionary of Philosophy*, ed. Robert Audi (Cambridge: Cambridge University Press, 1995), 852.

82.   Whitehead, *Process and Reality*, 18.

83.   Whitehead, *Adventures of Ideas*, 253.

84.   Whitehead, *Process and Reality*, 23.

85.   Ibid.

86.   Ibid., 21.

87.   Ibid., 18.

88.   Ibid.

89.   Stengers, *Thinking with Whitehead*, 452.

90.   Whitehead, *Process and Reality*, 348.

91.   In my view, Stengers interprets the significance of this well when she writes that "The theological figure of a creator God, omnipotent, perfect, paternal, omniscient, providential, and judge, never inspired anything but the strictest disapproval in Whitehead, right down to the end. Constructing a concept of God, he could not, of course, envisage repairing the historical disaster humanity had undergone, but he certainly undertook to create the means to fight against its consequences where this was possible for him: in philosophical thought." Stengers, *Thinking with Whitehead*, 451. Stengers's reference to the "historical disaster" of the omnipotent, paternal construction of God comes directly from Whitehead, who once declared, "I consider Christian theology to be one of the great disasters of the human race." See Lucien Price, ed., *Dialogues of Alfred North Whitehead* (Boston: Godine, 2001), 171.

92.   Whitehead, *Process and Reality*, 345.

93.   Stengers, *Thinking with Whitehead*, 449–501.

94.   Ibid.

95.   Conversation with Donald Crosby, among others, has helped me to clarify these points.

96.   George Allan, "In Defense of Secularizing Whitehead," *Process Studies* 39, no. 2 (Fall-Winter 2010), 332–333, italics added.

97.   Whitehead, *Religion in the Making* (New York: Macmillan, 1926), 16.

98.   Ibid., 59.

99.   Ibid., 60.

100. Ibid.

101. Ibid., 80. Recall that Whitehead's God functions as a conservator of cosmic value as well as an ontological location for the potential of novelty in the universe. Since actual occasions are perpetually perishing, and since actual occasions are the locus of value in Whitehead's cosmology, all value, apart from God, would seem to be lost. God's primordial aspect is home to cosmic possibility; God's consequent aspect is home to the passing of actuality. With Whitehead's God, everything is perpetually perishing, but nothing is lost; without Whitehead's God, everything is simply perpetually perishing. My point is that if "world-loyalty" is a condition of the religious sensibility as described by Whitehead, then this condition is better satisfied in a world without God than in a world with God. Loyalty to the world can be intensified by the sense that the value in and of the world is finite and passing. Of course, given the chiastic

entanglement of Whitehead's account of the God/world relation, there is really no point at which the world ends and God begins. But when novelty is interpreted as emergent rather than antecedent, and value as contingent rather than conserved, this chiasmus is, arguably, an unnecessary cosmic flourish.

102. Frankenberry, "Contingency All the Way Down," 109, 110, 111.

103. Charles Hartshorne, "On Some Criticisms of Whitehead's Philosophy," *Philosophical Review* 44, no. 4 (July 1935): 343.

104. Ibid., 344.

105. Eric Liu and Nick Hanauer, *The Gardens of Democracy: A New American Story of Citizenship, the Economy, and the Role of Government* (Seattle: Sasquatch, 2011), 9.

4. DIVINING IMMANENCE

1. For a technical scientific account of this, see Gerardo Ceballos, Paul R. Ehrlich, Anthony D. Barnosky, Andrés García, Robert M. Pringle, and Todd M. Palmer, "Accelerated Modern Human-Induced Species Losses: Entering the Sixth Mass Extinction," *Science Advances* 1, no. 5 (June 2015), doi:10.1126/sciadv.1400253. For a popular scientific, Pulitzer Prize–winning interpretation, see Elizabeth Kolbert, *The Sixth Extinction: An Unnatural History* (New York: Holt, 2014). And for an analysis of the sixth extinction in the context of a critique of capitalism, see Ashley Dawson, *Extinction: A Radical History* (New York: OR, 2016).

2. No contemporary philosopher has done more to theorize the generativity of difference in nature than Robert S. Corrington. As mentioned earlier (introduction, note 6), Corrington's philosophical naturalism prioritizes the phenomenology of difference within nature, difference that continuously erupts through the ontological contrast between nature naturing and nature natured. Corrington's emphasis on difference reflects his commitment to Justus Buchler's ordinal metaphysics rather than to a panpsychic process metaphysics such as Whitehead's. For an ordinal metaphysics, nature naturing is generative of innumerable "natural complexes," or complex orders of nature differentiated from one another by phenomenologically dynamic traits rather than ontologically static essences. Within the ordinal system, there is no generic trait that subsumes all others, and thus no order of natural complexes that contains all others. The importance of this, for Corrington, is threefold: it checks the imperial impulse in metaphysics to seek totalizing explanatory closure; it prevents the construction of hierarchies based on ontological essences; and it challenges a tendency to move from the idea that nature is all to the idea that nature is all the same, or homogenous. Given these commitments, Corrington rejects the Whiteheadian priority of internal over external relatedness. He argues that such a distinction "is too simplistic" insofar as it "envisions a web of total connectivity wherein all orders are internally (epistemically and literally) known to each other in a vast total super order, or via an underground extensive continuum." Corrington, *Nature's Sublime: An Essay in Aesthetic Naturalism* (New York: Lexington, 2013), 11. It is arguable, however, that an emergentist

nontheistic reading of Whitehead, such as the one I outlined in the previous chapter, can retain an emphasis on proximate internal relatedness while also avoiding the tendency to metaphysical closure that Corrington critiques. An emergentist interpretation of internal relatedness provides important context for the prismatic axiological theory I begin to articulate further along in this chapter, which is itself an important element of the philosophy of democracy I discuss in chapter 5. For more on this, see Buchler *Metaphysics of Natural Complexes*, 2nd expanded ed. (Albany: State University of New York Press, 1990).

3. John Dewey, *A Common Faith*, LW 9:1–59 (1986).

4. For an informative classic example that interprets American supernaturalist, idealist, romantic, and naturalist traditions running through the mid-twentieth century, see Henry Nelson Wieman and Bernard Eugene Meland, eds., *American Philosophies of Religion* (Chicago: Willett, Clark, 1936). Although the language and sources in this survey reflect the limitations of its historical context, it offers an informative view of the field of American philosophy of religion, in that historical moment, as seen through the lenses of the Chicago school of theology.

5. William Dean, *American Religious Empiricism* (Albany: State University of New York Press, 1986).

6. Loyal Rue, *Religion Is Not About God: How Spiritual Traditions Nurture Our Biological Nature and What to Expect When They Fail* (New Brunswick, NJ: Rutgers University Press, 2005).

7. William James, "The Chicago School," in *William James: Writings, 1902–1910*, ed. Bruce Kuklick (New York: Library of America, 1987), 1136–1137.

8. Ibid.

9. Informative historical treatments of the Chicago School theologians include Larry F. Axel, "Process and Religion: The History of a Tradition," *Process Studies* 8, no. 4 (Winter 1978): 231–239; Jerome A. Stone and W. Creighton Peden, eds., *The Chicago School of Theology—Pioneers in Religious Inquiry*, 2 vols. (Lewiston: Edwin Mellen, 1996); Gary Dorrien, *The Making of American Liberal Theology: Idealism, Realism, and Modernity*, vol. 2, *The Making of Modern Liberal Theology* (Louisville: Westminster John Knox, 2003), 151–285; Jerome A. Stone, *Religious Naturalism Today: The Rebirth of a Forgotten Alternative* (Albany: State University of New York Press, 2008), 59–100.

10. Henry Nelson Wieman, *Religious Experience and Scientific Method* (1926; Carbondale: Southern Illinois University Press, 1971), 32.

11. Henry Nelson Wieman, *Man's Ultimate Commitment* (1958; Lanham, MD: University Press of America, 1991), 11.

12. Henry Nelson Wieman, *The Source of Human Good* (Chicago: University of Chicago Press, 1946), 56.

13. Ibid., 299–300.

14. Ibid., 69, 74.

15. Bernard M. Loomer, "The Size of God," *American Journal of Theology and Philosophy* 8, nos. 1 and 2 (January and May 1987): 20.

16. Ibid., 26.

17. Ibid., 20.

18. I allude here to Whitehead's well-known airplane metaphor. At the opening of *Process and Reality*, where he is describing his version of speculative philosophy, and contrasting it in particular with the unimaginative strictures of Baconian science, he writes that "The true method of discovery is like the flight of an aeroplane. It starts from the ground of particular observation; it makes a flight in the thin air of imaginative generalization; and it again lands for renewed observation rendered acute by rational interpretation." Whitehead, *Process and Reality*, corrected ed. (New York: Free, 1978), 5.

19. Loomer, "The Size of God," 25.

20. Ibid., 41.

21. Ibid., 29.

22. Ibid., 29, 42.

23. A fuller statement of Meland's idea is as follows: "We experience more than we know, and we know more than we can think; and we think more than we can say; and language therefore lags behind the intuitions of immediate experience." Bernard E. Meland, "Response to Paper by Professor Beardslee," *Encounter* 36 (1975): 340.

24. Roy Rapport, *Ritual and Religion in the Making of Humanity* (Cambridge: Cambridge University Press, 1999), 451.

25. Ibid., 452.

26. Thomas Homer-Dixon coins this term and makes a forceful case for this idea in his book *The Upside of Down: Catastrophe, Creativity, and the Renewal of Civilization* (Toronto: Random House, 2006), 265–308.

27. The use of the concept of *resilience* has exploded in recent years. Emerging through the study of systems in psychosocial and socioecological fields, *resilience* is now referenced across a range of disciplines. Important critical analyses of why and how this has occurred include Jeremy Walker and Melinda Cooper, "Genealogies of Resilience: From Systems Ecology to the Political Economy of Crisis Adaptation," *Security Dialogue* 42, no. 2 (2011): 143–160; Brad Evans and Julian Reid, *Resilient Life: The Art of Living Dangerously* (Cambridge: Polity, 2014); David Chandler, *Resilience: The Governance of Complexity* (London: Routledge, 2014); and David Chandler and Julian Reid, *The Neoliberal Subject: Resilience, Adaptation and Vulnerability* (Lanham, MD: Rowman and Littlefield, 2016). According to these critiques, the emergence of resilience discourse is an effect of the contraction of the social welfare and security functions of the state under neoliberal policy regimes. Furthermore, these critiques argue that resilience discourse is politically disempowering to the extent that it prioritizes adaptation over mitigation and survivability over system change. While there are important insights in these critiques, they are flawed in two ways. First, their critical target is a concept of resilience in which it is assumed that resilience is morally normative and intrinsically good. As I define it, however, resilience is a nonmoral concept that describes a quality of system functioning. The relevance of the critiques, then, is limited to cases in which resilience is treated as sufficiently normative, as a moral or political telos "in itself." In contrast, I argue that the moral and political value of resilience depends upon understanding it as a nonmoral analytic concept. Interpreted and leveraged this way, it is a

concept that can help us to analyze the durability of unjust systems in order to know better where and how to critique and disrupt them. Constructively, this concept of resilience can help us more effectively to build sustainable moral communities and movements for social and environmental justice. Second, the critiques seem to assume a passive understanding of adaptation. But adaptation is not a merely responsive process. It is not only about a system's (or an organism's, community's, or social movement's) acceptance of the status quo of its environment. Resilient adaptive systems can also actively change their environments by resisting threats and transforming conditions. I will put this concept of *resilience* to constructive use in chapter 5.

28. Charles H. Long, *Significations: Signs, Symbols, and Images in the Interpretation of Religion* (Philadelphia: Fortress, 1986), 7.

29. Ibid.

30. Grace M. Jantzen, *Becoming Divine: Towards a Feminist Philosophy of Religion* (Bloomington: Indiana University Press, 1999), 254. Among the many sources Jantzen draws from in her work, she briefly discusses process philosophy and process theology. See especially pp. 255–259. She is drawn to a dipolar and dynamic concept of God, but she questions the "realism" in Whitehead's philosophy and his alleged indifference to the constructions of new religious symbolics. In my view, Jantzen's reservations about Whitehead are misdirected and are largely rooted in an engagement with Whitehead's theistic interpreters and neglect his important work on symbolism.

31. Ibid.

32. Rue, *Religion Is Not About God.*

33. Ursula Goodenough uses this concept in a similar way. See, for example, Goodenough, *The Sacred Depths of Nature* (Oxford: Oxford University Press, 1998); and Goodenough "Religiopoiesis," *Zygon: Journal of Religion and Science* 35 (September 2000): 561–566. I have interpreted Goodenough and the concept of *religiopoiesis* at length in *The Promise of Religious Naturalism* (Lanham, MD: Rowman and Littlefield, 2010).

34. William David Hart, "Neville's Metaphysics," *American Journal of Theology and Philosophy* 37, no. 3 (September 2016), 255. Hart's reference to the human as a "god who shits" is an allusion to Ernest Becker, *The Denial of Death* (New York: Free, 1997), 58.

35. Justus Buchler, "Probing the Idea of Nature," *Process Studies* 8, no. 3 (Fall 1978): 157. Also included as appendix 4 in Buchler, *Metaphysics of Natural Complexes.*

36. The paragraph that follows is especially informed by the classic intellectual history of Western concepts of nature in R. G. Collingwood, *The Idea of Nature* (1945; Oxford: Oxford University Press, 1960). There are of course many other important and valuable resources that examine diverse concepts of nature. Of these many others, significant historical, and comparative resources include J. Baird Callicott and Roger T. Ames, eds., *Nature in Asian Traditions of Thought: Essays in Environmental Philosophy* (Albany: State University of New York Press, 1989), which attends to the diversity of concepts of nature in Chinese, Japanese, and Indian philosophy and religion; R. Bruce Hall, *Infinite Nature* (Chicago: University of Chicago Press, 2006), which makes a very compelling argument for the enviropolitical significance of "pluralizing" the concept of nature; and Phillipe Descola, *Beyond Nature and Culture*, trans. Janet Lloyd (Chicago:

University of Chicago Press, 2013), which presents a field-reshaping, global anthropology of four distinct, cultural systems of nature.

37. As this book went to press, a recently published study in *The Astrophysical Journal* concluded that there are two trillion galaxies in the observable universe, which is upward of ten times the number of galaxies previously thought. See Davide Castelvicci, "Universe Has Ten Times More Galaxies Than Previously Thought," *Nature: International Weekly Journal of Science*, October 14, 2016, www.nature.com/news/universe-has-ten -times- more-galaxies-than-researchers-thought-1.20809.

38. For example, this argument was powerfully made by the German Jewish philosopher Hans Jonas. See, especially, Jonas, *The Imperative of Responsibility: In Search of an Ethics for the Technological Age* (Chicago: University of Chicago Press, 1984), 79–90. Originally published as *Das Prinzip Verantwortung: Versuch einer Ethik für die technologische Zivilisation* (Frankfurt: Insel, 1979). For my own analysis of this argument, see Michael S. Hogue, *The Tangled Bank: Towards an Ecotheological Ethic of Responsible Participation* (Eugene, OR: Wipf and Stock, 2008).

39. Carol Wayne White, *Black Lives and Sacred Humanity: Toward an African American Religious Naturalism* (New York: Fordham University Press, 2016), 40.

40. Wieman, *Religious Experience and Scientific Method*, 38–39.

41. Ibid.

42. Hans Jonas, "The Outcry of Mute Things," in *Mortality and Morality: A Search for the Good After Auschwitz*, ed. Lawrence Vogel, Northwestern University Studies in Phenomenology and Existential Philosophy (Chicago: Northwestern University Press, 1996), 201–202.

43. Ann Gibbons, "World's Oldest Homo Sapiens Found in Morocco," *Science*, www .sciencemag.org/news/2017/06/world-s-oldest-homo-sapiens-fossils-found-morocco. This website article by Gibbons summarizes findings published by Jean-Jacques Hublin et al., "New Fossils from Jebel Irhoud, Morocco, and the Pan-African Origins of Homo Sapiens," *Nature* 546 (June 8, 2017): 289–292, doi:10.1038/nature22336.

5. TOWARD A THEOPOLITICS OF RESILIENT DEMOCRACY

1. James Boggs and Grace Lee Boggs, *Revolution and Evolution in the Twentieth Century* (1974; New York: Monthly Review Press, 2008), viii.

2. Ibid.

3. Ibid.

4. Ursula Goodenough and Terrence Deacon, "The Sacred Emergence of Nature," in *Oxford Handbook of Religion and Science*, ed. Philip Clayton (Oxford: Oxford University Press, 2006), 854. "Something more from nothing but" is one of the ways Goodenough and Deacon explain the concept of emergence. They say it would be more accurate, although less euphonious, to describe emergence as "something else from nothing but."

5.   Boggs and Boggs, *Revolution and Evolution*, 212.

6.   Paul Hawken, *Blessed Unrest: How the Largest Movement in the World Came Into Being and Why No One Saw It Coming* (New York: Penguin, 2007), 4.

7.   Among many other example, see the "Our Power Campaign" project of the Climate Justice Alliance (www.ourpowercampaign.org) and the "Stop the Dakota Access Pipeline" (DAPL) blockade and encampment at the Standing Rock Sioux Reservation, www.standingrock.org.

8.   For information about the commoning movement, see www.onthecommons.org. For history, analysis, and philosophy of commoning, excellent sources include David Bollier, *Thinking Like a Commoner: Introduction to the Life of the Commons* (Garbriola Island, British Columbia: New Society, 2014); and Peter Linebaugh, *The Magna Carta Manifesto: Liberties and Commons for All* (Berkeley: University of California Press, 2008).

9.   On the importance of "honor codes" in relation to social and political change, see Kwame Anthony Appiah, *The Honor Code: How Moral Revolutions Happen* (New York: Norton, 2010). Sharon Welch, *After the Protests Are Heard: An Ethic of Power, Professionalism and Risk* (New York: New York University Press, 2018), explores and advances the shift in "honor codes" emerging through new approaches to social change.

10. Alfred North Whitehead, *Adventures of Ideas* (1933; New York: Free, 1967), 7.

11. Sheldon S. Wolin, *Politics and Vision: Continuity and Innovation in Western Political Thought*, expanded ed. (Princeton: Princeton University Press, 2004), 603.

12. Sheldon S. Wolin, *Fugitive Democracy, and Other Essays*, ed. Nicholas Xenos (Princeton: Princeton University Press, 2016), 112. Wolin's earlier formulation of these ideas appears in "Fugitive Democracy," *Constellations* 1, no. 1 (1994), later collected in *Democracy and Difference: Contesting the Boundaries of the Political*, ed. Seyla Benhabib (Princeton: Princeton University Press, 1996).

13. For a cogent take on the relevance of Whitehead to undoing ethnoracial and cultural hierarchies, see Henry James Young, *Hope in Process: A Theology of Social Pluralism* (Minneapolis: Fortress, 1990). Working from Whitehead's ontology of internal relatedness, Young makes a compelling case for a social ethics that aims for unity-in-diversity rather than unity-in-conformity with dominant social groups.

14. Alfred North Whitehead, *Symbolism: Its Meaning and Effect* (1927; New York: Fordham University Press, 1985), 88.

15. Wilfrid Sellars, "Philosophy and the Scientific Image of Man," in *Frontiers of Science and Philosophy*, ed. Robert G. Colodny (Pittsburgh: University of Pittsburgh Press, 1962), 37.

16. C. S. Holling, "Understanding the Complexity of Economic, Ecological, and Social Systems," *Ecosystems* 4 (2001): 392.

17. Thomas Homer-Dixon, *The Upside of Down: Catastrophe, Creativity, and the Renewal of Civilization* (Toronto: Random House, 2006), 230.

18. Roger Boyd, "Panarchy: Implications for Economic and Social Policy," *Humanity's Test* (blog), December 2, 2014, www.humanitystest.com/?s=panarchy.

19. As I interpret this, James O'Connor, John Bellamy Foster, and Jason W. Moore represent, respectively, three prominent lines of thinking about this. O'Connor argues that

there are two contradictions, social and ecological. Foster argues that there is one meta-bolic rift, with interrelated social and environmental dimensions. Moore rejects the distinction between social and ecological relations and talks about relations between human and nonhuman natures. Moore also locates the historical origins of the meta-bolic rift in the sixteenth century rather than in the "second agricultural revolution" of the nineteenth century. See, for example, O'Conner, *Natural Causes: Essays in Ecological Marxism* (Vermont: Guilford, 1997); Foster, *Marx's Ecology: Materialism and Nature* (New York: Monthly Review Press, 2000); Foster, *The Ecological Rift: Capitalism's War on Nature* (New York: Monthly Review Press, 2011); and Moore, *Capitalism in the Web of Life: Ecology and the Accumulation of Capital* (New York: Verso, 2015).

20. Foster, *The Ecological Rift.*

21. Furthermore, the Act ensures that "If the discoverer dies before perfecting proof of discovery or fully complying with the provisions of section 1412 of this title, his widow, heir, executor, or administrator shall be entitled to the benefits of such discovery." Legal Information Institute at Cornell University School of Law, www.law.cornell.edu /uscode/text/48/1411.

22. See data sources cited in chapter 2.

23. O'Connor, *Natural Causes*, esp. 267–323.

24. Foster, "Capitalism and Ecology: The Nature of the Contradiction," *Monthly Review* 54, no. 4 (September 2002).

25. Anthony Giddens, *Runaway World*, rev. ed. (New York: Routledge, 2003), 26.

26. Ibid.

27. Ulrich Beck, *Ecological Enlightenment: Essays on the Politics of the Risk Society* (Amherst, NY: Prometheus, 1995), 2. See also Beck, *Risk Society: Toward a New Moder-nity* (London: Sage, 1992); Beck, *World at Risk* (Cambridge: Polity, 2009); and, most recently, Beck, *The Metamorphosis of the World* (Cambridge: Polity, 2016).

28. Beck, *Ecological Enlightenment*, 2.

29. "CFC Substitutes: Good for the Ozone Layer, Bad for Climate?," *Science Daily Web*, February 24, 2012, www.sciencedaily.com/releases/2012/02/120224110737.htm.

30. As this book went to press, an important amendment to the Montreal Protocol was just being finalized that could lead to the gradual elimination of HFCs as well. The unin-tended negative effects of HFC replacements remain to be seen.

31. The philosophical literature on "vulnerability" is quickly growing. See, for example, Judith Butler, *Precarious Life: The Powers of Mourning and Violence* (New York: Verso, 2004); and Butler, *Notes Toward a Performative Theory of Assembly* (Cam-bridge: Harvard University Press, 2015); Catriona Mackenzie, Wendy Rogers, and Susan Dodds, eds., *Vulnerability: New Essays in Ethics and Feminist Philosophy* (Oxford: Oxford University Press, 2014); Martha Albertson Fineman, "The Vulnerable Sub-ject: Anchoring Equality in the Human Condition," *Yale Journal of Law and Feminism* 20, no. 1 (2008); and Martha Albertson Fineman and Anna Grear, eds., *Vulnerability: Reflections on a New Ethical Foundation for Law and Politics* (Burlington, VT: Ashgate, 2013). Within this literature, there is an important debate about whether vulnerability should be treated as universal or differentiated. Fineman argues for vulnerability as

universal. She writes, "I want to claim the term 'vulnerable' for its potential in describing a universal, inevitable, enduring aspect of the human condition that must be at the heart of our concept of social and state responsibility." Fineman, "The Vulnerable Subject," 8. Fineman's argument is rooted in foundationalist reasoning that she takes to be necessary to the overturning of liberal political and legal theories of the subject. Mackenzie, Rogers, and Dodds, on the other hand, make a case for differentiating between inherent (that is, universal), situational (that is, context specific), and pathogenic (that is, systemic) sources of vulnerability and dispositional (that is, potential) and occurrent (manifest) states of vulnerability. See Mackenzie, Rogers, and Dodds, *Vulnerability*, 1–10. By distinguishing between "creatural" and "contingent" vulnerability, I think it is possible and important to affirm (along with Mackenzie, Rogers, and Dodds) that vulnerability is a human universal and that some humans in some times and places are, for diverse systemic and situational reasons, more vulnerable than others.

32. In addition to examples cited earlier, the "transition" and "degrowth" movements are also illustrative of this work. For more about the "transition" movement, see www.transitionus.org/, transitionnetwork.org/, and work by Rob Hopkins, the founder of the movement, including Hopkins, *The Power of Just Doing Stuff: How Local Action Can Change the World* (Cambridge: UIT Cambridge, 2013). On "degrowth," see Serge Latouche, "Why Less Should Be So Much More: Degrowth Economics," *Le Monde Diplomatique*, November 2004, http://mondediplo.com/2004/11/14latouche; and Latouche, *Degrowth: A Vocabulary for a New Era*, ed. Giacomo D'Alisa, Federico Demaria, and Giorgos Kallis (New York: Routledge, 2014).

33. For example, Chantal Mouffe advocates for an "agonistic" democratic politics. See Mouffe, *The Democratic Paradox* (New York: Verso, 2000); Mouffe, *On the Political* (New York: Routledge, 2005); and Mouffe, *Agonistics: Thinking the World Politically* (New York: Verso, 2013). Along similar lines, John Medearis has recently argued that "The democratic path . . . simply is continuous oppositional exertion, without any expectation of transcendent victory." At the core of his idea of democracy as oppositional is the view that democracy fundamentally "opposes alienation, opposes the tendency of our common activities to escape our common control, and reproduce malign social structures." See John Medearis, *Why Democracy Is Oppositional* (Cambridge: Harvard University Press, 2015), 2, 4, 129–168.

34. William E. Connolly, for example, argues convincingly for the democratic spirit of "presumptive generosity." See Connolly, *Why I Am Not a Secularist* (Minneapolis: University of Minnesota Press, 2000); Connolly, *Pluralism* (Durham: Duke University Press, 2005); Connolly, *Capitalism and Christianity, American Style* (Durham: Duke University Press, 2008); and Connolly, *A World of Becoming* (Durham: Duke University Press, 2011).

35. Bernard Loomer, "Two Kinds of Power," *Process Studies* 6, no. 1 (Spring 1976): 15–32. For a very clear, brief elaboration of Loomer's ideas about power, as influenced by Whitehead, see C. Robert Mesle, *Process-Relational Philosophy: An Introduction to Alfred North Whitehead* (West Conshohocken, PA: Templeton Foundation Press, 2008), 72–78.

36. As Sheldon Wolin perceptively argued several years ago, "The fact that democracy continues to be invoked in American political rhetoric and the popular media may be a tribute, not to its vibrancy, but to its utility in supporting a myth that legitimates the very formations of power which have enfeebled it. . . . Thus the paradox: while democracy is widely proclaimed as the political identity of the American system, the demos is becoming disenchanted with the form that claims it. Disaffiliation is one of the marks that identify the state not only as postdemocratic but as postrepresentative." See Sheldon Wolin, *Politics and Vision: Continuity and Innovation in Western Political Thought*, expanded ed. (Princeton: Princeton University Press, 2004), 601. The postdemocratic and postrepresentative nature of democracy in the United States was vividly illustrated in the 2016 presidential election. Although Hillary Clinton won the popular vote by a very large margin, nearly three million votes, Donald Trump won enough states to win the votes of the Electoral College and thereby to be elected president. But the rise of ethnonationalism and authoritarian populism, within the United States and globally, reflects something more dangerous than disenchantment. Some researchers have identified a precipitous "democratic deconsolidation" taking place around the world over the last several years. Beyond the disenchantment of the demos, deconsolidation refers to the antidemocratic turn of governing institutions in historically democratic states. See Amanda Tabu, "How Stable Are Democracies? 'Warning Signs are Flashing Red,'" *New York Times*, November 29, 2016, www.nytimes.com/2016/11/29/world/americas/western-liberal- democracy.html?_r=0, and the work of political scientist Yascha Mounk, http://www.yaschamounk.com/.

37. C. Douglas Lummis, *Radical Democracy* (Ithaca: Cornell University Press, 1996), 15.

38. See Paulina Ochoa Espejo, *The Time of Popular Sovereignty: Process and the Democratic State* (University Park: Penn State University Press, 2011). Espejo draws on process philosophy in innovative ways. As her title suggests, she engages the democratic ideal of "popular sovereignty" as a theoretical conundrum for practical democracy. She intervenes within this conundrum by turning to process philosophy in order to reimagine "the people" as an unfolding event rather than a unified aggregation. She argues that a process theory of popular sovereignty "makes internally coherent and compatible the claims that a people can constitute an electorate democratically, that a people creates and rules itself, . . . that the people can have continuity in time" and, in addition, can "legitimize the state democratically as the people changes composition" (197). This is a bold and innovative argument with which I am sympathetic. But my focus in this chapter is on the problem of structuring and sustaining democratic communities rather than the question of the democratic legitimacy of the state. That said, I am dealing at a deeper level with the religious and symbolic roots of the problem that rightly concerns Espejo. The problem of popular sovereignty conceived as unitary consent is, in part, a symptom of the more historically entrenched problem of a unitary ideality of power.

39. Dewey, "Democracy is Radical," LW 11:298 (1987), italics original.

40. Although other philosophers have made much of this idea—for example, Jacques Derrida's concept of *la démocratie à venir* (democracy to come)—my thinking about this is obviously more influenced by Dewey. As Dewey expresses the idea, "Since [the task

of democracy] is one that can have no end till experience itself comes to an end, the task of democracy is forever that of creation of a freer and more humane experience in which all share and to which all contribute." See Dewey, "Creative Democracy—the Task Before Us," LW 14:230 (1988). For Derrida, see, especially, Derrida, *Spectres of Marx: The State of the Debt, the Work of Mourning and the New International*, trans. Peggy Kamuf (New York: Routledge, 1994); and Derrida, *Rogues: Two Essays on Reason*, trans. Pascale-Anne Brault and Michael Naas (Stanford: Stanford University Press, 2005).

41.   Dewey, *The Public and Its Problems*, LW 2:325 (1984).

42.   See note 16 in chapter 3.

43.   Dewey, LW 14:226 (1988).

44.   Sheldon Wolin's work on "fugitive democracy," mentioned earlier, makes similar arguments against the limitations of formalized democracy. But where Dewey conceives of democracy as a "way of life," which I interpret as a "formless" set of embodied habits and practices, Wolin conceives of fugitive democracy as pluriform, momentary, and ephemeral. He writes, for example, that "democracy should be about forms rather than *a* form or constitution; and instead of an institutionalized process, it should be conceived as a moment of experience, a crystallized response to deeply felt grievances or needs. . . . Its moment is not just a measure of fleeting time but an action that protests actualities and reveals possibilities." See Wolin, *Politics and Vision: Continuity and Innovation in Western Political Thought*, expanded ed. (Princeton: Princeton University Press, 2004), 603, italics original. As previously noted, I affirm Wolin's localized concept of democracy as "anti-totality." And the idea that democracy emerges out of felt need is resonant with my commitments to the importance of "vulnerable power" and the "power of the vulnerable." But I would emphasize that the efficacy of democratic moments (of protest and possibility) depends on the prior embodiment of democratic habits and practices. Another way to put this would be to say that the possibility of "fugitive" democracy depends upon an actualized commitment to democracy as a way of life, formless but habitual.

45.   Dewey, LW 2:250.

46.   Dewey, LW 2:327, 328.

47.   Butler, *Precarious Life*, 26.

48.   Ibid., 20.

49.   Ibid., 20–23.

50.   Sheldon Wolin argued along similar lines, "The experience of which democracy is the witness is the realization that the political mode of existence is such that it can be, and is, periodically lost." Wolin, *Fugitive Democracy*, 111.

51.   Claude Lefort, *Democracy and Political Theory* (Minneapolis: University of Minnesota Press, 1988), 19.

52.   Benjamin Barber, "Foundationalism and Democracy," in *Democracy and Difference: Contesting the Boundaries of the Political*, ed. Seyla Benhabib (Princeton: Princeton University Press, 1996), 349.

53.   Benjamin Barber, *Strong Democracy* (Berkeley: University of California Press, 1984), 46.

54. Ibid., 54.

55. Ibid.

56. Ibid., 65.

57. Ibid.

58. Dewey, "Philosophy and Democracy," MW 11:50 (1982).

59. C. Douglas Lummis, *Radical Democracy* (Ithaca: Cornell University Press, 1996), 40. Lummis makes his point by way of contrast to Carl Schmitt: "For the radical democrat, the dictum will read, 'Sovereign are they who decide whether the "dictator's" decision really is a decision and not the pronouncements of a usurper or a crackpot'" (170n36). Jacques Rancière has also argued that democracy is the very principle of politics. He claims that "democracy is neither a society to be governed, nor a government of society, it is specifically this ungovernable [the power of the people] on which every government must ultimately find out it is based." His point, as I understand it, is quite the same as Lummis's. The power of the people is the foundation of any form of politics, even if that form of politics is one that subordinates the people. But the power of the people, prior to being formed politically, is ungovernable. The ungovernable democratic foundation for government is no foundation at all. See Rancière, *Hatred of Democracy* (New York: Verso, 2006). Jeffrey W. Robbins and Clayton Crockett make use of this idea in their book *Religion, Politics, and the Earth: The New Materialism* (New York: Palgrave Macmillan, 2012).

60. Lummis, *Radical Democracy*, 40.

61. David A. Hollinger, "From Identity to Solidarity," *Daedalus* (Fall 2006): 23.

62. Ibid., 24.

63. Ibid.

64. Ibid., 25.

65. This is the evocative title of Charles Eisenstein's book *The More Beautiful World Our Hearts Know Is Possible* (Berkeley: North Atlantic, 2013).

66. Whitehead, *Adventures of Ideas*, 265.

67. Ibid.

BIBLIOGRAPHY

Allan, George. "In Defense of Secularizing Whitehead." *Process Studies* 39, no. 2 (Fall-Winter 2010): 319–333.

Anderson, Scott. "Fractured Lands: How the Arab World Came Apart." *New York Times Magazine*, April 10, 2016.

Anderson, Victor. *Pragmatic Theology: Negotiating the Intersections of an American Philosophy of Religion and Public Theology.* Albany: State University of New York Press, 1988.

Appiah, Kwame Anthony. *The Honor Code: How Moral Revolutions Happen.* New York: Norton, 2010.

Asad, Talal. *Genealogies of Religion: Discipline and Reasons of Power in Christianity and Islam.* Baltimore: Johns Hopkins University Press, 1993.

"At O'Hare, President Says 'Get on Board.'" Remarks by President Bush to airline employees, O'Hare International Airport, Chicago, Illinois. National Archives and Records Administration. September 27, 2001. http://georgewbush-whitehouse.archives.gov/news/releases /2001/09/20010927–1.html.

Axel, Larry F. "Process and Religion: The History of a Tradition." *Process Studies* 8, no. 4 (Winter 1978): 231–239.

Baptist, Edward E. *The Half Has Never Been Told: Slavery and the Making of American Capitalism.* New York: Basic, 2014.

Barber, Benjamin. *Strong Democracy.* Berkeley: University of California Press, 1984.

Bauman, Whitney A. "Climate Weirding and Queering Nature: Getting Beyond the Anthropocene." *Religions* 6, no. 2 (2015): 742–754. doi:10.3390/rel6020742.

Beck, Ulrich. *Ecological Enlightenment: Essays on the Politics of the Risk Society.* Amherst, NY: Prometheus, 1995.

——. *The Metamorphosis of the World.* Cambridge: Polity, 2016.

——. *Risk Society: Toward a New Modernity.* London: Sage, 1992.

——. *World at Risk*. Cambridge: Polity, 2009.

Bellah, Robert. *The Broken Covenant: American Civil Religion in a Time of Trial*. New York: Seabury, 1975.

Benhabib, Seyla, ed. *Democracy and Difference: Contesting the Boundaries of the Political*. Princeton: Princeton University Press, 1996.

Biello, David. "Mass Deaths in Americas Start New CO2 Epoch." *Scientific American*, March 11, 2015. www.scientificamerican.com/article/mass-deaths-in-americas-start-new-co2-epoch/.

Boger, Julian. "'A Recipe for Scandal': Trump Conflicts of Interest Point to Constitutional Crisis." *Guardian*, November 27, 2016. www.theguardian.com/us-news/2016/nov/27/donald -trump-conflicts-interest- constitutional-crisis.

Boggs, James, and Grace Lee. *Revolution and Evolution in the Twentieth Century*. 1974; New York: Monthly Review Press, 2008.

Bollier, David. *Thinking Like a Commoner: Introduction to the Life of the Commons*. Garbriola Island, British Columbia: New Society, 2014.

Bonneuil, Christophe, and Jean-Baptiste Fressoz. *The Shock of the Anthropocene*. Translated by David Fernbach. London: Verso, 2016.

Boyd, Roger. "Panarchy: Implications for Economic and Social Policy." *Humanity's Test* (blog), December 2, 2014. www.humanitystest.com/panarchy-implications-for-economic-social -policy/.

Buchler, Justus. *Metaphysics of Natural Complexes*. 2nd expanded ed. Edited by Kathleen Wallace and Armen Marsoobian with Robert S. Corrington. Albany: State University of New York Press, 1990.

——. "Probing the Idea of Nature." *Process Studies* 8, no. 3 (Fall 1978): 157–168.

Bullard, Robert D. *Dumping in Dixie: Race, Class, and Environmental Quality*. Boulder: Westview, 2000.

Bullard, Robert D., Paul Mohai, Robin Sana, and Beverly Wright. *Toxic Wastes and Race at Twenty, 1987–2007: A Report Prepared for the United Church of Christ Justice and Witness Ministries*. Cleveland: United Church of Christ, 2007.

Butler, Judith. *Notes Toward a Performative Theory of Assembly*. Cambridge: Harvard University Press, 2015.

——. *Precarious Life: The Powers of Mourning and Violence*. New York: Verso, 2004.

Callicott, J. Baird, and Roger T. Ames, eds. *Nature in Asian Traditions of Thought: Essays in Environmental Philosophy*. Albany: State University of New York Press, 1989.

Cama, Timothy. "$220 Million Flint Aid Package Included in Water Bill." *Hill*, April 26, 2016. http://thehill.com/policy/energy-environment/277664–220-million-flint-aid-package -included-in-water-bill.

Carbon Dioxide Information Analysis Center (CDIAC) Database. United States Department of Energy. http://cdiac.ornl.gov/.

Carrington, Damian. "Fossil Fuels Subsidized by $10m a Minutes, says IMF." *Guardian*, May 18, 2015. www.theguardian.com/environment/2015/may/18/fossil-fuel-companies-getting -10m-a-minute-in- subsidies-says-imf.

Castelvicci, Davide. "Universe Has Ten Times More Galaxies Than Previously Thought." *Nature: International Weekly Journal of Science*, October 14, 2016. www.nature.com/news /universe-has-ten-times-more- galaxies-than-researchers-thought-1.20809.

Ceballos, Gerardo, Paul R. Ehrlich, Anthony D. Barnosky, Andrés García, Robert M. Pringle, and Todd M. Palmer. "Accelerated Modern Human-Induced Species Losses: Entering the Sixth Mass Extinction." *Science Advances* 1, no. 5 (June 2015). doi: 10.1126/sciadv .1400253.

"CFC Substitutes: Good for the Ozone Layer, Bad for Climate?" *Science Daily Web*, February 24, 2012. www.sciencedaily.com/releases/2012/02/120224110737.htm.

Chakrabarty, Dipesh. "The Climate of History: Four Theses." *Critical Inquiry* 35 (Winter 2009): 197–222.

Chandler, David. *Resilience: The Governance of Complexity*. London: Routledge, 2014.

Chandler, David, and Julian Reid. *The Neoliberal Subject: Resilience, Adaptation and Vulnerability*. Lanham, MD: Rowman and Littlefield, 2016.

"Citizens United vs. Federal Election Commission," *SCOTUSblog*. www.scotusblog.com/case -files/cases/citizens-united-v-federal-election-commission/.

Clark, Zoe. "In First Executive Order, Snyder Splits Up the State Department of Natural Resources and Environment." *Michigan Radio*, January 5, 2011. http://michiganradio.org /post/first-executive-order-snyder- splits-state-department-natural-resources-and-envir onment#stream/o.

Climate Justice Alliance. "Our Power Campaign." www.ourpowercampaign.org.

Coady, David, Ian Parry, Louis Sears, and Baoping Shang. "How Large Are Global Energy Subsidies?" International Monetary Fund. Working Paper 15/105. www.imf.org/external /pubs/cat/longres.aspx?sk=42940.0.

Coates, Ta-Nehisi. *Between the World and Me*. New York: Spiegel and Grau, 2015.

Cobb, John. *Process Theology as Political Theology*. Philadelphia: Westminster, 1982.

Collingwood, R. G. *The Idea of Nature*. 1945; Oxford: Oxford University Press, 1960.

Collomb, Jean-Daniel. "The Ideology of Climate Change Denial in the United States." *European Journal of American Studies* 9, no. 1 (Spring 2014). doi:10.4000/ejas.10305.

"Comparing the New Emergency Manager Law with the One Repealed by Voters." *Michigan Radio*, March 28, 2013. http://michiganradio.org/post/comparing-new-emergency-manager -law-one-repealed-voters#stream/o.

Connolly, William E. *Christianity and Capitalism, American Style*. Durham: Duke University Press, 2008.

——. *Pluralism*. Durham: Duke University Press, 2005.

——. *The Terms of Political Discourse*. 2nd ed. Princeton: Princeton University Press, 1983.

——. *Why I Am Not a Secularist*. Minneapolis: University of Minnesota Press, 2000.

——. *A World of Becoming*. Durham: Duke University Press, 2011.

Corrington, Robert S. *Deep Pantheism: Toward a New Transcendentalism*. New York: Lexington, 2016.

——. *Ecstatic Naturalism: Signs of the World*. Bloomington: Indiana University Press, 1994.

——. *Introduction to C. S. Peirce: Philosopher, Semiotician, Ecstatic Naturalist*. Lanham, MD: Rowman and Littlefield, 1993.

——. *Nature and Spirit: An Essay in Ecstatic Naturalism*. New York: Fordham University Press, 1992.

——. *Nature's Religion*. Lanham, MD: Rowman and Littlefield, 1997.

——. *Nature's Sublime: An Essay in Aesthetic Naturalism*. New York: Lexington, 2013.

——. *A Semiotic Theory of Theology and Philosophy*. New York: Cambridge University Press, 2004.

Crist, Eileen. "On the Poverty of Our Nomenclature." In *Anthropocene or Capitalocene: Nature, History, and the Crisis of Capitalism*, edited by Jason W. Moore, 14–33. Oakland, CA: Kairos, PM, 2016.

Crockett, Clayton. "The Conception of Insurrections." Columbia University Press Blog. March 25, 2013. www.cupblog.org/?p=9760.

——. *Radical Political Theology: Religion and Politics After Liberalism*. New York: Columbia University Press, 2013.

Crockett, Clayton, and Jeffrey W. Robbins. *Religion, Politics, and the Earth: The New Materialism*. New York: Palgrave, 2012.

Crosby, Donald L. *Living with Ambiguity: Religious Naturalism and the Menace of Evil*. Albany: State University of New York, 2009.

——. *A Religion of Nature*. Albany: State University of New York, 2002.

Cummings, Robert Neville. *On the Scope and Truth of Theology: Theology as Symbolic Engagement*. New York: T and T Clark, 2006.

D'Alisa, Giacomo, Federico Demaria, and Giorgos Kallis, eds. *Degrowth: A Vocabulary for a New Era*. New York: Routledge, 2014.

"Dan Wyant Group Executive of DEQ, DNR and Agriculture and Rural Development." *Farm Progress*, December 2, 2010. http://farmprogress.com/story-dan-wyant-group-executive-of -deq-dnr-and-agriculture- rural-development-9-44349.

Davies, William. "The New Neoliberalism." *New Left Review* 101 (September-October 2016): 121–134.

Dawson, Ashley. *Extinction: A Radical History*. New York: OR Books, 2016.

Dean, William. *American Religious Empiricism*. Albany: State University of New York Press, 1986.

Dempsey, Dave. "Snyder Appointments: Better Lock the Henhouse." *Lansing City Pulse*, December 8, 2010. http://lansingcitypulse.com/search-articles-better+lock+the+henhouse. html.

Derrida, Jacques. *Rogues: Two Essays on Reason*. Translated by Pascale-Anne Brault and Michael Naas. Stanford: Stanford University Press, 2005.

——. *Spectres of Marx: The State of the Debt, the Work of Mourning and the New International*. Translated by Peggy Kamuf. New York: Routledge, 1994.

Descola, Phillipe. *Beyond Nature and Culture*. Translated by Janet Lloyd. Chicago: University of Chicago Press, 2013.

Dewey, John. *The Collected Works of John Dewey, 1882–1953*. Edited by Jo Ann Boydston. 37 vols. Carbondale: Southern Illinois University Press, 1969–1991.

Dorrien, Gary. *The Making of American Liberal Theology: Idealism, Realism, and Modernity*. Vol. 2, *The Making of Modern Liberal Theology*. Louisville: Westminster John Knox, 2003.

Dubuisson, Daniele. *The Western Construction of Religion: Myths, Knowledge, and Ideology*. Translated by William Sayers. Baltimore: Johns Hopkins University Press, 2003.

Eames, S. Morris. *Pragmatic Naturalism: An Introduction*. Carbondale: Southern Illinois University Press, 1977.

Egan, Paul. "Amid Denials, State Workers in Flint Got Clean Water." *Detroit Free Press*, January 29, 2016. www.freep.com/story/news/local/michigan/flint-water-crisis/2016/01/28/amid
-denials-state-workers-flint-got-clean-water/79470650/.

Eisenstein, Charles. *The More Beautiful World Our Hearts Know Is Possible*. Berkeley, CA: North Atlantic, 2013.

"Environmental Justice." US Environmental Protection Agency. www.epa.gov/environ
mentaljustice.

Espejo, Paulina Ochoa. *The Time of Popular Sovereignty: Process and the Democratic State*. University Park: Pennsylvania State University Press, 2011.

Evans, Brad, and Julian Reid. *Resilient Life: The Art of Living Dangerously*. Cambridge: Polity, 2014.

Farrell, Justin. "Network Structure and Influence of the Climate Change Counter-Movement." *Nature Climate Change* 6 (2016): 370–374. doi:10.1038/nclimate2875.

Fineman, Martha Albertson. "The Vulnerable Subject: Anchoring Equality in the Human Condition." *Yale Journal of Law and Feminism* 20, no. 1 (2008).

Fineman, Martha Albertson, and Anna Grear, eds. *Vulnerability: Reflections on a New Ethical Foundation for Law and Politics*. Burlington, VT: Ashgate, 2013.

Finnegan, William. "The Economics of Empire: Notes on the Washington Consensus." *Harper's*, May 2003.

Flint Water Advisor Task Force. "Flint Water Advisor Task Force: Final Report." March 2016. http://mediad.publicbroadcasting.net/p/michigan/files/201603/taskforce_report.pdf?
_ga=1.147700144.60 9033213.1458749402.

Fonger, Ron. "General Motors Shutting Off Flint River at Engine Plant Due to Corrosion Worries." *MLive*, January 17, 2015. www.mlive.com/news/flint/index.ssf/2014/10/general_motors
_wont_use_flint.html.

Foster, John Bellamy. "Capitalism and Ecology: The Nature of the Contradiction." *Monthly Review* 54, no. 4 (September 2002): 6–16.

——. *The Ecological Rift: Capitalism's War on Nature*. New York: Monthly Review Press, 2011.

——. *Marx's Ecology: Materialism and Nature*. New York: Monthly Review Press, 2000.

Frankenberry, Nancy. "Contingency All the Way Down: Whitehead Among the Pragmatists." In *Thinking with Whitehead and the Pragmatists: Experience and Reality*, edited by Brian G. Henning, William T. Myers, and Joseph D. John, 97–116. Lanham, MD: Lexington, 2015.

——. *Religion and Radical Empiricism*. Albany: State University of New York Press, 1987.

Friedrich, Johannes, and Thomas Damassa. "The History of Carbon Dioxide Emissions." World Resources Institute Blog, May 21, 2014. www.wri.org/blog/2014/05/history-carbon
-dioxide-emissions.

Gardiner, Stephen M. *A Perfect Moral Storm: The Ethical Tragedy of Climate Change*. Oxford: Oxford University Press, 2011.

Giddens, Anthony. *Runaway World*. Rev. ed. New York: Routledge, 2003.

Goodenough, Ursula. "Religiopoiesis." *Zygon: Journal of Religion and Science* 35 (September 2000): 561–566.

——. *The Sacred Depths of Nature*. Oxford: Oxford University Press, 1998.

Goodenough, Ursula, and Terrence Deacon. "The Sacred Emergence of Nature." In *Oxford Handbook of Religion and Science*, edited by Philip Clayton, 853–871. Oxford: Oxford University Press, 2006.

Goodman, Amy, and Denis Moynihan. "The Terror of Flint's Poisoned Water." *Democracy Now*, February 4, 2016. www.democracynow.org/2016/2/4/the_terror_of_flint_s_poisoned.

Graham, David A. "Who Is to Blame for Flint's Lead Crisis?" *Atlantic*, March 24, 2016. www.theatlantic.com/politics/archive/2016/03/flint-task-force-rick-snyder-blame/475182/.

"Guano Islands Act (US Code of Law, Title 48, Chapter 8)." Legal Information Institute at Cornell University School of Law. www.law.cornell.edu/uscode/text/48/1411.

Halcom, Chad. "Dan Wyant's Foundation Work an Asset as He Joins Gov.-Elect Snyder's Team." Crain's Detroit Business, December 8, 2010. www.crainsdetroit.com/article/20101208/SUB01/312089996/dan-wyants-foundation-work-an-asset-as-he-joins-gov-elect-snyders.

Hall, R. Bruce. *Infinite Nature*. Chicago: University of Chicago Press, 2006.

Hamilton, Clive. "Getting the Anthropocene So Wrong." *Anthropocene Review* 2, no. 2 (August 2015): 101–107. doi:10.1177/2053019615590922.

Hart, William David. "Neville's Metaphysics." *American Journal of Theology and Philosophy* 37, no. 3 (September 2016): 248–262.

Hartshorne, Charles. "On Some Criticisms of Whitehead's Philosophy." *Philosophical Review* 44, no. 4 (July 1935): 323–344.

Harvey, David. *A Brief History of Neoliberalism*. Oxford: Oxford University Press, 2005.

Hawken, Paul. *Blessed Unrest: How the Largest Movement in the World Came Into Being and Why No One Saw It Coming*. New York: Penguin, 2007.

Hervieu-Léger, Daniele. *Religion as a Chain of Memory*. New Brunswick, NJ: Rutgers University Press, 2000.

Hodgson, Godfrey. *The Myth of American Exceptionalism*. New Haven: Yale University Press, 2009.

Hoffman, Andrew J. *How Culture Shapes the Climate Debate*. Stanford: Stanford University Press, 2015.

Hogue, Michael S. *The Promise of Religious Naturalism*. Lanham, MD: Rowman and Littlefield, 2010.

——. *The Tangled Bank: Towards an Ecotheological Ethic of Responsible Participation*. Eugene, OR: Wipf and Stock, 2008.

Holling, C. S. "Understanding the Complexity of Economic, Ecological, and Social Systems." *Ecosystems* 4 (2001): 390–405.

Hollinger, David A. "From Identity to Solidarity." *Daedalus* (Fall 2006): 23–31.

Homer-Dixon, Thomas. *The Upside of Down: Catastrophe, Creativity, and the Renewal of Civilization*. Toronto: Random House, 2006.

Hopkins, Rob. *The Power of Just Doing Stuff: How Local Action Can Change the World*. Cambridge: UIT Cambridge, 2013.

Hovey, Craig, Jeffrey Bailey, and William Cavanaugh, eds. *An Eerdmans Reader in Contemporary Political Theology*. Grand Rapids, MI: Eerdmans, 2012.

Hughes, Richard T. *Myths America Lives By*. Urbana: University of Illinois Press, 2004.

Jackson, Andrew. First Annual Message to Congress, December 8, 1829. American Presidency Project. University of California Santa Barbara. www.presidency.ucsb.edu/ws/index.php ?pid=29471.

James, William. *Essays in Radical Empiricism*. Vol. 5, *The Works of William James*, edited by Fredson Bowers and Ignas K. Skrupskelis. Cambridge: Harvard University Press, 1976.

——. *Pragmatism and the Meaning of Truth*. Vol. 11, *The Works of William James*, edited by Fredson Bowers and Ignas K. Skrupskelis. Cambridge: Harvard University Press, 1978.

——. *Pragmatism: The Works of William James*. Edited by Bruck Kuklick. Cambridge: Harvard University Press, 1975.

——. *The Principles of Psychology*. Vol. 1. New York: Holt, 1890.

——. *William James: Writings, 1902–1910*. Edited by Bruce Kuklick. New York: Library of America, 1987.

Jamieson, Dale. *Reason in a Dark Time: Why the Struggle Against Climate Change Failed—and What It Means for Our Future*. Oxford: Oxford University Press, 2014.

Jantzen, Grace M. *Becoming Divine: Towards a Feminist Philosophy of Religion*. Bloomington: Indiana University Press, 1999.

Jefferson, Thomas. *Notes on the State of Virginia*. New York: Penguin, 1998.

Jennings, Francis. *The Invasion of America: Indians, Colonialism, and the Cant of Conquest*. New York: Norton, 1976.

Jonas, Hans. *The Imperative of Responsibility: In Search of an Ethics for the Technological Age*. Chicago: University of Chicago Press, 1984. Originally published as *Das Prinzip Verantwortung: Versuch einer Ethik für die technologische Zivilisation*. Frankfurt: Insel, 1979.

——. "The Outcry of Mute Things." In *Mortality and Morality: A Search for the Good After Auschwitz*, edited by Lawrence Vogel, 198–202. Northwestern University Studies in Phenomenology and Existential Philosophy. Chicago: Northwestern University Press, 1996.

Keller, Catherine. *Cloud of the Impossible: Negative Theology and Planetary Entanglement*. Insurrections: Critical Studies in Religion, Politics, and Culture. New York: Columbia University Press, 2014.

——. *God and Power: Counter-Apocalpytic Journeys*. Minneapolis: Fortress, 2005.

Kelly, Colin P., Shahrzad Mohtadib, Mark A. Canec, Richard Seagerc, and Yochanan Kushnirc. "Climate Change in the Fertile Crescent and Implications of the Recent Syrian Drought." *Proceedings of the National Academy of Sciences of the United States of America* 112, no. 11:3241–3246. doi:10.1073/pnas.1421533112.

King, Thomas. *The Truth About Stories*. Toronto: House of Anansi, 2003.

Kitcher, Philip. *Preludes to Pragmatism: Towards a Reconstruction of Philosophy*. Oxford: Oxford University Press, 2012.

Kolbert, Elizabeth. *The Sixth Extinction: An Unnatural History*. New York: Holt, 2014.

Krikorian, Yervant H., ed. *Naturalism and the Human Spirit*. New York: Columbia University Press, 1944.

Latouche, Serge. "Why Less Should Be So Much More: Degrowth Economics." *Le Monde Diplomatique*, November 2004. http://mondediplo.com/2004/11/14latouche.

Lawrence, William. "The Relation of Wealth to Morals." In *God's New Israel: Religious Inter-pretations of American Destiny*, edited by Conrad Cherry, 249–259. Chapel Hill: University of North Carolina Press, 1998.

Lefort, Claude. *Democracy and Political Theory*. Minneapolis: University of Minnesota Press, 1988.

Lennard, Natasha, and Adrian Parr. "Our Crimes Against the Planet, and Ourselves." *New York Times*, May 18, 2016. www.nytimes.com/2016/05/18/opinion/our-crime-against-the -planet-and-ourselves.html.

Lewis, Simon L., and Mark A. Maslin. "Anthropocene Began with Species Exchange Between Old and New Worlds." *Conversation*, March 11, 2015. https://theconversation.com/anthro-pocene-began-with-species- exchange-between-old-and-new-worlds-38674.

——. "Defining the Anthropocene." *Nature* 519 (March 12, 2015): 171–180. doi:10.1038/ nature14258.

Linebaugh, Peter. *The Magna Carta Manifesto: Liberties and Commons for All*. Berkeley: University of California Press, 2008.

"List of Annex I Parties to the Convention." United Nations Framework Convention on Climate Change. http://unfccc.int/parties_and_observers/parties/annex_i/items/2774.php.

Liu, Eric, and Nick Hanauer. *The Gardens of Democracy: A New American Story of Citizen-ship, the Economy, and the Role of Government*. Seattle: Sasquatch, 2011.

"Local Financial Stability and Choice Act (Act 436 of 2012)." Michigan Legislature. www .legislature.mi.gov/(S(af3qncmzllaneqgnylc1mlqe))/mileg.aspx?page=GetObject&object name= mcl-act-436-of-2012.

Locke, John. *Two Treatises of Government*. Edited by Peter Laslett. Cambridge: Cambridge University Press, 1988.

Long, Charles H. *Significations: Signs, Symbols, and Images in the Interpretation of Religion*. Philadelphia: Fortress, 1986.

Loomer, Bernard M. "The Size of God." *American Journal of Theology and Philosophy* 8, nos. 1 and 2 (January and May 1987): 20–51.

——. "Two Kinds of Power." *Process Studies* 6, no. 1 (Spring 1976): 15–32.

Lovelock, James. *Gaia: A New Look at Life on Earth*. Oxford: Oxford University Press, 1979.

Lummis, C. Douglas. *Radical Democracy*. Ithaca: Cornell University Press, 1996.

Mackenzie, Catriona, Wendy Rogers, and Susan Dodds, eds. *Vulnerability: New Essays in Eth-ics and Feminist Philosophy*. Oxford: Oxford University Press, 2014.

Marsh, James L. *Process, Praxis and Transcendence*. Albany: State University of New York, 1999.

Marshall, George. *Don't Even Think About It: Why Our Brains Are Wired to Ignore Climate Change*. New York: Bloomsbury, 2014.

Masuzawa, Tomoku. *The Invention of World Religions: Or, How European Universalism Was Preserved in the Language of Pluralism*. Chicago: University of Chicago Press, 2005.

McCarraher, Eugene. "The Heavenly City of Business." In *The Short American Century*, edited by Andrew J. Bacevich, 187–230. Cambridge: Harvard University Press, 2012.

McCright, Aaron M., and Riley E. Dunlap. "The Politicization of Climate Change and Polar-ization in the American Public's Views of Global Warming, 2001–2010." *Sociological Quar-terly* 52 (2011): 155–194.

McKibben, Bill. *The End of Nature*. New York: Random House, 1989.

McNeill, John R., and Peter Engelke. *The Great Acceleration: An Environmental History of the Anthropocene Since 1945*. Cambridge: Harvard University Press, 2016.

Medearis, John. *Why Democracy Is Oppositional*. Cambridge: Harvard University Press, 2015.

Meland, Bernard E. "Response to Paper by Professor Beardslee." *Encounter* 36 (1975): 331–341.

Mesle, C. Robert. *Process-Relational Philosophy: An Introduction to Alfred North Whitehead*. West Conshohocken, PA: Templeton Foundation Press, 2008.

Moore, Jason W. *Capitalism in the Web of Life: Ecology and the Accumulation of Capital*. New York: Verso, 2015.

Morris, Ian. *Foragers, Farmers and Fossil Fuels: How Human Values Evolve*. Princeton: Princeton University Press, 2015.

Morton, Timothy. *Hyperobjects: Philosophy and Ecology After the End of the World*. Minnesota: University of Minnesota Press, 2013.

Mouffe, Chantal. *Agonistics: Thinking the World Politically*. New York: Verso, 2013.

——. *The Democratic Paradox*. New York: Verso, 2000.

——. *On the Political*. New York: Routledge, 2005.

Mounk, Yascha. Personal website. www.yaschamounk.com/.

Neville. Robert Cummings. *The Highroad Around Modernism*. Albany: State University of New York Press, 1992.

"New Data Brings New Answers on Climate Migration." United Nations Climate Change Newsroom. May 19, 2016. http://newsroom.unfccc.int/unfccc-newsroom/human-mobility-and-the-paris-agreement/.

Niebuhr, H. Richard. *The Kingdom of God in America*. 1937; Middletown, CT: Wesleyan University Press, 1988.

Nongbri, Brent. *Before Religion: A History of a Modern Concept*. New Haven: Yale University Press, 2013.

O'Conner, James. *Natural Causes: Essays in Ecological Marxism*. Vermont: Guilford, 1997.

On the Commons (Commons Movement Strategy Center). www.onthecommons.org.

Oreskes, Naomi, and Erik M. Conway. *Merchants of Doubt: How a Handful of Scientists Obscured the Truth on Issues from Tobacco Smoke to Global Warming*. London: Bloomsbury, 2010.

O'Sullivan, John L. "Annexation." Making of America Series, Cornell University. Originally published in *United States Democratic Review* 17, no. 85 (July-August 1845). http://ebooks.library.cornell.edu/cgi/t/text/text-idx?c=usde;cc=usde;view=toc;subview=short;idno=usde0017-1.

——. "Editorial." *New York Morning News*, December 27, 1845.

——. "The Great Nation of Futurity." Making of America Series, Cornell University. Originally published in *United States Democratic Review* 6, no. 23 (November 1839). http://ebooks.library.cornell.edu/cgi/t/text/text-idx?c=usde;cc=;view=toc;subview=short;idno=usde0006-4.

Painter, James. *Poles Apart: The International Reporting of Climate Scepticism*. Reuters Institute for the Study of Journalism. Oxford: Oxford University Press, 2011.

Parr, Adrian. *The Wrath of Capital: Neoliberalism and Climate Change Politics*. New York: Columbia University Press, 2013.

Peirce, Charles Sanders. "How to Make Our Ideas Clear." In *Collected Papers of Charles Sanders Peirce*, edited by Charles Hartshorne and Paul Weis, 5:388–410. Cambridge: Harvard University Press, 1935.

Phillips, Elizabeth. *Political Theology: A Guide for the Perplexed*. New York: T and T Clark, 2012.

"President Outlines War Effort," Remarks by President Bush at the California Business Association Breakfast, Sacramento Memorial Auditorium, Sacramento, California. National Archives and Records Administration. October 17, 2001. http://georgewbush-whitehouse.archives.gov/news/releases/2001/10/20011017-15.html.

Purdy, Jedediah. *After Nature: A Politics for the Anthropocene*. Cambridge: Harvard University Press, 2015.

——. "Anthropocene Fever." *Aeon*, March 31, 2015. https://aeon.co/essays/should-we-be-suspicious-of-the-anthropocene-idea.

Rancière, Jacques. *Hatred of Democracy*. Translated by Steve Corcoran. New York: Verso, 2006.

Raposa, Michael. *Peirce's Philosophy of Religion*. Bloomington: Indiana University Press, 1989.

Rapport, Roy. *Ritual and Religion in the Making of Humanity*. Cambridge: Cambridge University Press, 1999.

Robbins, Jeffrey W. *Radical Democracy and Political Theology*. New York: Columbia University Press, 2013.

Roy, Siddhartha. "Lead Testing Results from Two Worst Case Homes in Flint (Before and After Water Switch)." Flint Water Study Updates, December 11, 2015. http://flintwaterstudy.org/2015/12/lead-testing-results-from-two-worst-case-homes-in-flint-before-and-after-water-switch/.

Rue, Loyal. *Religion Is Not About God: How Spiritual Traditions Nurture Our Biological Nature, and What to Expect When They Fail*. New Brunswick, NJ: Rutgers University Press, 2005.

Ryder, John. *The Things in Heaven and Earth: An Essay in Pragmatic Naturalism*. New York: Fordham University Press, 2013.

Saxton, Alexander. *The Rise and Fall of the White Republic: Class Politics and Mass Culture in Nineteenth-Century America*. London: Verso, 1991.

Schmitt, Carl. *Political Theology: Four Chapters on the Concept of Sovereignty*. Translated by George Schwab. Chicago: University of Chicago Press, 1985. Originally published as *Politische Theologie: Vier Kapitel zur Lehre von der Souveranitat*. Berlin: Duncker und Humblot, 1922.

Scott, Peter, and William T. Cavanaugh, eds. *Blackwell Companion to Political Theology*. Oxford: Blackwell, 2004.

Sellars, Wilfrid. "Philosophy and the Scientific Image of Man." In *Frontiers of Science and Philosophy*, edited by Robert G. Colodny, 35–78. Pittsburgh: University of Pittsburgh Press, 1962.

Sherburne, Donald W. "Whitehead, Alfred North." In *The Cambridge Dictionary of Philosophy*, edited by Robert Audi, 851–853. Cambridge: Cambridge University Press, 1995.

"Snyder Splits DEQ, DNR." *CBS Detroit*, November 30, 2010. http://detroit.cbslocal.com/2010/11/30/snyder-splits-deq-dnr/.

Spanos, William V. *Redeemer Nation in the Interregnum: An Untimely Meditation on the American Vocation.* New York: Fordham University Press, 2016.

Spinoza, Baruch. *A Spinoza Reader: The Ethics and Other Works.* Translated and edited by Edwin Curley. Princeton: Princeton University Press, 1994.

Stannard, David E. *American Holocaust: Columbus and the Conquest of the New World.* Oxford: Oxford University Press, 1992.

Şteffen, Will, Wendy Broadgate, Lisa Deutsch, Owen Gaffney, and Cornelia Ludwig. "The Trajectory of the Anthropocene: The Great Acceleration." *Anthropocene Review* 2, no. 1 (April 2015): 81–98.

Steffen, Will, Jacques Ginevald, Paul Crutzen, and John McNeill. "The Anthropocene: Conceptual and Historical Perspectives." *Philosophical Transactions of the Royal Society A* (2011). doi:10.1098/rsta.2010.0327.

Stengers, Isabelle. *Thinking with Whitehead: A Free and Wild Creation of Concepts.* Translated by Michael Chase. Cambridge: Harvard University Press, 2011.

Stiles, Ezra. "The United States Elevated to Glory and Honor." In *God's New Israel: Religious Interpretations of American Destiny*, edited by Conrad Cherry, 82–92. Chapel Hill: University of North Carolina Press, 1998.

Stone, Jerome A. *Religious Naturalism Today: The Rebirth of a Forgotten Alternative.* Albany: State University of New York, 2008.

Stone, Jerome A., and W. Creighton Peden, eds. *The Chicago School of Theology—Pioneers in Religious Inquiry.* 2 vols. Lewiston, NY: Edwin Mellen, 1996.

"Stop the Dakota Access Pipeline" (DAPL) main page. Standing Rock Sioux Reservation. www.standingrock.org.

Stout, Jeffrey. *Democracy and Tradition.* Princeton: Princeton University Press, 2004.

Sturm, Douglas. *Solidarity and Suffering.* Albany: State University of New York, 1988.

Tabu, Amanda. "How Stable Are Democracies? 'Warning Signs are Flashing Red.'" *New York Times*, November 29, 2016. www.nytimes.com/2016/11/29/world/americas/western-liberal-democracy.html?_r=0.

Tainter, Joseph. *The Collapse of Complex Societies.* Cambridge: Cambridge University Press, 1988.

Taylor, Charles. *A Secular Age.* Cambridge: Harvard University Press, 2007.

Transition Network. https://transitionnetwork.org/.

Transitions US. www.transitionus.org/.

Tuveson, Ernest Lee. *Redeemer Nation: The Idea of America's Millennial Role.* 1968; Chicago: University of Chicago Press, 1980.

US Department of State. *The National Security Strategy of the United States.* Washington, DC: US Department of State, 2002. www.state.gov/documents/organization/63562.pdf.

Walker, Jeremy, and Melinda Cooper. "Genealogies of Resilience: From Systems Ecology to the Political Economy of Crisis Adaptation." *Security Dialogue* 42, no. 2 (2011): 143–160.

Welch, Sharon. *After the Protests Are Heard: An Ethic of Power, Professionalism and Risk.* New York: New York University Press, 2018.

Wendle, John. "The Ominous Story of Syria's Climate Refugees." *Scientific American*, December 17, 2015. www.scientificamerican.com/article/ominous-story-of-syria-climate-refugees/.

White, Carol Wayne. *Black Lives and Sacred Humanity: Toward an African American Religious Naturalism*. New York: Fordham University Press, 2016.

Whitehead, Alfred North. *Adventures of Ideas*. 1933; New York: Free, 1967.

——. *Dialogues of Alfred North Whitehead*. Edited by Lucien Price. Boston: Godine, 2001.

——. *Modes of Thought*. 1938; New York: Free, 1968.

——. *Process and Reality*. Corrected ed. Edited by David Ray Griffin and Donald W. Sherburne. New York: Free, 1978.

——. *Religion in the Making*. New York: Macmillan, 1926.

——. *Symbolism: Its Meaning and Effect*. 1927; New York: Fordham University Press, 1985.

"Why Are CAFO's Bad?" Sierra Club—Michigan Chapter. www.sierraclub.org/michigan/cafo-facts.

Wieman, Henry Nelson. *Man's Ultimate Commitment*. 1958; Lanham, MD: University Press of America, 1991.

——. *Religious Experience and Scientific Method*. 1926; Carbondale: Southern Illinois University Press, 1971.

——. *The Source of Human Good*. Chicago: University of Chicago Press, 1946.

Wieman, Henry Nelson, and Bernard Eugene Meland, eds. *American Philosophies of Religion*. Chicago: Willett, Clark, 1936.

Wildman, Wesley. "Religious Naturalism: What It Can Be, and What It Need Not Be." *Philosophy, Theology, and the Sciences* 1, no. 1 (2014): 36–58.

Williams, Raymond. *Keywords: A Vocabulary of Culture and Society*. Rev. ed. New York: Oxford University Press, 1983.

Winthrop, John. "A Model of Christian Charity." In *The American Bible: How Our Words Unite, Divide, and Define a Nation*, edited by Stephen Prothero, 34–51. New York: HarperCollins, 2012.

Wolin, Sheldon S. *Fugitive Democracy, and Other Essays*. Edited by Nicholas Xenos. Princeton: Princeton University Press, 2016.

——. *Politics and Vision: Continuity and Innovation in Western Political Thought*. Expanded ed. Princeton: Princeton University Press, 2004.

Working Group II. "Climate Change 2014: Impacts, Adaptation and Vulnerability." Assessment Report 5, Intergovernmental Panel on Climate Change (IPCC). www.ipcc.ch/report/ar5/wg2/.

Young, Henry James. *Hope in Process: A Theology of Social Pluralism*. Minneapolis: Fortress, 1990.

Zalasiewicz, Jan, Mark Williams, Will Steffen, and Paul Crutzen. "The New World of the Anthropocene." *Environmental Science and Technology* 44, no. 7 (2010): 2228–2231.

Zimring, Carl A. *Clean and White: A History of Environmental Racism in the United States*. New York: New York University Press, 2015.

INDEX

Bacon, Francis, 142
Baptist, Edward E., 44
Barber, Benjamin, 175–76
Beauty, 182–84
Beck, Ulrich, 164, 165
Being, 86
Bellah, Robert, 1, 31, 32
Berlin, Germany, 174
Berlin wall, 52
Beveridge, Albert J., 33
Biblical covenant, 76
Biello, David, 57
Bifocal political theology, 5, 6, 16, 121
Bifurcation of nature, 76, 78, 99, 132, 162
Big Bang, 141
Big Oil, 74
Big Tobacco, 74
Biocide, 118
Black Lives Matter movement, 4, 155
Black Power movement, 152
Boggs, Grace Lee, 152, 164, 178, 179, 180
Boggs, James, 152
Bonneuil, Christophe, 64
Borer, Julian, 50
Boyd, Roger, 161
Bucer, Martin, 35
Buchler, Justus, 141
Buddhists, 138
Bush, George W., 46, 47–48
Butler, Judith, 173–74

Calvin, John, 35
Capital, accumulation of, 161–62, 191n28
Capitalism: American, 49; contradictions of, 162; in eighteenth century, 50; global ascendancy of American, 44; industrial, 44; logic of, 30. See also Neoliberal capitalism
Capitalocene, 63
Case, Shirley Jackson, 123
Causal efficacy, 100, 102, 105, 108
Central bank interventions, 161

Certainty: aftermath of, 74, 116, 135; end of, 75, 76, 115, 175, 179; quest for, 120, 175; spirit of resistance to, 91
CFCs. See Chlorofluorocarbons
Chakrabarty, Dipesh, 64, 66
Chicago School of theology, 123; community of temper associated with, 125; early concerns of, 124
Chlorofluorocarbons (CFCs), 165
Christianity, 33, 138
Christian realism, 49
Civic rituals, 97
Civil religion, 1
Civil rights movement, 2
Civil War, 1, 34, 44
Class conflict, 162
Classical theism, 14, 168; God of, 169
Class prejudice, 45
Class privilege, 86
Climate, viscosity of, 73, 75
Climate crisis, 28; anthropogenic, 4; human-centered patterns of thinking leading to, 7; main drivers of, 59; morality and, 67–68; phenomenology of, 55; responsibility for, 63; wickedness of, 163
Climate denialists, 73–74, 190n24
Climate Justice movement, 4
Climate wickedness, 74, 98; moral phenomenology of, 115; phenomenology of, 65
Climatic feedback loop, 67
Cluster concepts, 6
CO_2 emissions, 67, 163; explosion of, 58; wealthy nations responsible for, 63
Coates, Ta-Nehisi, 30, 44
Cognitive understanding, 104
Coherentist theories of knowledge, 90
Collaborative spirit, 167
Collapse of Complex Societies, The (Tainter), 69
Colonial exploitation, 32
Columbian Exchange, 57

Wickedness, 156; of climate crisis, 163
Wicked problems, 71, 165; scale and
    complexity of, 65; vulnerable
    communities affected by, 66; wickedness
    of, 156
Wieman, Henry Nelson, 12, 124–26, 149
Wildman, Wesley, 12, 130, 186n4, 190n22
Williams, Raymond, 6

Winthrop, John, 29, 35–36, 37
Women's rights, 2
Working class, 45; disempowerment, 47
World Bank, 59
World-in-process, 90, 177
World loyalty, 6, 13, 130, 154
World War II, 59
Wyant, Dan, 24; resignation of, 27